THE
BIG BOOK
OF
FANTASTIC
FACTS

BARNES
&NOBLE
BOOKS
NEW YORK

CONTENTS

Earth and Universe

The Living World

This edition published by Barnes & Noble Inc., by arrangement with Orpheus Books Ltd.

Copyright © 2000 Orpheus Books Ltd

ISBN 0-7607-2200-5

Library of Congress Cataloging Data available upon request.

The material in this book was previously published in 1997 as four separate volumes entitled: *Earth and Universe*, *The Living World*, *People and Places*, and *Machines and Inventions*.

Created and produced by Nicholas Harris, Joanna Turner, and Claire Aston, Orpheus Books Ltd

Text written by Storm Dunlop, David Lambert, Neil Grant and Peter Lafferty

Illustrations by Mike Atkinson (*Garden Studio*), Janos Marffy, Alan Weston, David Wright (*Kathy Jakeman Illustration*), Shane Marsh, David More, Sebastian Quigley (*Linden Artists*), Alessandro Bartolozzi, Simone Boni, Luigi Galante, Rosanna Rea (*The McRae Agency*), Betti Ferrero (*Milan Illustration Agency*), Tim Hayward (*Bernard Thornton Artists*), John Morris (*Wildlife Art Agency*), Julian Baker, Stephen Conlin, Gary Hincks, Steven Kirk, Colin Rose, Roger Stewart, Martin Woodward

Printed and bound in Spain

People and Places

Machines and Inventions

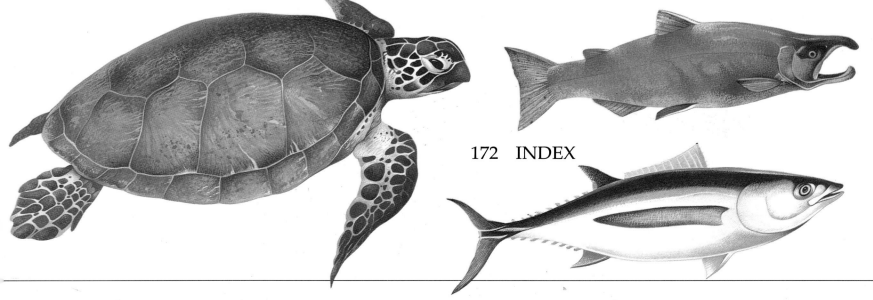

Earth and Universe

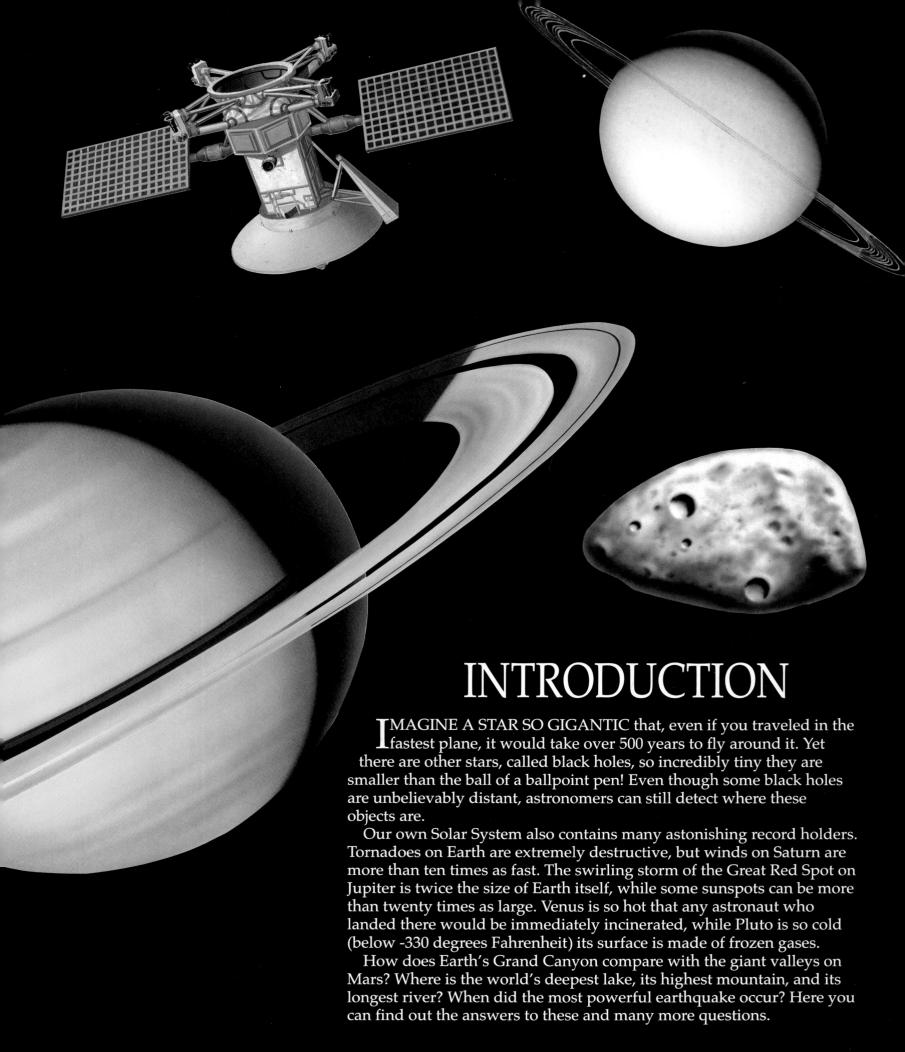

INTRODUCTION

IMAGINE A STAR SO GIGANTIC that, even if you traveled in the fastest plane, it would take over 500 years to fly around it. Yet there are other stars, called black holes, so incredibly tiny they are smaller than the ball of a ballpoint pen! Even though some black holes are unbelievably distant, astronomers can still detect where these objects are.

Our own Solar System also contains many astonishing record holders. Tornadoes on Earth are extremely destructive, but winds on Saturn are more than ten times as fast. The swirling storm of the Great Red Spot on Jupiter is twice the size of Earth itself, while some sunspots can be more than twenty times as large. Venus is so hot that any astronaut who landed there would be immediately incinerated, while Pluto is so cold (below -330 degrees Fahrenheit) its surface is made of frozen gases.

How does Earth's Grand Canyon compare with the giant valleys on Mars? Where is the world's deepest lake, its highest mountain, and its longest river? When did the most powerful earthquake occur? Here you can find out the answers to these and many more questions.

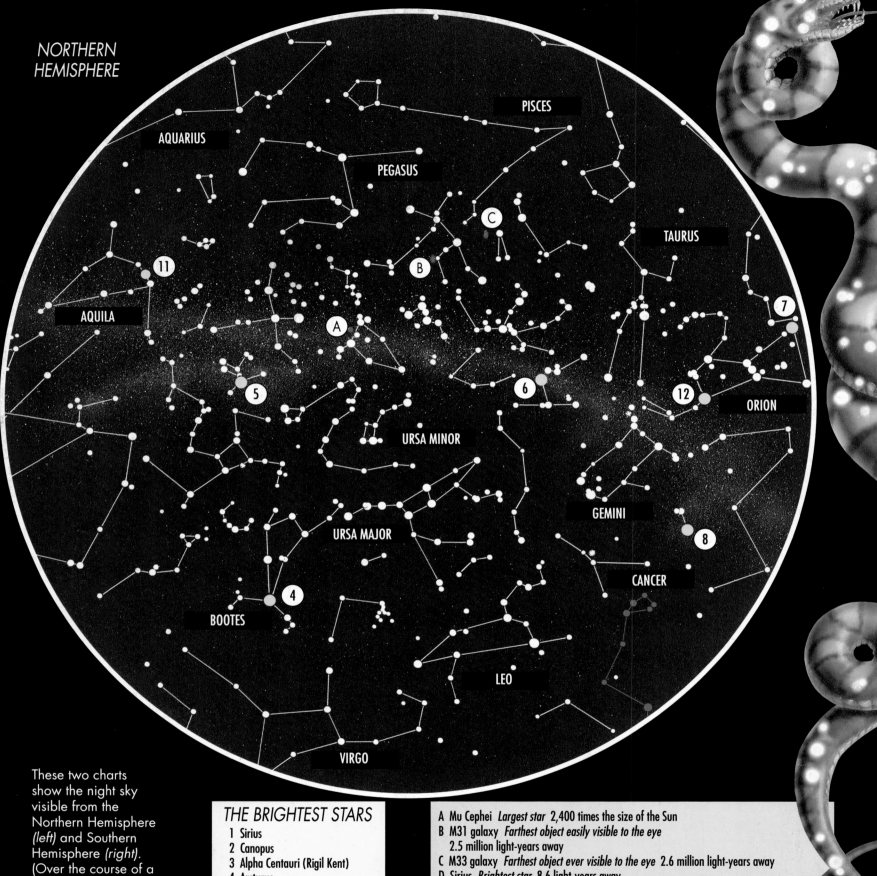

NORTHERN HEMISPHERE

PISCES

AQUARIUS

PEGASUS

TAURUS

C

11

B

AQUILA

A

ORION

12

5

6

URSA MINOR

GEMINI

8

URSA MAJOR

CANCER

4

BOOTES

LEO

VIRGO

These two charts show the night sky visible from the Northern Hemisphere *(left)* and Southern Hemisphere *(right)*. (Over the course of a year, the part you can see varies.) The brighter stars are shown as larger spots. The lines between the stars link those stars together in the same constellation.

THE BRIGHTEST STARS

1 Sirius
2 Canopus
3 Alpha Centauri (Rigil Kent)
4 Arcturus
5 Vega
6 Capella
7 Rigel
8 Procyon
9 Achernar
10 Hadar
11 Altair
12 Betelgeuse

A Mu Cephei *Largest star* 2,400 times the size of the Sun
B M31 galaxy *Farthest object easily visible to the eye*
    2.5 million light-years away
C M33 galaxy *Farthest object ever visible to the eye* 2.6 million light-years away
D Sirius *Brightest star* 8.6 light-years away
E Hydra *Largest constellation*
F Large Magellanic Cloud *Second nearest galaxy* 169,000 light-years away
G Eta Carinae *Most massive star* 200 times the mass of the Sun
H Crux *Smallest constellation*
J Proxima Centauri *Nearest star* 4.2 light-years away
K Alpha Centauri (Rigil Kent) *Second nearest star and nearest visible to the eye*
    4.4 light-years away
L Sagittarius Dwarf Galaxy *Nearest galaxy* 50,000 light-years away

STARS OF NORTHERN & SOUTHERN SKIES
A GUIDE TO STELLAR RECORD HOLDERS

IMAGINE FLYING in the Concorde at its cruising speed of 1,450 miles per hour. It would take nearly 200,000 years to reach the nearest star! Distances in the Universe are so vast that we have to use a special measure called light-years. Light moves at 186,290 miles per second (it would take the Concorde nearly five-and-a-half days to cover the same distance). In a year, light travels about 6 trillion miles, so we can use this distance, a *light-year*, instead of reckoning in millions and millions of miles. Powerful telescopes can detect quasars, central regions of galaxies throwing out enormous amounts of light and heat far out in the Universe. They are the farthest objects known. The most distant quasar so far discovered is about 13,200,000 light-years away!

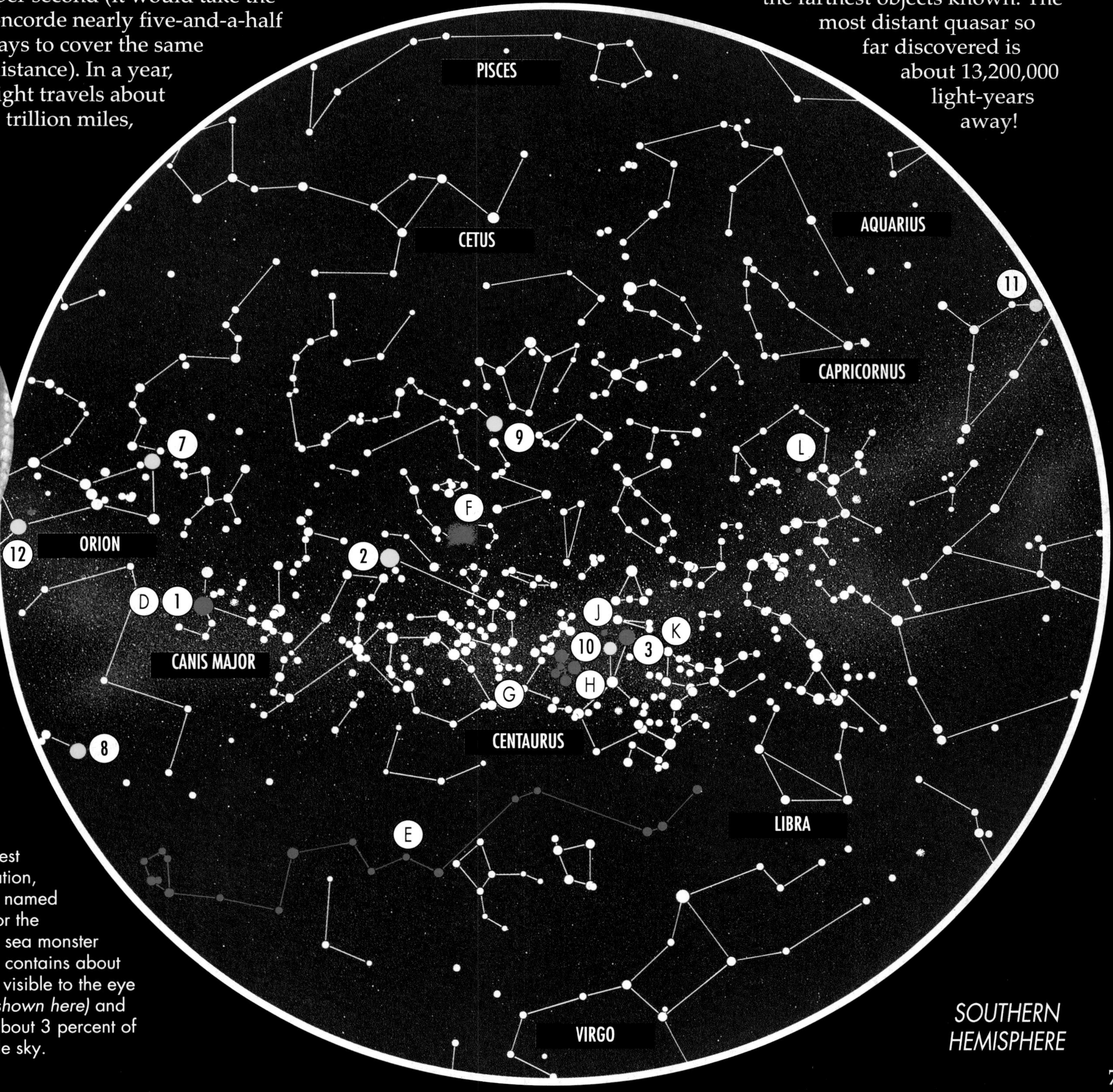

PISCES

CETUS

AQUARIUS

CAPRICORNUS

7

9

L

F

12

ORION

2

D 1

J

K

10 3

CANIS MAJOR

H

G

CENTAURUS

8

LIBRA

E

The largest constellation, which is named Hydra for the mythical sea monster *(above)*, contains about 68 stars visible to the eye *(not all shown here)* and covers about 3 percent of the whole sky.

VIRGO

SOUTHERN HEMISPHERE

7

THE LARGEST VISIBLE STAR
BETELGEUSE, THE SIZE OF 800 SUNS

THEY MAY LOOK like tiny points of light in the night sky, but stars can be enormous – sometimes millions of times the size of Earth. The very largest stars, called supergiants, are unbelievably huge! Betelgeuse, the bright red star in the constellation Orion, is the largest one visible without a telescope. About 620 million miles across, it is 800 times the size of the Sun, our own "local" star.

It is very difficult to measure the sizes of stars because they are so far away. Astronomers do not always agree which is the largest of all. It is probably Mu Cephei, a star about 2,400 times the size of the Sun.

Supergiant stars are so big that perhaps the only way to imagine just how big they are is to compare them with the orbits of planets in our Solar System *(below)*. Betelgeuse would engulf Mercury, Venus, Earth, and Mars – all the inner planets circling the Sun. The supergiant Mu Cephei would consume Jupiter and Saturn, as well!

THE LIFE AND DEATH OF A STAR

Stars are formed when clouds of gas and dust in space (1) shrink and become dense "blobs" called protostars (2). The same force that keeps us firmly on the ground – gravity – causes this to happen. The core of the new protostar becomes so hot that nuclear reactions *(see page 12)* start deep inside it. Gas and dust are blown away by a violent "wind" from the star (3). Sometimes a spinning disk of dust, gas, and ice results (4). This may eventually become the birthplace of planets.

The fuel that powers the nuclear

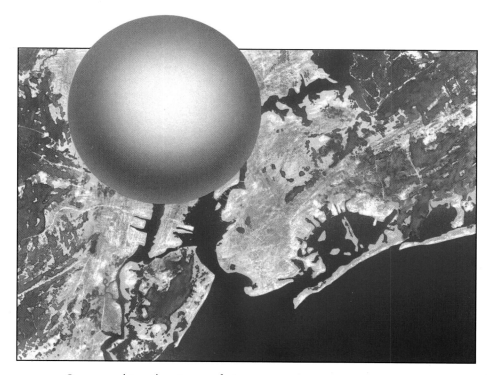

THE SMALLEST STARS

Stars like the Sun are so small when compared with giants and supergiants that astronomers call them dwarfs. A teaspoonful of material from the Sun is as heavy as a spoonful of syrup. After the Sun swells to become a red giant (in about five billion years) it will lose its outer layers. Just the small, very hot, dead core will remain. Called a white dwarf, it will measure about 6,200 miles across (roughly the size of Earth) and be extremely dense. A teaspoonful of white-dwarf material would weigh 5.5 tons.

The core that remains after a supernova explosion is a tiny star no more than 16 miles across. It is a neutron star, the smallest type of star that exists. A teaspoonful would weigh an incredible 1.1 billion tons!

Compared to other types of stars, neutron stars are incredibly small. Here *(above)* one compares in size with a view of New York City as seen from the air.

reactions lasts billions of years (5). When it runs out, the core collapses, and the outer regions grow into red giants (6). Most stars, including our Sun, are destined to become red giants, but some much heavier ones become supergiants (7).

When its nuclear "fuel" runs out, a supergiant's core will collapse in a split-second. The outside explodes as a supernova, the greatest explosion known in all nature (8). For a fraction of a second, a supernova will give off more energy than all the billions of stars – in every one of the billions of galaxies – all put together! All that is left behind after the explosion is a dense neutron star (9) or a black hole (see page 10).

9

BLACK HOLES
THE DENSEST OBJECTS IN THE UNIVERSE

COMPLETELY INVISIBLE, black holes are the strangest objects in the Universe. Like neutron stars *(see page 9)* they are all that remains of stars that have blown up in supernova explosions.

All bodies in space have a force of gravity, the force that attracts other things toward them. It is this force that holds stars together, keeps the planets in their orbits around the Sun, and causes all objects to fall to the ground on Earth. To escape from a star or planet, you would have to travel at very high speeds to overcome the force of gravity. A rocket launched from Earth must go faster than 25,050 miles per hour to escape from Earth's gravitational pull.

After a supernova explosion, the central core collapses until it is a tiny fraction of the size it used to

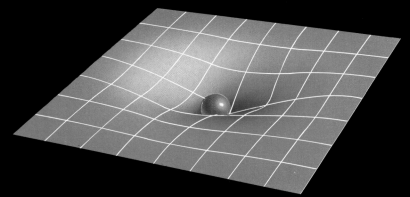

You can think of the force of gravity being like a ball on a rubber sheet. A star or a planet "bends" space: Anything close by will fall toward them. If the ball got so heavy that part of the sheet stretched into a long, thin tube, you would have a black hole.

be. No more than a tiny pinpoint in space, it is nevertheless surrounded by a force of gravity more powerful than any normal star in the Universe. In order to escape from here, you would have to travel faster than the speed of light: 186,290 miles per second! In fact, escape would be impossible because nothing can travel faster than the speed of light. That is why these mysterious, invisible objects are called "black holes": Nothing, not even light, can escape them.

No one has ever seen a black hole, but astronomers believe that they exist because they can detect their powerful gravitational force.

The pair of stars called Cygnus X-1 almost certainly contains a black hole. We can see a supergiant star *(above)* circling something invisible with an enormous gravitational pull. The star is losing gas, which swirls down into the black hole.

MASSIVE ENERGY MACHINES

Incredibly powerful, giant black holes, astronomers think, lurk in the centers of galaxies. In some galaxies, such as our own Milky Way, the black holes are fairly peaceful. In others, they are the scene of violent activity. As stars are sucked in toward them, they are torn apart into clouds of gas. Quasars, the most distant objects in the Universe, are probably the central regions of such violent galaxies. The energy they give out is so great they can still be detected even though the galaxies themselves are too far away to be visible.

THE NEAREST STAR
A SHIMMERING BALL OF GAS

THE NEAREST STAR to Earth is the Sun itself. A gigantic ball of extremely hot gases, mostly hydrogen and helium, it is big enough to contain nearly 1,400,000 bodies the size of our own planet. It dwarfs even the largest planet, Jupiter. In fact, the Sun contains more than 99 percent of all the matter in the Solar System. The Sun also provides most of the heat in the Solar System, and thus the warmth that makes life possible on Earth.

The surface, called the photosphere, is in constant motion, like water in a boiling kettle. Its temperature is about 11,000°F, but at the center this rises to an incredible 27 million°F! The core generates all the Sun's energy through what are known as nuclear reactions. At such high temperatures, hydrogen is changed into helium in a reaction that gives off an enormous amount of energy. (This is called nuclear fusion, the same process that scientists hope one day will drive the world's power stations.)

Incredibly, scientists have created temperatures far hotter than at the center of the Sun. Plasma, produced when gases are subjected to very high temperatures, is the hottest known matter. At the Princeton Plasma Physics Laboratory, New Jersey, scientists achieved a temperature of 920 million°F.

The Sun "burns" about 4.4 million tons of hydrogen every second, but it is so enormous that, fortunately for us, it will take another 5 billion years before it finally exhausts its supply!

Prominences *(above)* are clouds, tongues, or arches of glowing gas held above the Sun by magnetic fields. Some prominences last for weeks, but other, more violent ones last only hours. Many prominences are gigantic. The highest arches are often more than 370,000 miles high, twice the distance from Earth to the Moon.

Sudden explosions of energy, flares are the most violent events on the Sun's surface. In a few minutes the strongest eruptions release as much energy as the entire Sun does in a few seconds. One of the greatest flares of recent times happened on August 10, 1989. It blacked out the power supply in Québec, Canada.

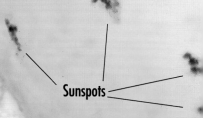

Sunspots

In this illustration of the Sun, a segment has been removed so that the layers inside are visible.

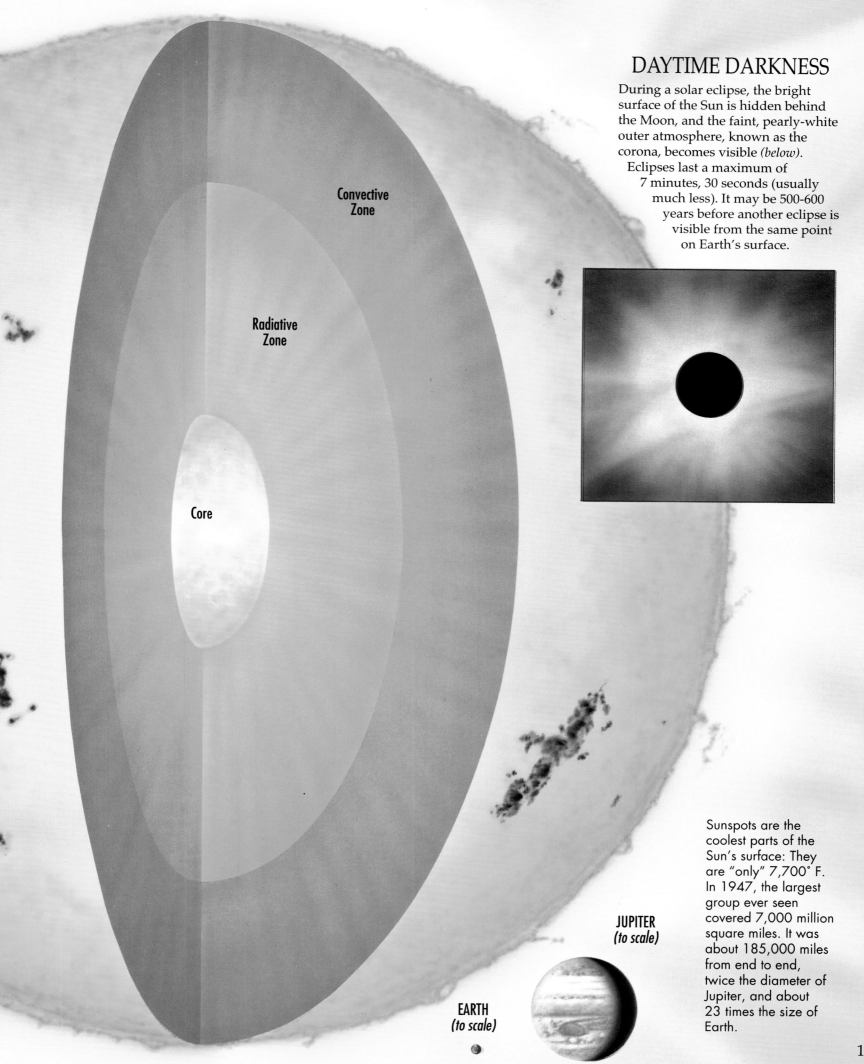

Convective Zone

Radiative Zone

Core

DAYTIME DARKNESS

During a solar eclipse, the bright surface of the Sun is hidden behind the Moon, and the faint, pearly-white outer atmosphere, known as the corona, becomes visible *(below)*. Eclipses last a maximum of 7 minutes, 30 seconds (usually much less). It may be 500-600 years before another eclipse is visible from the same point on Earth's surface.

Sunspots are the coolest parts of the Sun's surface: They are "only" 7,700° F. In 1947, the largest group ever seen covered 7,000 million square miles. It was about 185,000 miles from end to end, twice the diameter of Jupiter, and about 23 times the size of Earth.

JUPITER
(to scale)

EARTH
(to scale)

13

Mercury is bare and rocky. It is the closest planet to the Sun, and rushes around it in 88 days, the quickest orbit of any planet.

The hottest planet, Venus spins slowly, so it has the longest day. On its orbit, it comes closer to Earth than any other planet.

MERCURY

VENUS

EARTH

MARS

THE INNER PLANETS

MERCURY *Diameter* 3,031 miles *Day* 58.7 Earth days *Year* 88 days. No moons; bare, rocky surface
VENUS *Diameter* 7,521 miles *Day* 243 Earth days *Year* 224 days. No moons; hot, cloud-covered
EARTH *Diameter* 7,926 miles *Day* 24 hrs *Year* 365.26 days. 1 moon; extensive oceans
MARS *Diameter* 4,222 miles *Day* 24.6 hrs *Year* 687 Earth days. 2 moons; dry, dusty, little atmosphere

Mars is a very cold and dry planet. It has the highest mountain in the Solar System.

Jupiter is larger than all the other planets put together. It spins faster and has the shortest day of all.

SUN

JUPITER

Mercury
Venus
Earth
Mars

Asteroids

Jupiter

Saturn

Uranus

THE PLANETS
SOLAR SYSTEM RECORD HOLDERS

Saturn has the most moons (18) and the largest rings. It has the lowest density – even less than that of water.

SATURN

THE LARGEST PLANETS in the Solar System – Jupiter, Saturn, Uranus, and Neptune – are known as the gas giants because, unlike our rocky planet, they consist mostly of gases, particularly hydrogen and helium. Jupiter and Saturn probably have rocky cores, but the others may only have liquid water and methane beneath their gassy exteriors.

The gas giants all have many moons, some of which are larger than Mercury or Pluto, the two smallest planets. The giant planets also all have rings, although except for Saturn's, they are very faint. Saturn's bright rings extend for 170,000 miles, more than twice the diameter of the planet. They consist of millions of blocks of ice, the largest of which are about 33 feet across – the size of small houses.

The outermost and smallest planet, Pluto is mostly made of ice. Its orbit around the Sun is more elongated than those of the other planets, so that some of the time it is actually closer to the Sun than Neptune.

The four, small, inner planets – Mercury, Venus, Earth, and Mars – are mainly made of rock. Between Mars and Jupiter, thousands of asteroids (also called minor planets) orbit the Sun. Even the largest, Ceres, is only 620 miles across.

The Sun and planets are illustrated to scale

Uranus was the first planet to be discovered with the use of a telescope.

URANUS

Neptune is the farthest planet observed by any space probe.

THE OUTER PLANETS

JUPITER *Diameter* 88,736 miles
Day 9.8 hrs *Year* 11.8 Earth years.
16 moons; tiny ring
SATURN *Diameter* 74,900 miles
Day 10.2 hrs *Year* 29.4 Earth years.
18 moons; giant rings
URANUS *Diameter* 31,800 miles
Day 17.4 hrs *Year* 84 Earth years.
15 moons; 10 thin rings
NEPTUNE *Diameter* 31,400 miles
Day 16.1 hrs *Year* 164.8 Earth
years. 15 moons; 2 thin rings
PLUTO *Diameter* 1,430 miles
Day 6.4 days *Year* 247.7 Earth
years. 1 moon; mostly made of ice

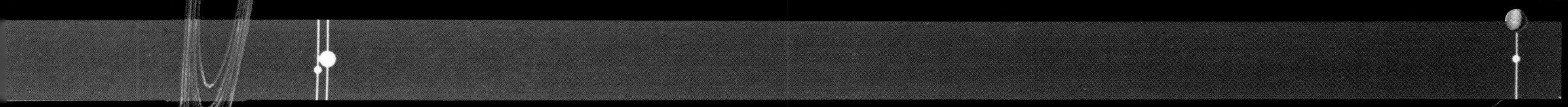

NEPTUNE

Pluto, the most distant planet, has a single moon, Charon. It is also the coldest and smallest planet.

PLUTO

Pluto Neptune
(when nearest the Sun)

This diagram shows the planets' relative distances from the Sun.

Pluto

15

TO THE CENTER OF JUPITER
GIANT AMONG PLANETS

WITH A DIAMETER more than 11 times that of our own planet, Jupiter – the largest of all the planets – could contain a thousand Earths! Its gravity (the force that attracts other things toward it) is so strong that it often alters the orbits of comets that pass close by *(see page 24)*, sometimes hurling them out of the Solar System altogether.

Jupiter's day is shorter than that of any other planet: just under 10 hours. Because it rotates so fast, it bulges at the equator and measures 5,300 miles less from pole to pole. Jupiter has no solid surface: Only its small core (with a diameter more than twice that of the whole Earth) is made of rock and metals. Most of the globe is liquid – not water, but a metallic form of hydrogen close to the core and, beneath the clouds near its surface, liquid hydrogen.

Like the other outer planets, Saturn, Uranus, and Neptune, Jupiter is surrounded by swirling clouds of gas. Divided into bright zones and dark belts, Jupiter's clouds are separated by bands of high-speed winds. Some reach speeds of 336 miles per hour. (Saturn holds the record, however, with winds of up to 1,100 miles per hour – faster than the speed of sound on Earth!)

Fast-moving clouds, the belts that circle Jupiter's globe, constantly change shape. A faint, dusty ring, probably only a few miles thick, also surrounds the planet. Jupiter's most famous feature is, however, the Great Red Spot, located here in the red box and seen in greater detail on the opposite page.

Metallic hydrogen region

Rocky, metallic core

This illustration shows what you would find if you were to tunnel through the Great Red Spot towards the center of Jupiter. A little way below the cloud layers there is liquid hydrogen and, deeper still, a strange "metallic" form of liquid hydrogen. Right at the center, there is a core made of rock, originally the "dust" that swirled in the vast cloud from which the Sun and planets were born *(see page 8)*.

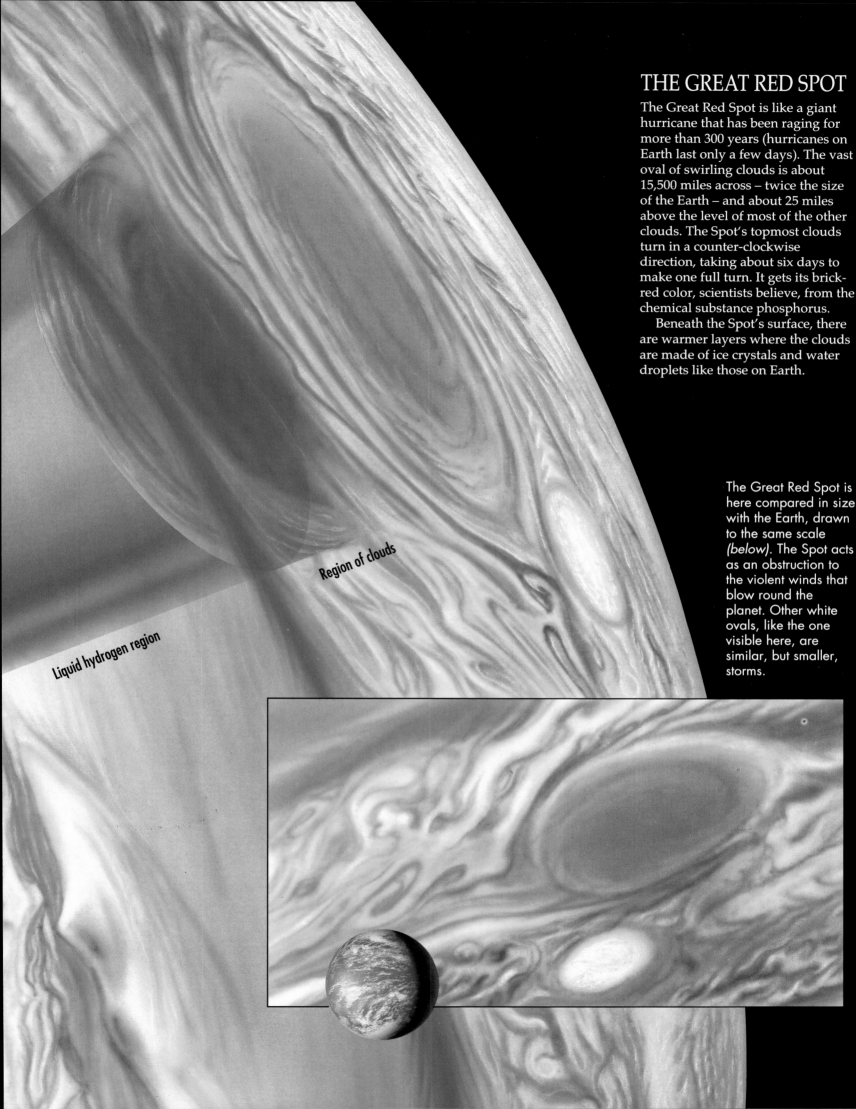

THE GREAT RED SPOT

The Great Red Spot is like a giant hurricane that has been raging for more than 300 years (hurricanes on Earth last only a few days). The vast oval of swirling clouds is about 15,500 miles across – twice the size of the Earth – and about 25 miles above the level of most of the other clouds. The Spot's topmost clouds turn in a counter-clockwise direction, taking about six days to make one full turn. It gets its brick-red color, scientists believe, from the chemical substance phosphorus.

Beneath the Spot's surface, there are warmer layers where the clouds are made of ice crystals and water droplets like those on Earth.

The Great Red Spot is here compared in size with the Earth, drawn to the same scale *(below)*. The Spot acts as an obstruction to the violent winds that blow round the planet. Other white ovals, like the one visible here, are similar, but smaller, storms.

Region of clouds

Liquid hydrogen region

THE HOTTEST PLANET
BENEATH THE SULFUROUS CLOUDS OF VENUS

VENUS IS THE NEAREST PLANET to Earth, but no world could be an unfriendlier place to visit! In any case, were you ever to set foot on its surface, you would be immediately incinerated. Venus is the hottest planet in the Solar System: Its average temperature of 915°F is easily enough to melt lead. It is even hotter than Mercury, although that planet is much closer to the Sun. This is because Venus's thick atmosphere of carbon dioxide – so dense that it would crush any person not already burnt to a cinder – prevents heat from escaping.

Most of the barren surface is covered by vast plains, studded with tens of thousands of volcanoes. The mountain known as Maxwell Montes is nearly 40,000 feet high, the second highest in the Solar System after Olympus Mons *(see page 20)* on Mars.

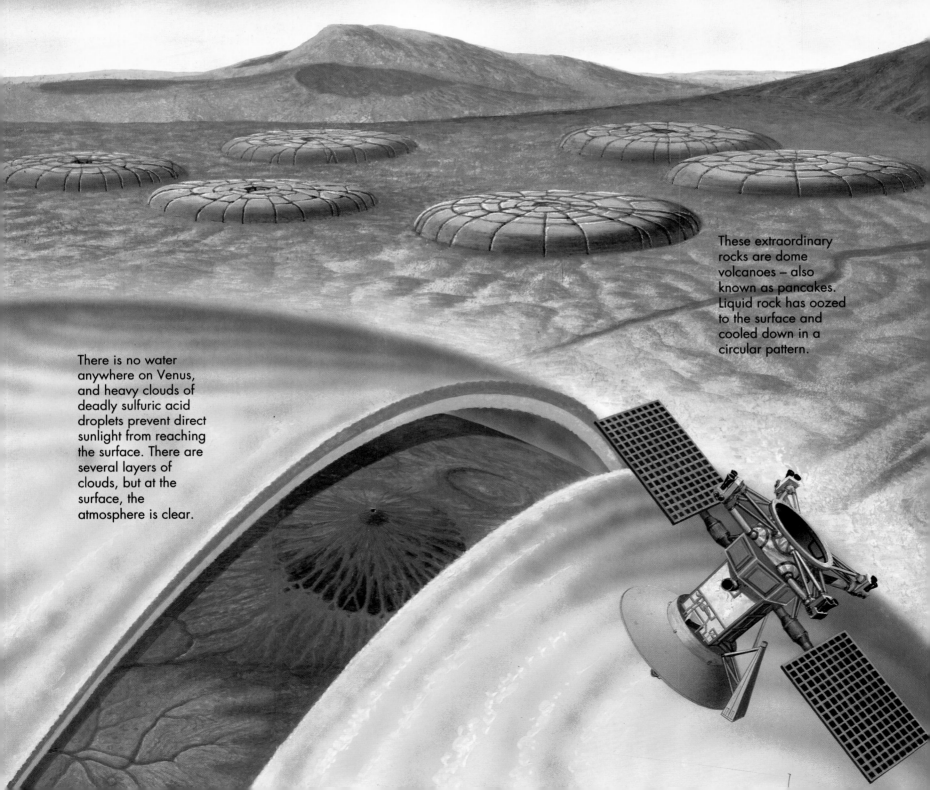

These extraordinary rocks are dome volcanoes – also known as pancakes. Liquid rock has oozed to the surface and cooled down in a circular pattern.

There is no water anywhere on Venus, and heavy clouds of deadly sulfuric acid droplets prevent direct sunlight from reaching the surface. There are several layers of clouds, but at the surface, the atmosphere is clear.

METEOROID BOMBARDMENT

Many meteoroids – fragments of rock and ice shooting around the Solar System – are completely destroyed in the dense atmosphere of Venus before they get near the ground. Some explode in mid-air, creating "splotches" where the shock wave from the explosion shatters the rocks on the surface below. The largest meteors smash into the ground with tremendous force, flinging rocks in all directions. The largest craters are about 68 miles across.

Modern technology has found a way to show us pictures of what Venus really looks like. An unmanned spacecraft called *Magellan (left)* has mapped the planet's surface beneath the clouds. It used radar, the same device ships and airplanes have to detect other craft out of direct vision.

OLYMPUS MONS
THE HIGHEST MOUNTAIN IN THE SOLAR SYSTEM

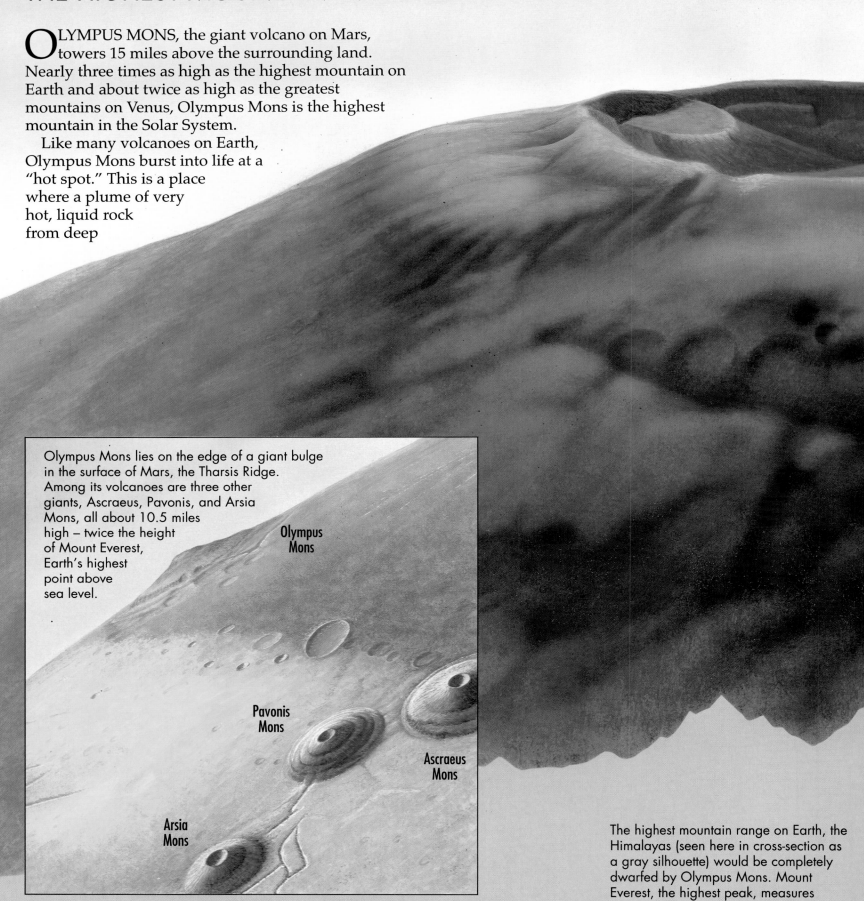

OLYMPUS MONS, the giant volcano on Mars, towers 15 miles above the surrounding land. Nearly three times as high as the highest mountain on Earth and about twice as high as the greatest mountains on Venus, Olympus Mons is the highest mountain in the Solar System.

Like many volcanoes on Earth, Olympus Mons burst into life at a "hot spot." This is a place where a plume of very hot, liquid rock from deep

Olympus Mons lies on the edge of a giant bulge in the surface of Mars, the Tharsis Ridge. Among its volcanoes are three other giants, Ascraeus, Pavonis, and Arsia Mons, all about 10.5 miles high – twice the height of Mount Everest, Earth's highest point above sea level.

Olympus Mons

Pavonis Mons

Ascraeus Mons

Arsia Mons

The highest mountain range on Earth, the Himalayas (seen here in cross-section as a gray silhouette) would be completely dwarfed by Olympus Mons. Mount Everest, the highest peak, measures

below the surface melts through a planet's outer crust. On Earth, the outer crust is constantly on the move, a fractured armor of "plates" sliding against, alongside, or beneath each other *(see page 32)*. Hot-spot volcanoes – like the Hawaiian Islands in the Pacific Ocean – appear at the surface in different places as a crustal plate wanders over the molten spot.

Unlike the Hawaiian volcanoes, Olympus Mons stayed put above its "hot spot." The eruptions and lava (liquid rock) flows have gone on for tens – perhaps hundreds – of millions of years. As each layer of rock cooled, the volcano grew larger and larger. It now measures about 370 miles across.

Area of inset
(opposite)

THE RED PLANET

Mars is the red planet. Its color comes from substances containing iron, similar to ordinary rust, in its surface rocks. Nearly 50 million miles farther from the Sun than Earth, Mars is a cold world. Sometimes the temperature reaches the melting point of water (32°F) at the equator in high summer. In winter, it plunges to below -180°F over the poles, which are capped by layers of frozen carbon dioxide and water ice. In the north, an expanse of water ice remains frozen in the summer. It is surrounded by the largest area of sand dunes known in the Solar System, stretching almost completely around the planet.

Now a dry and dusty place, a great deal of water once flowed over the Martian surface. Dried-up river beds are all that remain. One, Vallis Marineris, is a gigantic rift valley *(see page 35)* about 2,500 miles long, nearly enough to reach from coast to coast of the United States. Parts of it are about 3.7 miles deep, nearly four times as deep as Earth's greatest gorge, the Grand Canyon *(see page 36)*.

29,080 feet to Olympus Mons' 86,600 feet! And just five mountains the size of Olympus Mons placed side by side would be roughly as long as the entire Himalaya range *(see page 33)*.

21

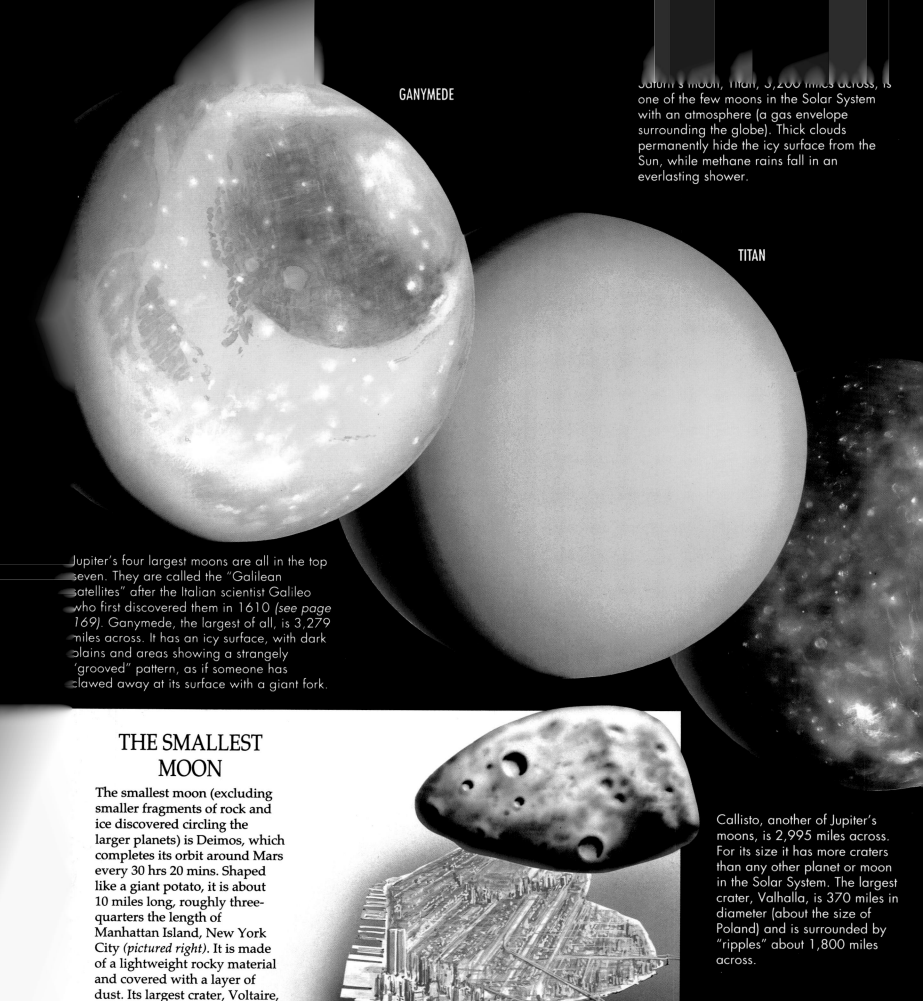

GANYMEDE

TITAN

Saturn's moon, Titan, 3,200 miles across, is one of the few moons in the Solar System with an atmosphere (a gas envelope surrounding the globe). Thick clouds permanently hide the icy surface from the Sun, while methane rains fall in an everlasting shower.

Jupiter's four largest moons are all in the top seven. They are called the "Galilean satellites" after the Italian scientist Galileo who first discovered them in 1610 *(see page 169)*. Ganymede, the largest of all, is 3,279 miles across. It has an icy surface, with dark plains and areas showing a strangely "grooved" pattern, as if someone has clawed away at its surface with a giant fork.

THE SMALLEST MOON

The smallest moon (excluding smaller fragments of rock and ice discovered circling the larger planets) is Deimos, which completes its orbit around Mars every 30 hrs 20 mins. Shaped like a giant potato, it is about 10 miles long, roughly three-quarters the length of Manhattan Island, New York City *(pictured right)*. It is made of a lightweight rocky material and covered with a layer of dust. Its largest crater, Voltaire, is 1.2 miles across.

Callisto, another of Jupiter's moons, is 2,995 miles across. For its size it has more craters than any other planet or moon in the Solar System. The largest crater, Valhalla, is 370 miles in diameter (about the size of Poland) and is surrounded by "ripples" about 1,800 miles across.

THE LARGEST MOONS
WORLDS OF ICE AND ROCK

MOONS, sometimes known as satellites, are small bodies that circle around the planets of the Solar System. Earth has one moon, of course, known simply as the Moon, but the larger planets have many more (Saturn has at least 18). The moons are as varied in size and form as the planets themselves and astronomers say there are two ways in which they came into being. Some are the result of fragments of rock and ice coming together to form a globe; others are old asteroids that have been "captured" by a planet's force of gravity *(see page 10)*. All seven largest moons illustrated here are larger than the smallest planet, Pluto. Mercury, the second smallest planet, with a diameter approximately the same as the distance across Canada and Alaska, is smaller than both Ganymede and Titan.

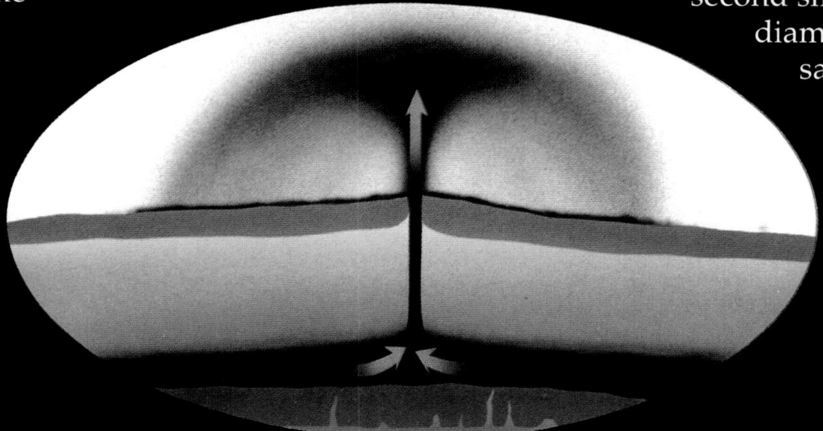

CALLISTO

Io's volcanoes erupt liquid sulfur in plumes which sometimes reach heights of 170 miles *(above)*. The ejected matter is blasted out at 2,200 mph, faster than a speeding rifle bullet.

Europa, Jupiter's fourth largest moon, is 1,943 miles across. The smoothest body in the Solar System, the largest "hills" on its icy crust measure only about 980 feet high.

Triton, Neptune's largest moon, is 1,690 miles across. Its surface is the coldest place known in the Solar System: Its temperature of -391°F is low enough to freeze oxygen and nitrogen in the air we breathe.

IO

Io, Jupiter's third largest moon, is 2,257 miles across. For its size, it is the most volcanically active body in the Solar System. At any one time, there are seven or eight eruptions in progress. Only Earth itself has more active volcanoes.

MOON

Our own Moon, Earth's nearest neighbor in space, is 2,160 miles across, the fifth largest moon in the Solar System. It would take 81 Moons to make up a body the size of Earth.

EUROPA

TRITON

HALLEY'S COMET

THE BRIGHTEST SHORT-PERIOD COMET

THE MOST FAMOUS of all comets is named after the English astronomer Edmond Halley (1656-1742). He was the first to predict that it would return to the night skies every 75-76 years.

Halley believed that comets, like the planets, traveled around the Sun in elliptical orbits (elongated circles). After examining the records of comets that had appeared in 1531 and 1607, he suggested that they, along with a comet he observed in the skies in 1682, were, in fact, all one and the same. On each occasion, people saw it passing close to Earth on its never-ending journey around the Sun. Halley did not live to see his prediction come true. What we now know as Halley's Comet was next sighted on Christmas Day 1758, 75 years after the astronomer had seen it.

Thousands of comets have been discovered. Those that complete their orbits in less than 200 years are called short-period comets. Halley's Comet is the brightest of these. The long-period comets (over 200 years) are often more spectacular, with longer tails. The record for the longest tail, measured at 199 million miles, is held by the Great Comet of 1843.

A COMETARY JOURNEY

Halley's orbit takes it from just outside Neptune's orbit to just within that of Venus. As it approaches the Sun, it heats up, brightens, and grows a spectacular tail of gas and dust, always pointing away from the Sun. The comet travels away from the Sun tail first. Eventually it fades and its tail disappears – until the next time it nears the Sun.

Halley's Comet last approached the Earth in 1986, but that year it was far away, and barely visible. A remote-controlled spacecraft called *Giotto* did, however, successfully photograph it at close range. You can make a note in your diaries for Halley's Comet's next visit – in the year 2062!

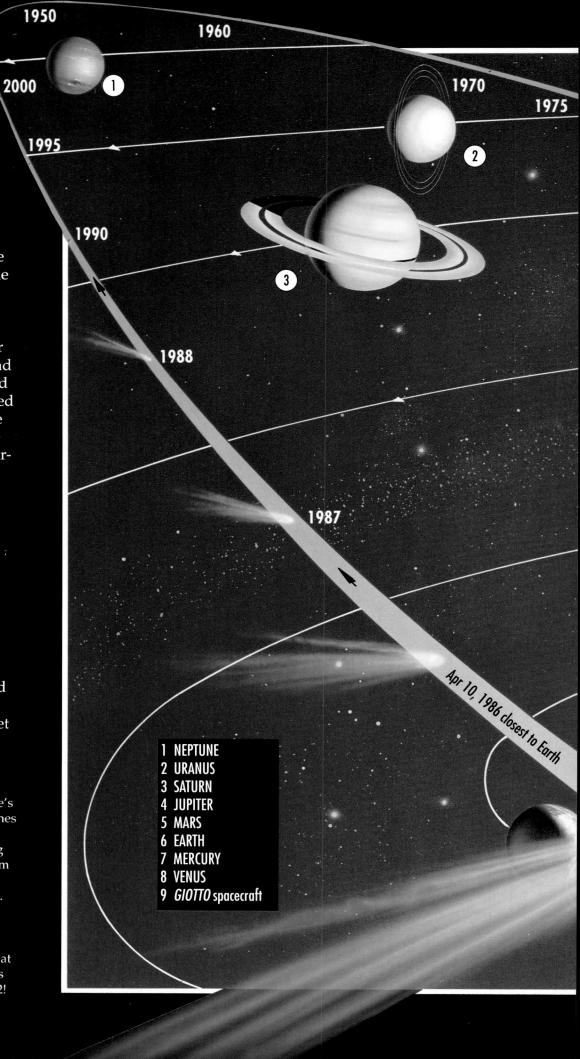

1 NEPTUNE
2 URANUS
3 SATURN
4 JUPITER
5 MARS
6 EARTH
7 MERCURY
8 VENUS
9 *GIOTTO* spacecraft

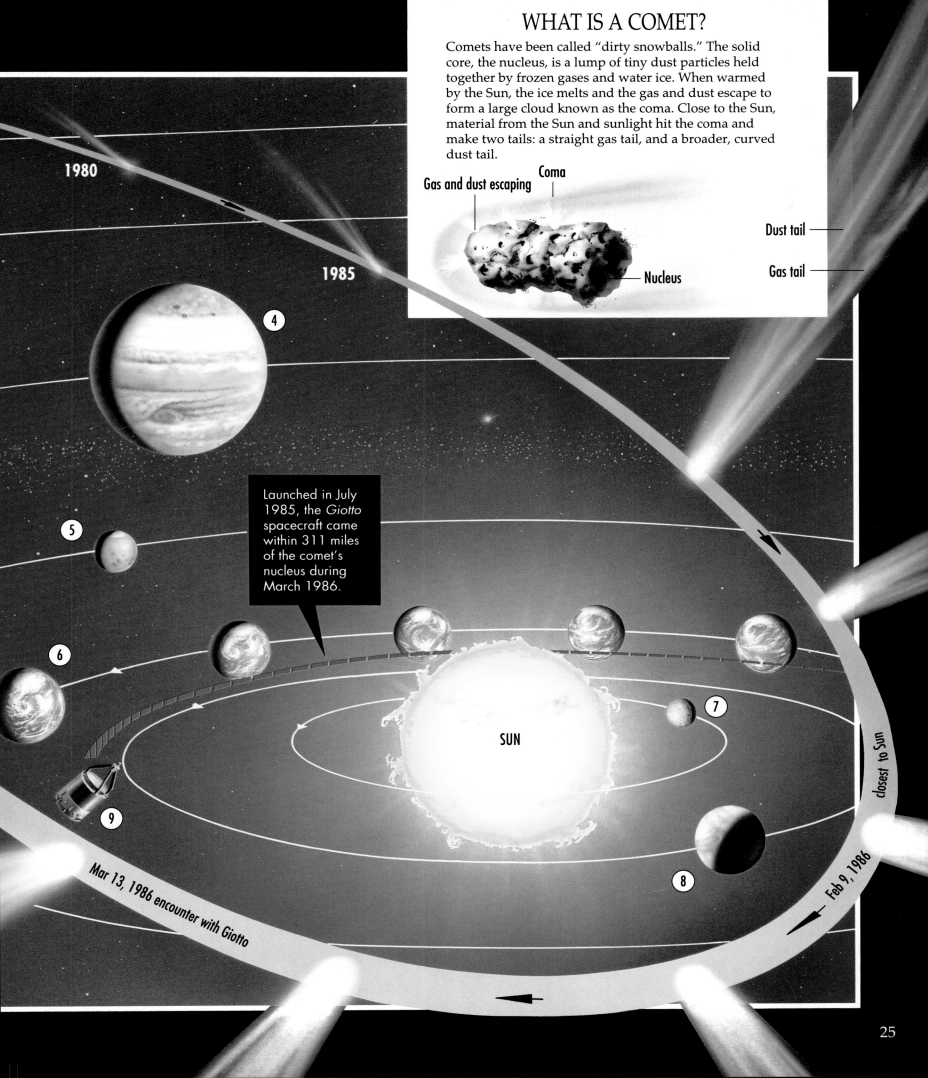

WHAT IS A COMET?

Comets have been called "dirty snowballs." The solid core, the nucleus, is a lump of tiny dust particles held together by frozen gases and water ice. When warmed by the Sun, the ice melts and the gas and dust escape to form a large cloud known as the coma. Close to the Sun, material from the Sun and sunlight hit the coma and make two tails: a straight gas tail, and a broader, curved dust tail.

Coma

Gas and dust escaping

Dust tail

Gas tail

Nucleus

1980

1985

Launched in July 1985, the *Giotto* spacecraft came within 311 miles of the comet's nucleus during March 1986.

SUN

closest to Sun

Mar 13, 1986 encounter with Giotto

Feb 9, 1986

EARTH RECORD HOLDERS
OUR HOME PLANET

OF ALL THE PLANETS in the Solar System, Earth has the most liquid water, its atmosphere contains the most oxygen, and it is the only planet that has any form of life. Without water, life could not have developed, and without plant life there would be no oxygen in the atmosphere. Without oxygen to breathe, no animals could exist.

The oceans amount to nearly three-quarters of Earth's surface. The largest ocean, the Pacific, accounts for half that area. More than one tenth of the land area is covered by permanent ice, mainly in the giant Antarctic and Greenland icecaps. About a third of the land surface forms the continent of Eurasia (Europe and Asia taken together), the largest landmass.

KEY

1   Grand Canyon, Arizona *Longest gorge* 217 miles
2   Yellowstone National Park, Wyoming *Tallest active geyser* 197-377 feet
3   Manitoulin Island, Lake Huron *Largest island in a lake* 1,076 sq miles
4   Landscape Arch, Utah *Longest natural arch* 289 feet
5   Mammoth Cave, Kentucky *Longest cave* 348 miles
6   Bay of Fundy, Canada *Greatest tides* 48 feet
7   Angel Falls, Venezuela *Highest waterfall* 3,212 feet
8   Lake Titicaca, Peru/Bolivia *Highest navigable lake* 12,504 feet
9   Amazon, South America *Largest river basin* 2,720,075 sq miles
10 Atacama Desert, Chile *Driest place* No rain for 400 years
11 Ojos de Salado, Chile/Argentina *Highest active volcano* 22,596 feet
12 Valdivia, Chile *Most powerful earthquake* (1960)
13 Scoresby Sund, Greenland *Longest fjord* 194 miles
14 Mid-Oceanic Ridge *Longest mountain range* 40,400 miles
15 Sahara, Africa *Largest desert* 3,243,000 miles
16 Al'Aziziyah, Libya *Hottest place* Highest temperature 136°F
17 Nile, Africa *Longest river* 4,145 miles
18 Great Rift Valley *Greatest rift valley* 3,977 miles
19 Pripet Marshes, Belarus *Largest swamp* 18,127 sq miles
20 Caspian Sea *Largest lake* 143,240 sq miles
21 Dead Sea, Israel/Jordan *Lowest point on land* 1,300 feet below sea level
22 Lake Baikal, Russia *Deepest lake* 5,371 feet
23 Tibet *Highest plateau* 15,995 feet
24 Cherrapunji, India *Wettest place* Recorded 1,042 inches in one year (1861)
25 Mount Everest, Nepal/Tibet *Highest mountain* 29,080 feet
26 Ganges/Brahmaputra, India/Bangladesh *Largest delta* 28,950 sq feet
27 Marianas Trench *Deepest point on Earth* 36,196 feet
28 Indonesia *Largest archipelago* More than 13,000 islands
29 Tambora, Indonesia *Greatest volcanic eruption* (1815)
30 Uluru (Ayers Rock), Australia *Largest fully exposed monolith* 1,142 ft high 1.9 miles long
31 Great Barrier Reef, Australia *Longest coral reef* 1,260 miles
32 Pole of Cold, Antarctica *Coldest place* Average temperature -72°F

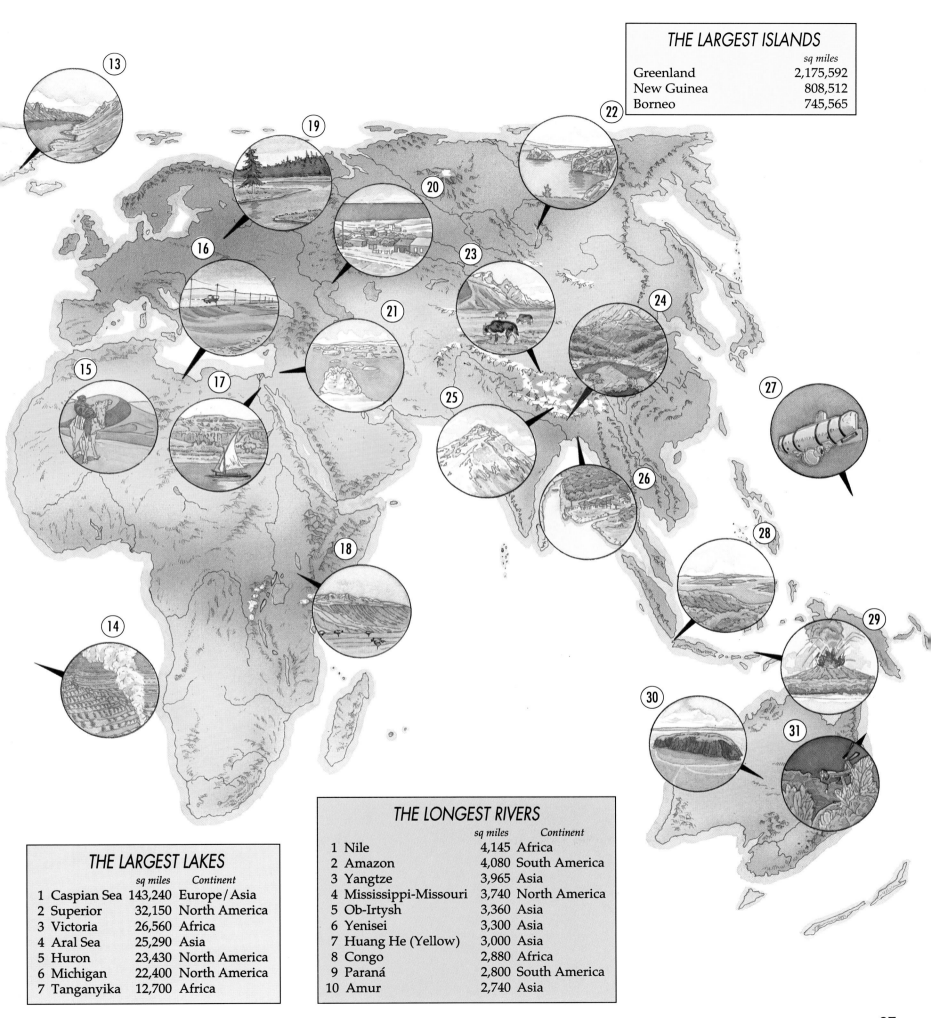

THE LARGEST ISLANDS

	sq miles
Greenland	2,175,592
New Guinea	808,512
Borneo	745,565

THE LONGEST RIVERS

		sq miles	Continent
1	Nile	4,145	Africa
2	Amazon	4,080	South America
3	Yangtze	3,965	Asia
4	Mississippi-Missouri	3,740	North America
5	Ob-Irtysh	3,360	Asia
6	Yenisei	3,300	Asia
7	Huang He (Yellow)	3,000	Asia
8	Congo	2,880	Africa
9	Paraná	2,800	South America
10	Amur	2,740	Asia

THE LARGEST LAKES

		sq miles	Continent
1	Caspian Sea	143,240	Europe/Asia
2	Superior	32,150	North America
3	Victoria	26,560	Africa
4	Aral Sea	25,290	Asia
5	Huron	23,430	North America
6	Michigan	22,400	North America
7	Tanganyika	12,700	Africa

THE GREATEST OCEAN
THE MIGHTY PACIFIC

Draining away all its waters would reveal the Pacific's deep ocean trenches, its vast seafloor plains peppered with volcanoes, and its steep continental slopes.

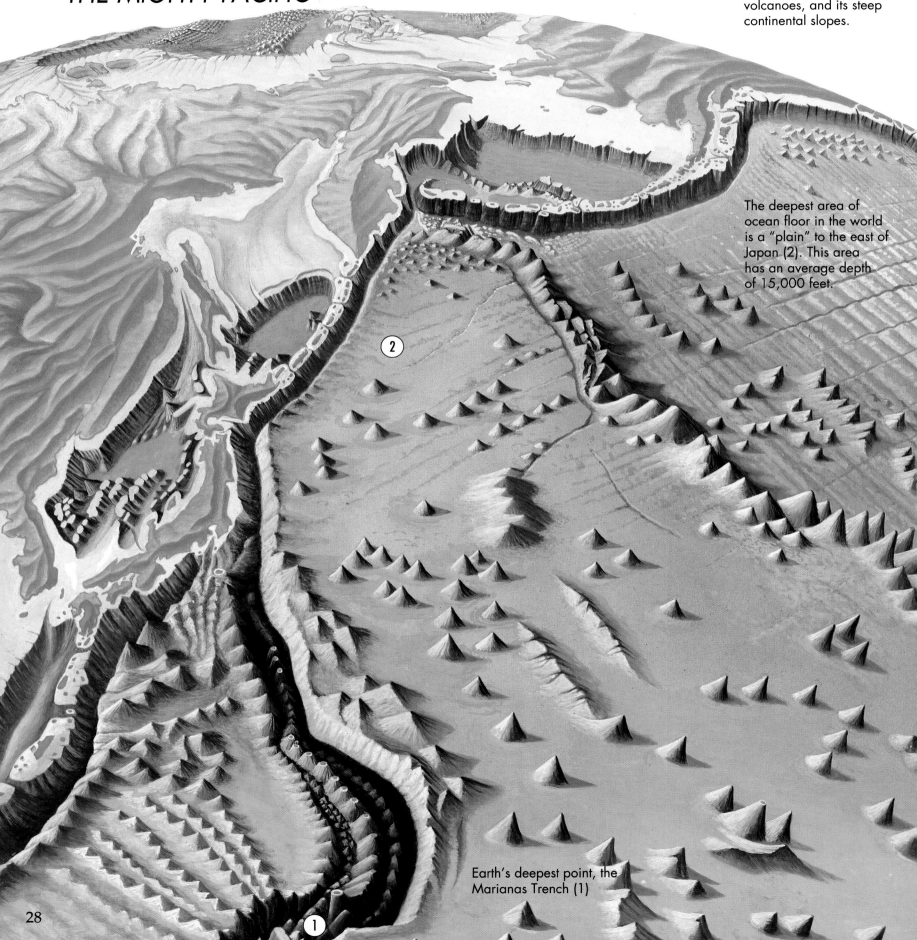

The deepest area of ocean floor in the world is a "plain" to the east of Japan (2). This area has an average depth of 15,000 feet.

Earth's deepest point, the Marianas Trench (1)

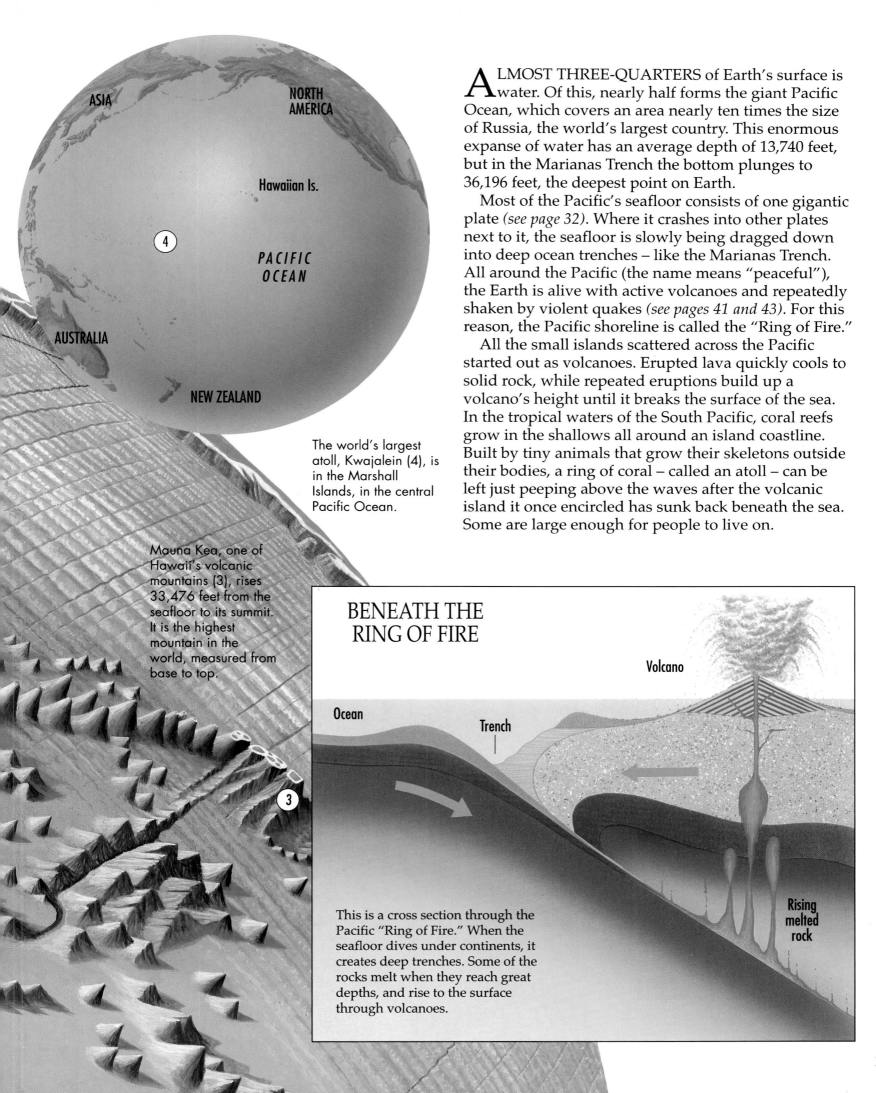

ASIA

NORTH AMERICA

Hawaiian Is.

(4)

PACIFIC OCEAN

AUSTRALIA

NEW ZEALAND

The world's largest atoll, Kwajalein (4), is in the Marshall Islands, in the central Pacific Ocean.

Mauna Kea, one of Hawaii's volcanic mountains (3), rises 33,476 feet from the seafloor to its summit. It is the highest mountain in the world, measured from base to top.

(3)

ALMOST THREE-QUARTERS of Earth's surface is water. Of this, nearly half forms the giant Pacific Ocean, which covers an area nearly ten times the size of Russia, the world's largest country. This enormous expanse of water has an average depth of 13,740 feet, but in the Marianas Trench the bottom plunges to 36,196 feet, the deepest point on Earth.

Most of the Pacific's seafloor consists of one gigantic plate *(see page 32)*. Where it crashes into other plates next to it, the seafloor is slowly being dragged down into deep ocean trenches – like the Marianas Trench. All around the Pacific (the name means "peaceful"), the Earth is alive with active volcanoes and repeatedly shaken by violent quakes *(see pages 41 and 43)*. For this reason, the Pacific shoreline is called the "Ring of Fire."

All the small islands scattered across the Pacific started out as volcanoes. Erupted lava quickly cools to solid rock, while repeated eruptions build up a volcano's height until it breaks the surface of the sea. In the tropical waters of the South Pacific, coral reefs grow in the shallows all around an island coastline. Built by tiny animals that grow their skeletons outside their bodies, a ring of coral – called an atoll – can be left just peeping above the waves after the volcanic island it once encircled has sunk back beneath the sea. Some are large enough for people to live on.

BENEATH THE RING OF FIRE

Volcano

Ocean

Trench

Rising melted rock

This is a cross section through the Pacific "Ring of Fire." When the seafloor dives under continents, it creates deep trenches. Some of the rocks melt when they reach great depths, and rise to the surface through volcanoes.

THE GREATEST MOUNTAIN RANGE
THE MID-OCEANIC RIDGE

HIDDEN BENEATH THE OCEANS is the world's greatest mountain range. Called the Mid-Oceanic Ridge, it starts in the Arctic Ocean and runs southward through the Atlantic before bending to the east, winding through the Indian and Pacific Oceans. It ends up near the west coast of North America after a journey of 40,400 miles. Some of its peaks are 13,700 feet high, but only a few break the ocean waters as tiny islands. Iceland has grown into a large island as volcanoes have erupted over and over again in the same place.

Beneath the Ridge, liquid rock or magma from the hot interior of Earth rises towards the surface. The seafloor bulges upward and cracks open. The magma, called lava as it bubbles out of the Earth's crust, seeps into the faults (long cracks) and pushes the rocks further apart. Every year, the faults running down the Ridge grow wider by an inch or so – about the speed that fingernails grow. Over millions of years, the ocean floor itself becomes wider and wider.

There are much longer faults cutting right across the Ridge at right-angles. These break up the seafloor into giant blocks, giving the Ridge a zigzag shape.

VOLCANOES UNDER THE SEA

Unlike the violent explosions of volcanoes like Santorini (*see page 40*), eruptions along the Ridge are fairly gentle. This is because the liquid rock flows easily. Along the center of the Ridge runs a rift valley, a strip of land between two parallel faults (*see page 35*). Most of the eruptions happen here, where lava finds its way to the seafloor through the faults.

Sometimes a volcano may erupt for long enough to reach the surface, where it forms an island in the ocean. Bouvet Island in the South Atlantic Ocean, the most remote island in the world – 1,050 miles from the nearest land – arose in this way.

Deep in the central valley that runs the length of the Mid-Oceanic Ridge, tall chimneys made of solidified minerals, called black smokers, blast hot smoke into the ocean waters. These smokers provide warmth and food for weird crabs, worms, and fishes found nowhere else on Earth.

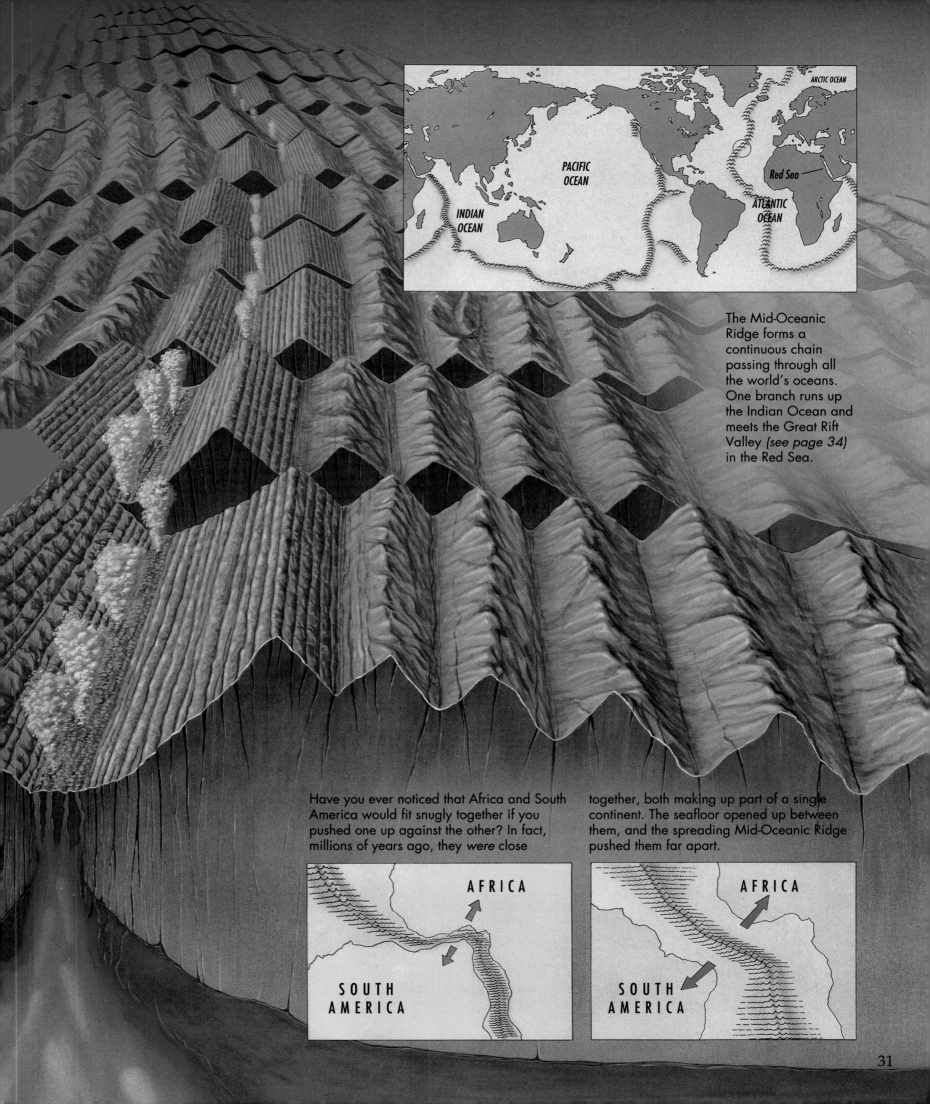

The Mid-Oceanic Ridge forms a continuous chain passing through all the world's oceans. One branch runs up the Indian Ocean and meets the Great Rift Valley *(see page 34)* in the Red Sea.

Have you ever noticed that Africa and South America would fit snugly together if you pushed one up against the other? In fact, millions of years ago, they *were* close together, both making up part of a single continent. The seafloor opened up between them, and the spreading Mid-Oceanic Ridge pushed them far apart.

ARCTIC OCEAN

PACIFIC OCEAN

INDIAN OCEAN

Red Sea

ATLANTIC OCEAN

AFRICA

SOUTH AMERICA

AFRICA

SOUTH AMERICA

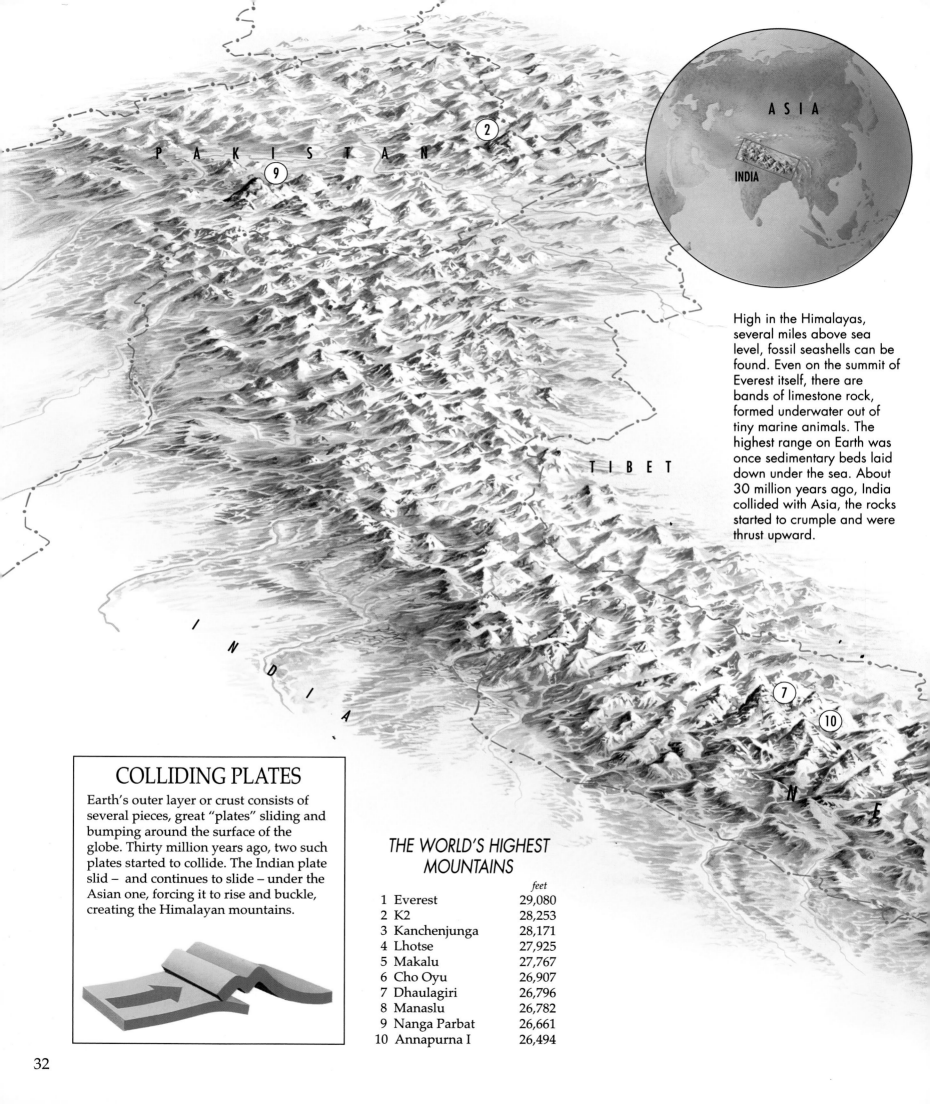

ASIA

INDIA

PAKISTAN

②

⑨

TIBET

INDIA

⑦

⑩

N

E

High in the Himalayas, several miles above sea level, fossil seashells can be found. Even on the summit of Everest itself, there are bands of limestone rock, formed underwater out of tiny marine animals. The highest range on Earth was once sedimentary beds laid down under the sea. About 30 million years ago, India collided with Asia, the rocks started to crumple and were thrust upward.

COLLIDING PLATES

Earth's outer layer or crust consists of several pieces, great "plates" sliding and bumping around the surface of the globe. Thirty million years ago, two such plates started to collide. The Indian plate slid – and continues to slide – under the Asian one, forcing it to rise and buckle, creating the Himalayan mountains.

THE WORLD'S HIGHEST MOUNTAINS

		feet
1	Everest	29,080
2	K2	28,253
3	Kanchenjunga	28,171
4	Lhotse	27,925
5	Makalu	27,767
6	Cho Oyu	26,907
7	Dhaulagiri	26,796
8	Manaslu	26,782
9	Nanga Parbat	26,661
10	Annapurna I	26,494

THE HIGHEST MOUNTAINS
THE TOWERING HIMALAYAS

THE HIMALAYA-KARAKORAM range is the greatest continental mountain range. It divides China in the north from Pakistan and India in the south. Nepal and Bhutan lie entirely within the Himalayas. The top ten summits, as well as about 90 percent of the world's 100 highest peaks, are found here. The highest peak of all (measured from sea level) is Mount Everest, which lies on the Tibet-Nepal border.

The Himalayas are getting still higher, as the forces that built up the mountain chain *(see panel, below left)* continue to grind on. Tibet, to the north, the world's highest and largest plateau, with an average height of 16,000 feet, was pushed up by the same processes. One day, some millions of years into the future, perhaps another peak may take Everest's place as the world's highest.

As the mountains "grow" they are attacked by wind, rain, frost, and ice. These forces of erosion produce the sharp, jagged peaks that make the mountain scenery so spectacular. Eventually, these peaks will be worn down to become low, rounded hills.

The Himalayan glaciers and rivers have cut the world's deepest gorges, those of the Kali Gandak (between Annapurna and Dhaulagiri) and the Arun (east of Everest). Both plunge more than 3 miles below neighboring summits.

The Everest and Lhotse peaks, first and fourth highest above sea level, form part of the same mountain massif. In this illustration *(right)*, Everest is in the left foreground, Lhotse to its right.

Named after Colonel Sir George Everest (1790-1866), Surveyor-General of India, Everest is known to the Tibetans as Qomolangma and to the Nepalese as Sagarmatha.

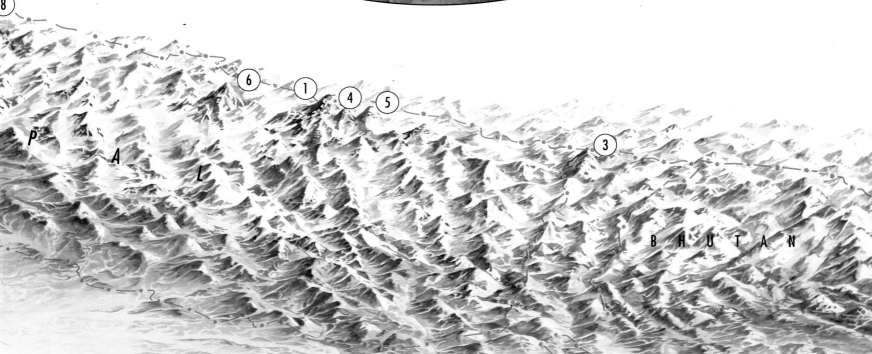

THE GREATEST RIFT
AND THE LONGEST RIVER

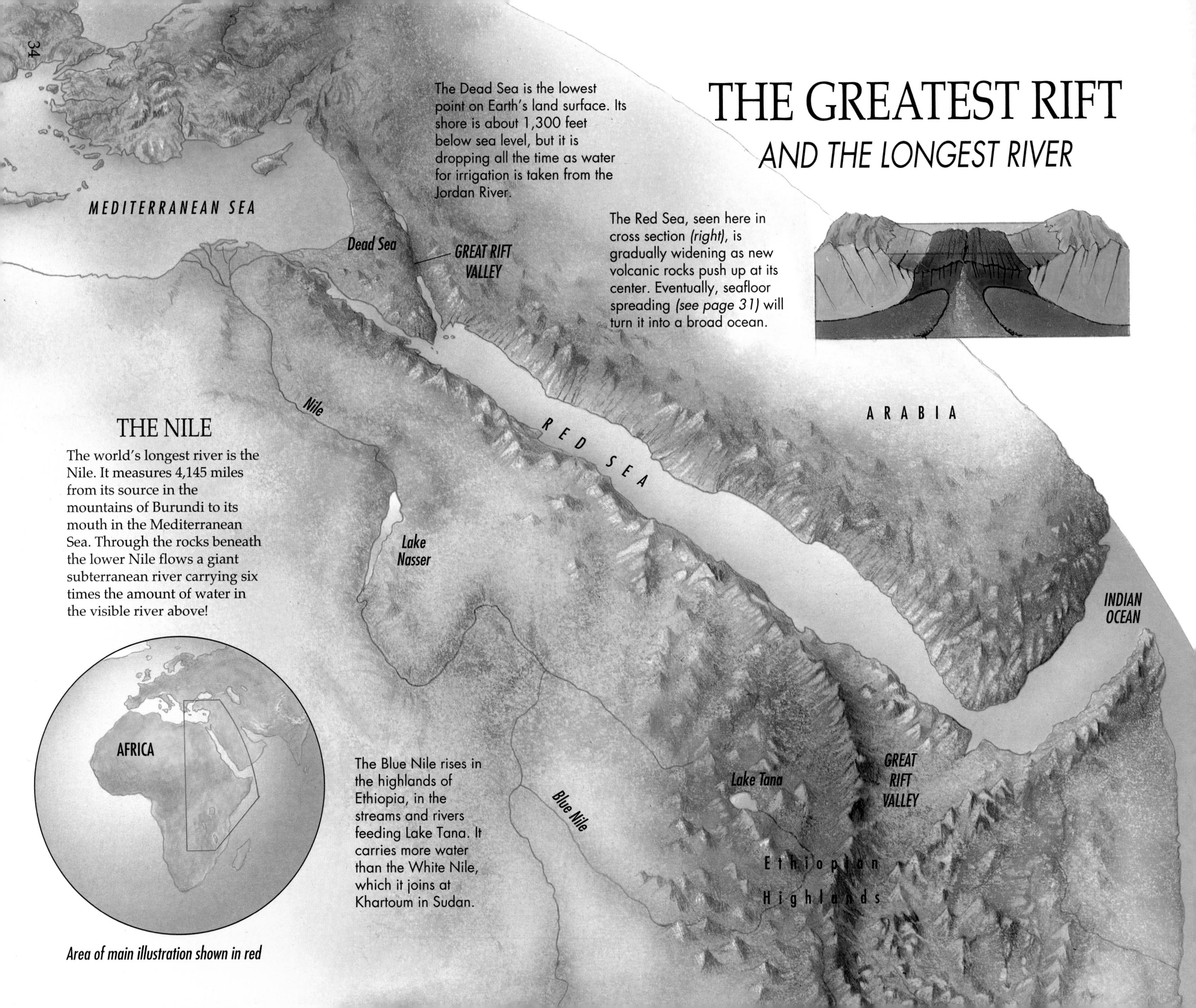

The Dead Sea is the lowest point on Earth's land surface. Its shore is about 1,300 feet below sea level, but it is dropping all the time as water for irrigation is taken from the Jordan River.

The Red Sea, seen here in cross section (right), is gradually widening as new volcanic rocks push up at its center. Eventually, seafloor spreading (see page 31) will turn it into a broad ocean.

THE NILE

The world's longest river is the Nile. It measures 4,145 miles from its source in the mountains of Burundi to its mouth in the Mediterranean Sea. Through the rocks beneath the lower Nile flows a giant subterranean river carrying six times the amount of water in the visible river above!

The Blue Nile rises in the highlands of Ethiopia, in the streams and rivers feeding Lake Tana. It carries more water than the White Nile, which it joins at Khartoum in Sudan.

ARABIA

INDIAN OCEAN

GREAT RIFT VALLEY

Lake Tana

Ethiopian Highlands

RED SEA

Blue Nile

GREAT RIFT VALLEY

Dead Sea

Nile

Lake Nasser

MEDITERRANEAN SEA

AFRICA

Area of main illustration shown in red

Lake Turkana

GREAT RIFT
VALLEY

Kilimanjaro

Lake
Malawi

Lake
Victoria

Source of
the Nile

GREAT RIFT
VALLEY

White Nile

Lake
Tanganyika

This is a view of the Great Rift Valley in East Africa (*above*). It was here that, scientists believe, our human ancestors first appeared.

EAST AFRICA SPLITS APART

THE GREAT RIFT VALLEY cuts a path through East Africa. Two branches run northward on either side of Lake Victoria. They meet and the valley runs on through Ethiopia, the Red Sea, the Dead Sea, finally ending up in southern Syria. The greatest cleft in Earth's surface above sea level (the rift in the Mid-Oceanic Ridge is longer, *see page 30*), the Great Rift Valley runs for 3,975 miles.

A giant block of country, hundreds of miles wide in places, has, over millions of years, dropped down between gigantic faults, deep cracks in Earth's crust. On each side, high cliffs tower above the valley floor. Volcanoes spew out lava, red-hot liquid rock from deep inside Earth that has forced its way up through the cracks (*see page 41*). One day, an arm of the Indian Ocean might fill the valley, turning East Africa into an island. This has already happened in a stretch of the valley to the north, now lying beneath the Red Sea.

The source of the White Nile (the longest branch) lies south of the Equator in Burundi, in mountains bordering Lake Tanganyika, the world's second deepest lake (greatest depth 4,823 feet). From there it flows into and out of Lake Victoria on its long journey to the coast.

THE LARGEST GORGE
THE SPECTACULAR GRAND CANYON

THE GRAND CANYON in Arizona is the largest gorge on Earth. It twists and turns across dry, rocky land for 218 miles. Averaging 10 miles in width and 1 mile in depth, this vast chasm has been carved by the savage force of the Colorado River and its tributaries. And the process continues today. On a normal day, the river carries off about half a million tons of sediment (mud and gravel pulled along by the current). When it is in flood, large boulders are swept downstream.

The Colorado has been at work for millions of years, cutting downward as the land beneath it has gradually risen higher and higher. Over a period of about 5 million years, the land has increased in height by more than 3,900 feet. In the meantime, the Colorado has carved through to rocks buried deep below the ground that once formed the lower slopes of ancient mountains standing 53,000 feet high – almost twice the height of Mount Everest.

A cross section through the Grand Canyon, showing the different layers of rock.

Colorado R.

HISTORY IN THE ROCKS

As near a complete display of Earth's history as you are ever likely to see is revealed on the slopes of the Grand Canyon. As the land lay under the sea for hundreds of millions of years, coatings of sediment have been laid down, one on top of the other like blankets on a bed. Each layer turned to stone, the different types reflecting the climates and life-forms of their age. The oldest rocks of all in the Grand Canyon, found in the deepest part of the gorge, are 1.7 billion years old.

An aerial view *(below)* of the Grand Canyon, and its location in Arizona.

Colorado River

USA

The Colorado River once flowed gently across the desert (1). Then, between 10 and 12 million years ago, the land beneath it began to rise (2). It did so only by about 0.01 inch a year, but the river kept pace with it, cutting a deeper channel to preserve its downward course to the sea. It carved through different layers of rock, some hard, some soft. The soft rock wore away more easily than the hard, which today stands out as vertical cliff faces (3).

This is a bird's-eye view of the Grand Canyon, showing the arid terrain and characteristic step-like slopes. The Grand Canyon exists only because the climate has always been extremely dry. (The Colorado River's water comes from the distant Rockies.) If there had been more rainfall, most of the softer, upper layers of rock would have been washed away.

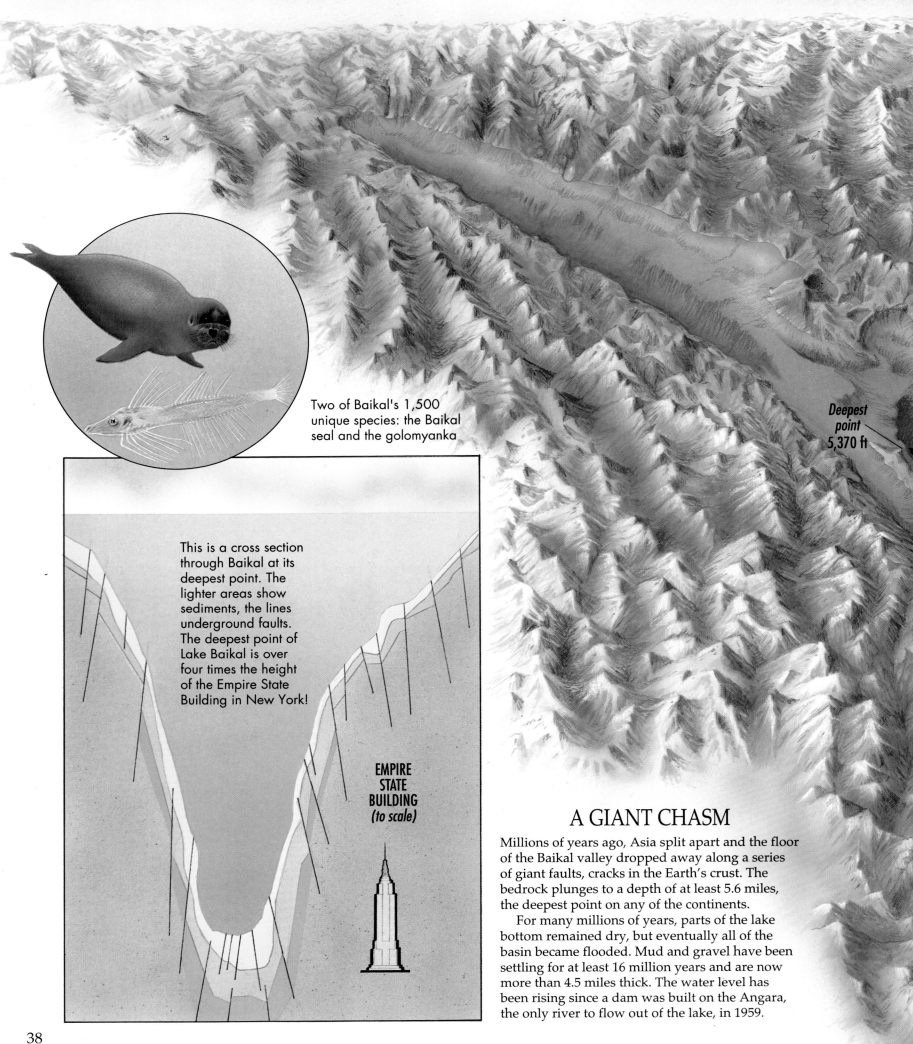

Two of Baikal's 1,500 unique species: the Baikal seal and the golomyanka

This is a cross section through Baikal at its deepest point. The lighter areas show sediments, the lines underground faults. The deepest point of Lake Baikal is over four times the height of the Empire State Building in New York!

EMPIRE
STATE
BUILDING
(to scale)

Deepest point 5,370 ft

A GIANT CHASM

Millions of years ago, Asia split apart and the floor of the Baikal valley dropped away along a series of giant faults, cracks in the Earth's crust. The bedrock plunges to a depth of at least 5.6 miles, the deepest point on any of the continents.

For many millions of years, parts of the lake bottom remained dry, but eventually all of the basin became flooded. Mud and gravel have been settling for at least 16 million years and are now more than 4.5 miles thick. The water level has been rising since a dam was built on the Angara, the only river to flow out of the lake, in 1959.

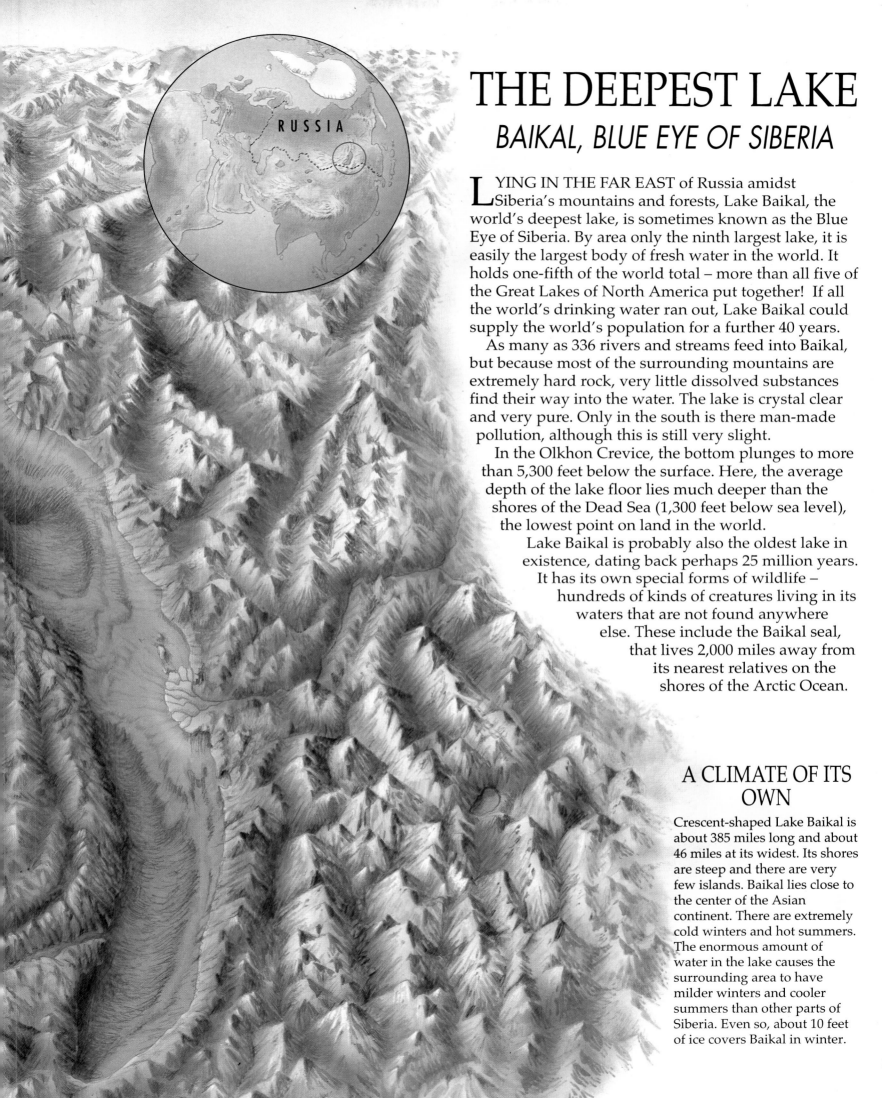

THE DEEPEST LAKE
BAIKAL, BLUE EYE OF SIBERIA

LYING IN THE FAR EAST of Russia amidst Siberia's mountains and forests, Lake Baikal, the world's deepest lake, is sometimes known as the Blue Eye of Siberia. By area only the ninth largest lake, it is easily the largest body of fresh water in the world. It holds one-fifth of the world total – more than all five of the Great Lakes of North America put together! If all the world's drinking water ran out, Lake Baikal could supply the world's population for a further 40 years.

As many as 336 rivers and streams feed into Baikal, but because most of the surrounding mountains are extremely hard rock, very little dissolved substances find their way into the water. The lake is crystal clear and very pure. Only in the south is there man-made pollution, although this is still very slight.

In the Olkhon Crevice, the bottom plunges to more than 5,300 feet below the surface. Here, the average depth of the lake floor lies much deeper than the shores of the Dead Sea (1,300 feet below sea level), the lowest point on land in the world.

Lake Baikal is probably also the oldest lake in existence, dating back perhaps 25 million years. It has its own special forms of wildlife – hundreds of kinds of creatures living in its waters that are not found anywhere else. These include the Baikal seal, that lives 2,000 miles away from its nearest relatives on the shores of the Arctic Ocean.

A CLIMATE OF ITS OWN

Crescent-shaped Lake Baikal is about 385 miles long and about 46 miles at its widest. Its shores are steep and there are very few islands. Baikal lies close to the center of the Asian continent. There are extremely cold winters and hot summers. The enormous amount of water in the lake causes the surrounding area to have milder winters and cooler summers than other parts of Siberia. Even so, about 10 feet of ice covers Baikal in winter.

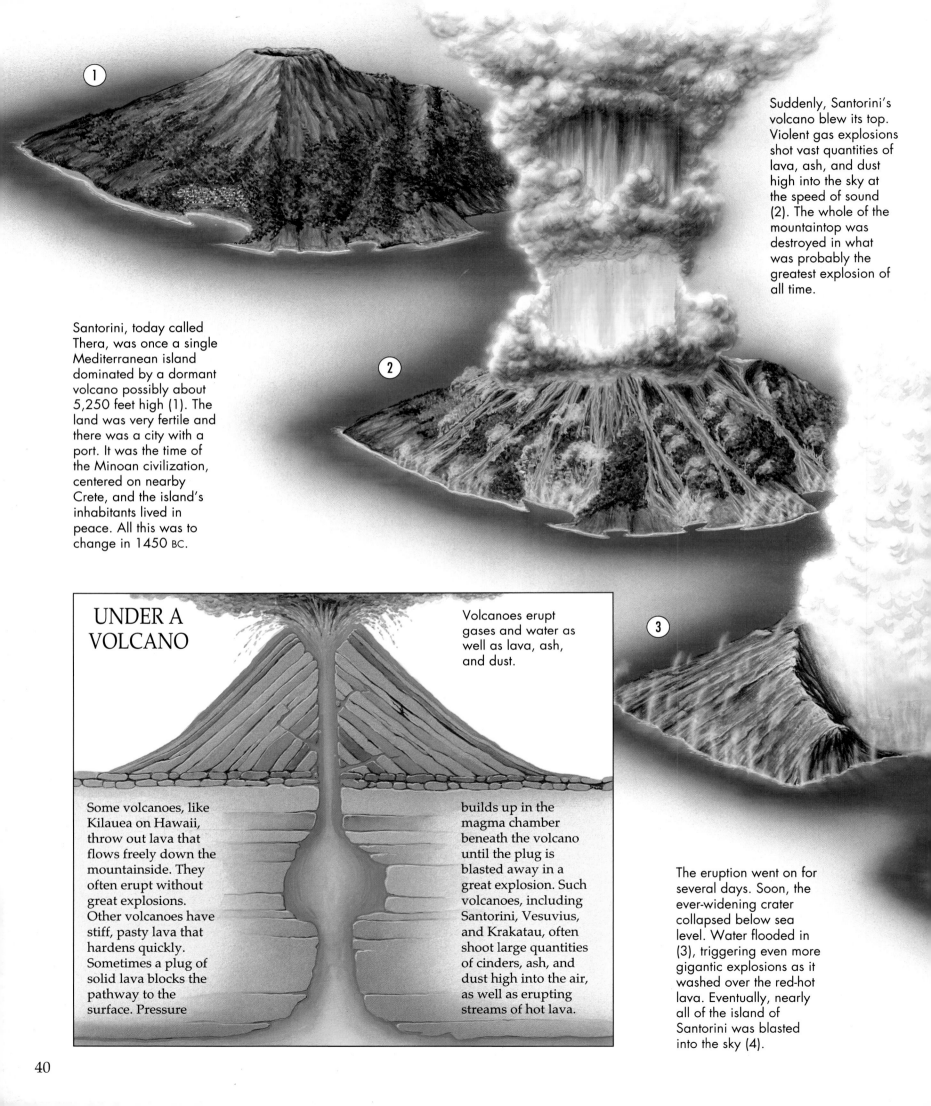

Santorini, today called Thera, was once a single Mediterranean island dominated by a dormant volcano possibly about 5,250 feet high (1). The land was very fertile and there was a city with a port. It was the time of the Minoan civilization, centered on nearby Crete, and the island's inhabitants lived in peace. All this was to change in 1450 BC.

Suddenly, Santorini's volcano blew its top. Violent gas explosions shot vast quantities of lava, ash, and dust high into the sky at the speed of sound (2). The whole of the mountaintop was destroyed in what was probably the greatest explosion of all time.

UNDER A VOLCANO

Volcanoes erupt gases and water as well as lava, ash, and dust.

Some volcanoes, like Kilauea on Hawaii, throw out lava that flows freely down the mountainside. They often erupt without great explosions. Other volcanoes have stiff, pasty lava that hardens quickly. Sometimes a plug of solid lava blocks the pathway to the surface. Pressure builds up in the magma chamber beneath the volcano until the plug is blasted away in a great explosion. Such volcanoes, including Santorini, Vesuvius, and Krakatau, often shoot large quantities of cinders, ash, and dust high into the air, as well as erupting streams of hot lava.

The eruption went on for several days. Soon, the ever-widening crater collapsed below sea level. Water flooded in (3), triggering even more gigantic explosions as it washed over the red-hot lava. Eventually, nearly all of the island of Santorini was blasted into the sky (4).

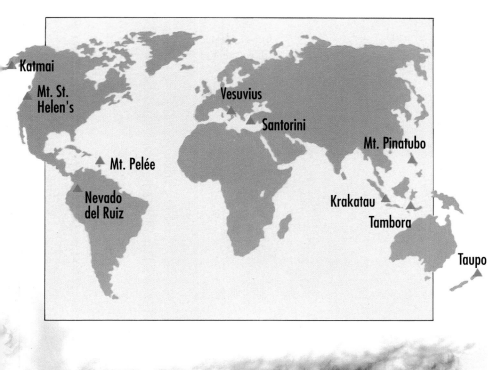

THE GREATEST EXPLOSION
A VOLCANO BLOWS

VOLCANIC ERUPTIONS, the most powerful explosions on Earth, are incredibly destructive. During the eruption of Krakatau in 1883, about 5 cubic miles of rock (nearly the entire exploded mountain) was blasted high into the air. The noise of the explosion, the greatest in modern times, was heard 3,000 miles away in India, China, and Australia. Probably three times as much was ejected during the eruption of Santorini around 1450 BC.

Greater still was the eruption of Tambora, on the island of Sumbawa in Indonesia in 1815, when about 40 cubic miles was blasted away. Pulverized rock was hurled at least 30 miles high into Earth's atmosphere. Dust blankets drifted around the globe, shutting off the Sun's rays and causing temperatures to drop. The year after the Tambora eruption, 1816, was known as "Eighteen hundred and froze to death."

FAMOUS VOLCANIC ERUPTIONS OF THE PAST

	Date
Santorini, Greece	c. 1450 BC
Vesuvius, Italy	AD 79
Taupo, New Zealand	c. AD 150
Tambora, Sumbawa	1815
Krakatau, Java	1883
Mont Pelée, Martinique	1902
Katmai, Alaska	1912
Mt. St. Helen's	1980
Nevado del Ruiz, Colombia	1985
Mt. Pinatubo, Philippines	1991

(Volcanoes located on map, above left)

All that remains today is a ring of five small islands (5). One day the volcanic islands in the center of the bay may build up into a new, large volcano.

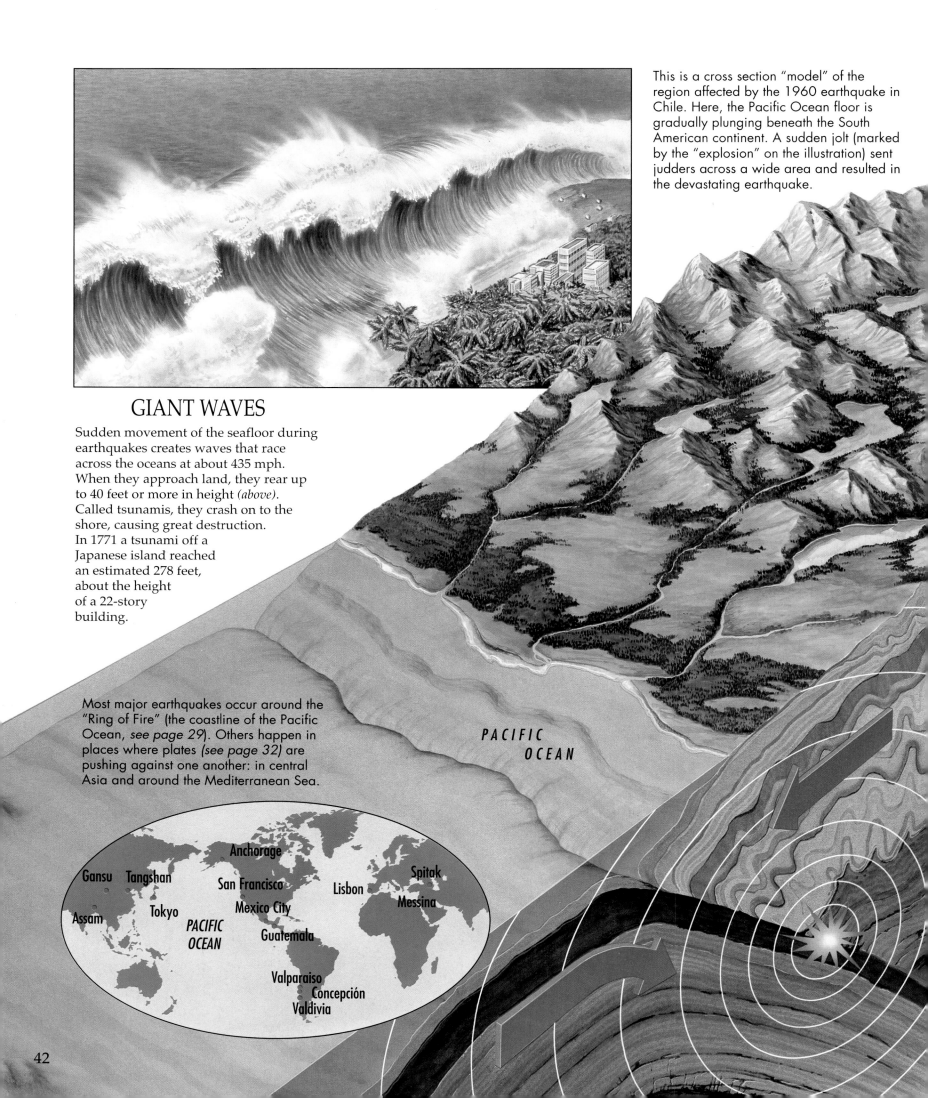

This is a cross section "model" of the region affected by the 1960 earthquake in Chile. Here, the Pacific Ocean floor is gradually plunging beneath the South American continent. A sudden jolt (marked by the "explosion" on the illustration) sent judders across a wide area and resulted in the devastating earthquake.

GIANT WAVES

Sudden movement of the seafloor during earthquakes creates waves that race across the oceans at about 435 mph. When they approach land, they rear up to 40 feet or more in height *(above)*. Called tsunamis, they crash on to the shore, causing great destruction. In 1771 a tsunami off a Japanese island reached an estimated 278 feet, about the height of a 22-story building.

Most major earthquakes occur around the "Ring of Fire" (the coastline of the Pacific Ocean, *see page 29*). Others happen in places where plates *(see page 32)* are pushing against one another: in central Asia and around the Mediterranean Sea.

PACIFIC OCEAN

Anchorage
Gansu   Tangshan
Spitak
San Francisco
Lisbon
Tokyo   Messina
Assam
Mexico City
PACIFIC OCEAN
Guatemala
Valparaiso
Concepción
Valdivia

THE GREATEST EARTHQUAKE
THE GREAT CHILEAN QUAKE

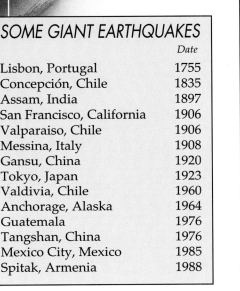

ON MAY 22, 1960, a giant fault, some 370 miles long, deep beneath the ground in western South America suddenly slipped about 65 feet. A vast area of land in southern Chile was violently shaken for nearly four minutes. In the town of Valdivia, buildings were reduced to rubble. The ocean floor dropped away, causing the sea to rush away from the shore, then return in several giant waves, 33 feet high, which smashed into the shore and flung ships far inland. It was the most powerful earthquake ever recorded.

A smaller tremor about ten minutes earlier had sent most people rushing into the streets. This saved many lives when the main quake came, although around 5,000 people were killed. This is a small number when compared with the most deadly earthquake of recent times. A quake which occurred on July 28, 1976, killed about 750,000 people in Tangshan, China.

The force of earthquakes is often described on the Richter scale: The larger the number, the worse the earthquake. The Chilean earthquake measured 9.5, and the Tangshan one, 7.8.

In the Chilean earthquake over 400,000 houses were destroyed in minutes as the ground rocked beneath them. Giant cracks and holes opened up in the surface and split the foundations of buildings. Afterward, Valdivia and a vast area of the surrounding countryside had sunk by nearly 7 feet.

SOME GIANT EARTHQUAKES

	Date
Lisbon, Portugal	1755
Concepción, Chile	1835
Assam, India	1897
San Francisco, California	1906
Valparaiso, Chile	1906
Messina, Italy	1908
Gansu, China	1920
Tokyo, Japan	1923
Valdivia, Chile	1960
Anchorage, Alaska	1964
Guatemala	1976
Tangshan, China	1976
Mexico City, Mexico	1985
Spitak, Armenia	1988

THE MOST POWERFUL STORM

THE DEADLY TORNADO

THE ATMOSPHERE, the envelope of gases that surrounds the globe, can be extremely violent. Hurricanes (otherwise known as cyclones or typhoons) are destructive circular storms where wind speeds sometimes reach 180 mph.

Even more powerful, although the damage they cause usually only affects a narrow strip of land, are tornadoes. A twisting column of air with wind speeds of more than 250 mph (the highest wind speeds on Earth), a tornado completely destroys everything in its path.

Ordinary thunderstorms are also incredibly powerful. Every day around the world there are 44,000 thunderstorms; every second there are 100 lightning strikes, each with a force of 100 million volts or more. The amount of power generated daily by such storms would be enough to supply the whole of the United States – twice over!

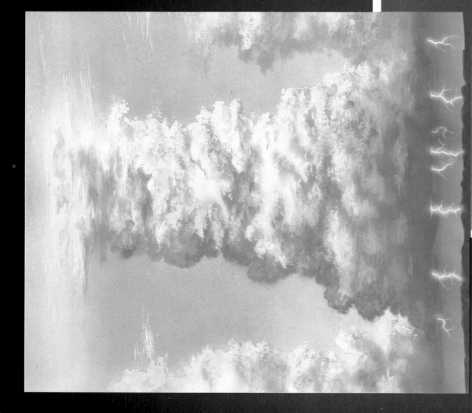

The tallest clouds are giant cumulonimbus *(above)*, which, in the tropics, may reach 12 miles into the sky from their bases at around 1,600 feet above ground level. Air currents shoot up inside them at 100 mph or more, and can keep hailstones weighing as much as 1 pound suspended in the air! Clusters of cumulonimbus clouds can produce thunderstorms and torrential rain, and may, in some parts of the world, spawn destructive tornadoes.

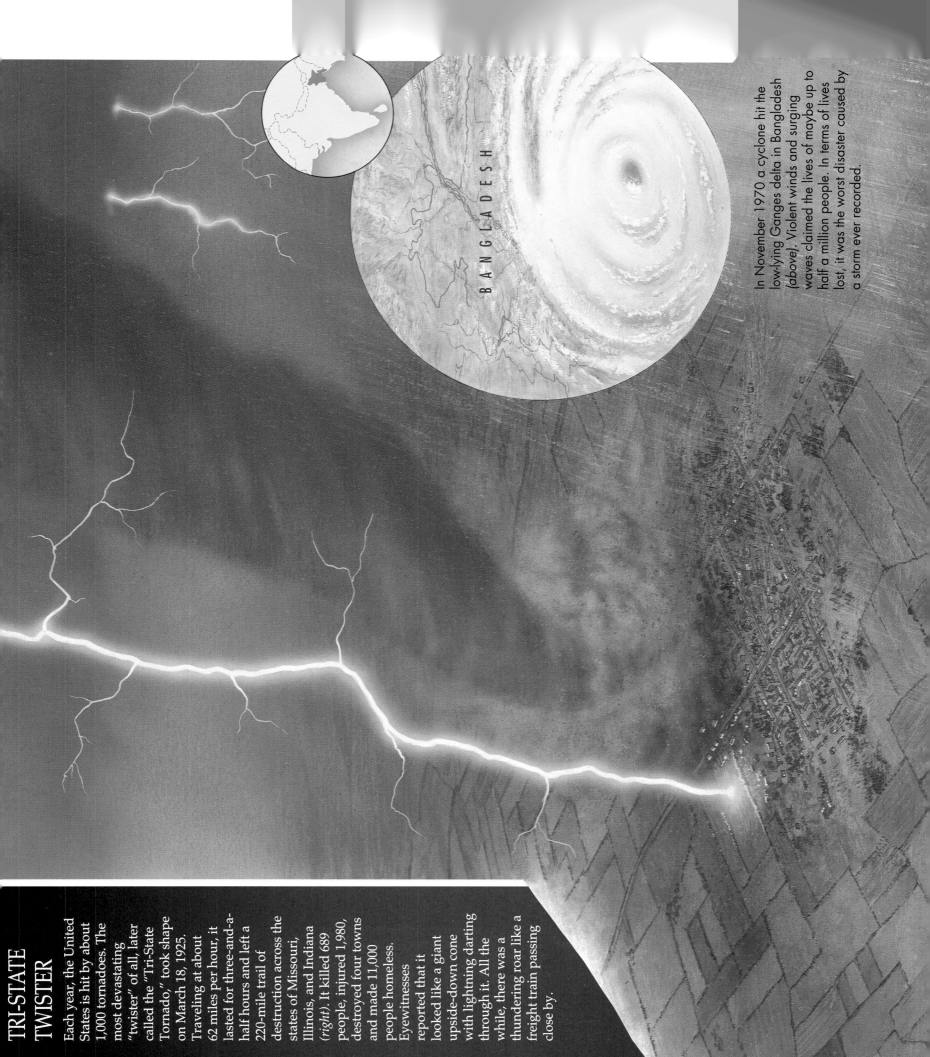

TRI-STATE TWISTER

Each year, the United States is hit by about 1,000 tornadoes. The most devastating "twister" of all, later called the "Tri-State Tornado," took shape on March 18, 1925. Traveling at about 62 miles per hour, it lasted for three-and-a-half hours and left a 220-mile trail of destruction across the states of Missouri, Illinois, and Indiana (*right*). It killed 689 people, injured 1,980, destroyed four towns and made 11,000 people homeless. Eyewitnesses reported that it looked like a giant upside-down cone with lightning darting through it. All the while, there was a thundering roar like a freight train passing close by.

BANGLADESH

In November 1970 a cyclone hit the low-lying Ganges delta in Bangladesh (*above*). Violent winds and surging waves claimed the lives of maybe up to half a million people. In terms of lives lost, it was the worst disaster caused by a storm ever recorded.

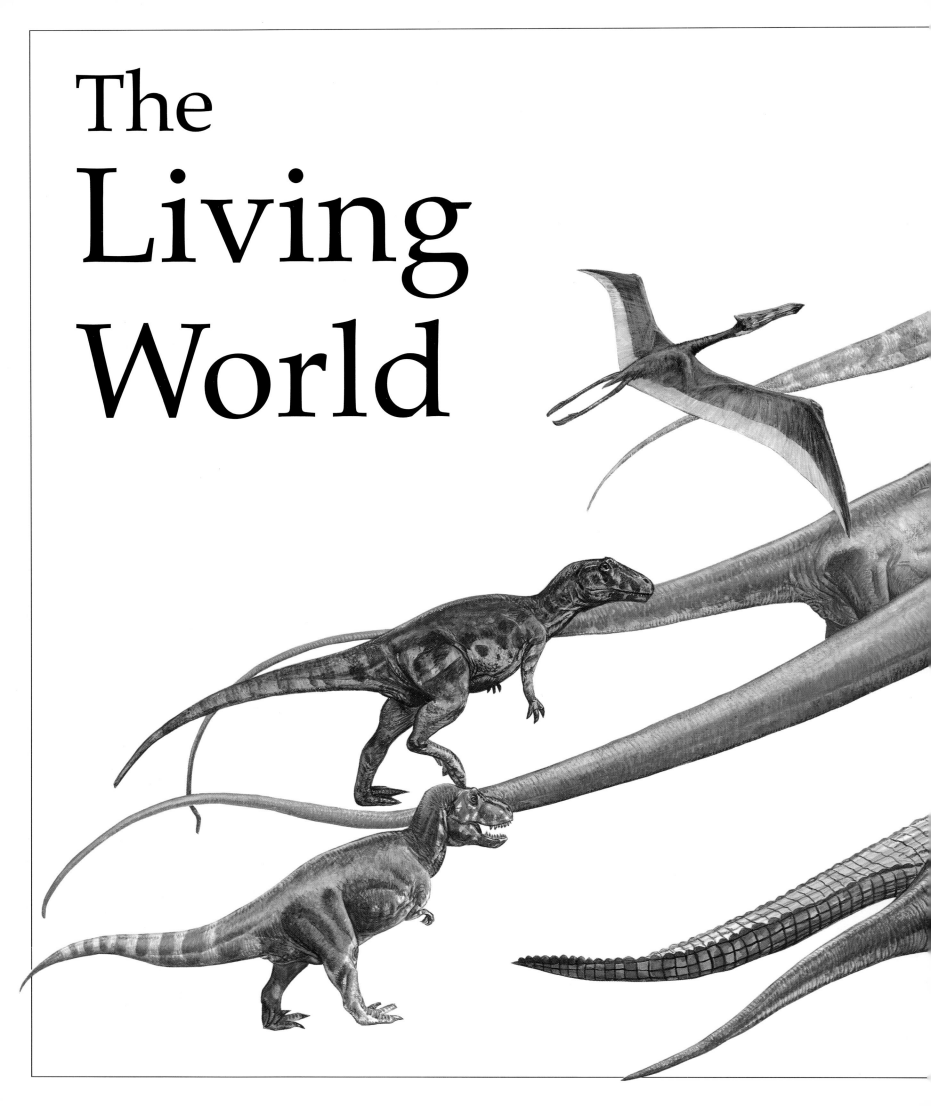

The Living World

INTRODUCTION

A T LEAST 275,000 KINDS OF FLOWERING PLANTS are alive today. There may be as many as 10 million kinds of animals. Thousands, perhaps millions more, died out long ago. Among these teeming numbers, a few stand out from the rest because they are, or were, the largest or smallest, or special in some other way. Have you ever wondered – if you could hold a competition among all living things – which ones would win the prizes?

Here you can find out many of the answers. You will discover that the heaviest whale, the blue whale, can weigh as much as 1,800 people, yet it would take more than a dozen of these giant animals to outweigh a giant sequoia tree, the heaviest living thing on Earth. You will come across a living tree older than the pyramids of Egypt, and a mammal that can dive almost two miles beneath the surface of the ocean.

Here are the greatest and smallest dinosaurs, the biggest-ever land mammals, the tallest animals that ever lived, and the tallest and shortest peoples. Here, too, are the speediest creatures on Earth, the animals that make the longest journeys around the world, and those that live to the greatest ages.

Welcome to the record breakers of the living world!

Arandaspis, one of the first known fish, lived 480 million years ago. It had no fins and could not shut its mouth.

Eusthenopteron was one of the first fish to breathe with lungs and use fins as legs to help it move about.

The small reptile *Euparkeria (right)* might have been the first animal to walk on two feet. It lived in southern Africa 240 million years ago.

Waterproof skin and waterproof eggs made *Hylonomus (above)* at home on land. This small reptile, one of the earliest known, lived 320 million years ago in Canada.

Eoraptor was one of the first dinosaurs, a two-legged flesh-eating beast no bigger than a large dog. *Eoraptor* hunted small reptiles. It lived 228 million years ago in Argentina.

THE EARLIEST ANIMALS
FIRST OF THEIR KIND

ALL ANIMALS have prehistoric ancestors whose fossil remains are found in ancient rocks. Scientists studying these fossils can work out when each living group of animals appeared. Over the thousands of millions of years since life began, the fossil history tells us, animals have – very gradually – changed: For example, they have grown a fin or a tail, developed wings, or lost teeth. We call this process *evolution*. When a new kind of animal has evolved, an older one may die out, or become extinct. Jellyfishlike creatures, among the very earliest fossils, appeared about 600 million years ago. Fifty million years later, the seas teemed with shellfish, worms, and animals with jointed legs. Later still, eel-like beasts with bony teeth appeared. These were probably the ancestors of fish, the earliest-known backboned animals.

By about 400 million years ago, fish with lungs and fleshy fins began to move around on land. Forty million years on, these animals had evolved into the first four-legged backboned creatures, the amphibians. These animals could live on land but they returned to the water to lay their eggs. It took a further 80 million years for the first backboned animals to live and breed on land – the reptiles – to evolve.

The illustrations are not drawn to scale

Ichthyostega (right) was one of the earliest four-legged animals. This amphibian crawled through warm, swampy forests that existed in Greenland about 360 million years ago.

One of the earliest-known birds was *Archaeopteryx*. This crow-sized creature had feathered wings and was probably able to fly. But its teeth, claws, and bony tail were like those of a small flesh-eating dinosaur. *Archaeopteryx* lived in Germany about 150 million years ago.

THE FIRST MAMMAL

A mammal is an animal whose females produce milk to feed their young. The earliest-known mammals were tiny shrew-like creatures such as *Kuehneotherium* and *Megazostrodon*. They lived 220 million years ago in the shadows of the early dinosaurs, probably hunting for insects by night. *Megazostrodon* lived in southern Africa, while its relative *Kuehneotherium* lived in Britain.

THE GREATEST DINOSAURS
LARGEST-EVER LAND ANIMALS

MOST DINOSAURS are known only from a few bones, so experts have had to guess just how big these creatures were. As for the question of which was the biggest, they disagree. It depends on whether the measure is height, length, or weight. The only fact upon which everyone is agreed is that the dinosaurs were certainly the largest land animals that ever lived.

The heaviest and tallest dinosaur known from a complete skeleton was *Brachiosaurus* ("arm lizard"). A plump *Brachiosaurus* might have weighed more than 44 tons, or as much as eight African elephants.

Mamenchisaurus ("Mamen Brook lizard") had the longest neck of all dinosaurs but the longest dinosaur was *Seismosaurus* ("earth-shaking lizard"), perhaps longer than two tennis courts laid end to end! With its snaky neck, whiplike tail and hollowed-out spinal bones, *Seismosaurus* was probably lighter than some shorter, but more heavily built, dinosaurs.

All these dinosaurs were plant-eaters. The flesh-eaters, which needed to be quick on their feet, were smaller. Even so, the largest of them, *Giganotosaurus* grew to be heavier than an elephant.

The illustrations are approximately to scale

PARADE OF THE GIANTS

If all the reptile record holders were gathered together, this *(below)* is how they would compare in size. All those shown here, pterosaurs, crocodiles, and dinosaurs, belonged to the same group, called archosaurs ("ruling reptiles").

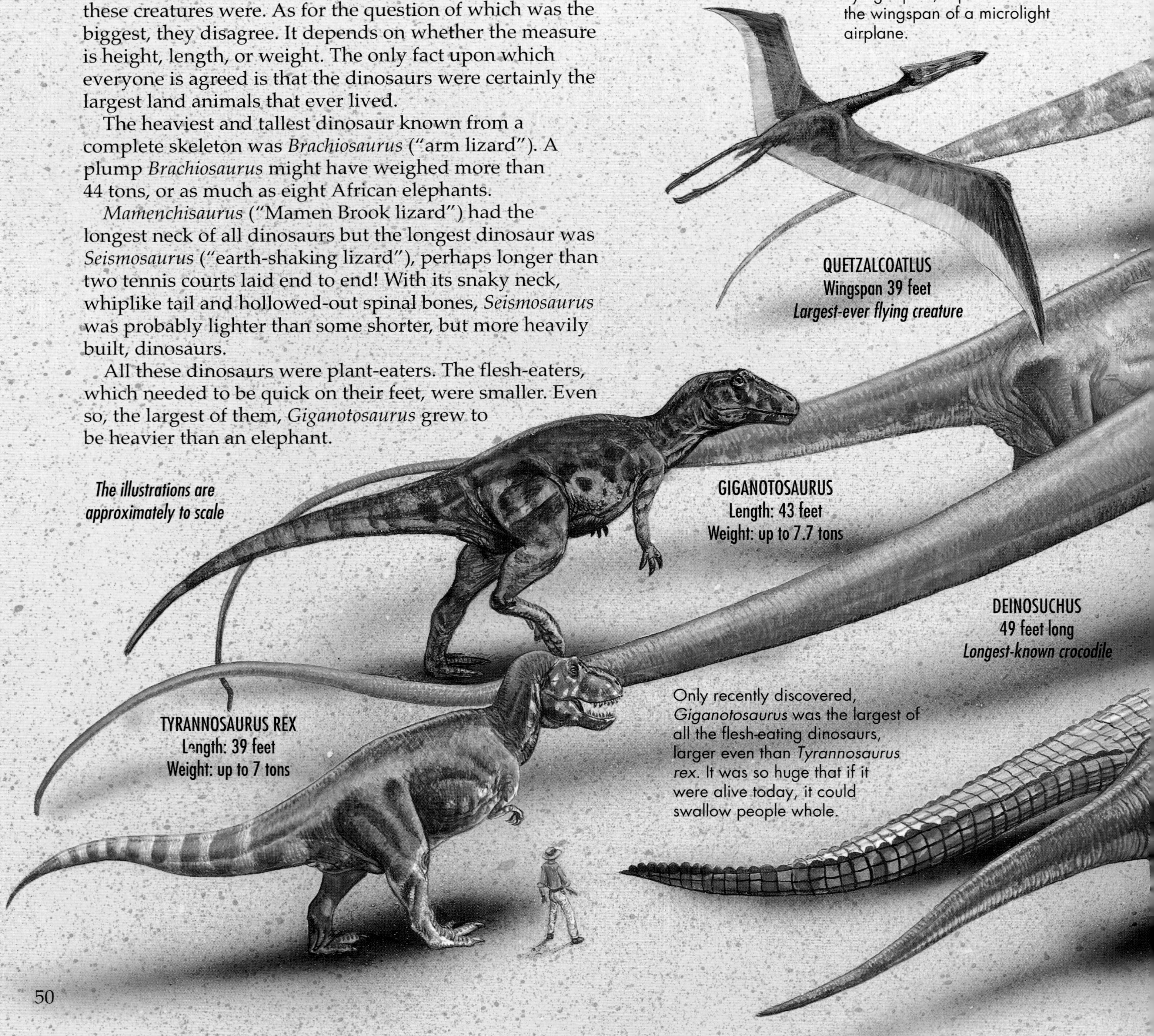

Quetzalcoatlus ("feathered serpent") was a skin-winged flying reptile, a pterosaur with the wingspan of a microlight airplane.

QUETZALCOATLUS
Wingspan 39 feet
Largest-ever flying creature

GIGANOTOSAURUS
Length: 43 feet
Weight: up to 7.7 tons

DEINOSUCHUS
49 feet long
Longest-known crocodile

Only recently discovered, *Giganotosaurus* was the largest of all the flesh-eating dinosaurs, larger even than *Tyrannosaurus rex*. It was so huge that if it were alive today, it could swallow people whole.

TYRANNOSAURUS REX
Length: 39 feet
Weight: up to 7 tons

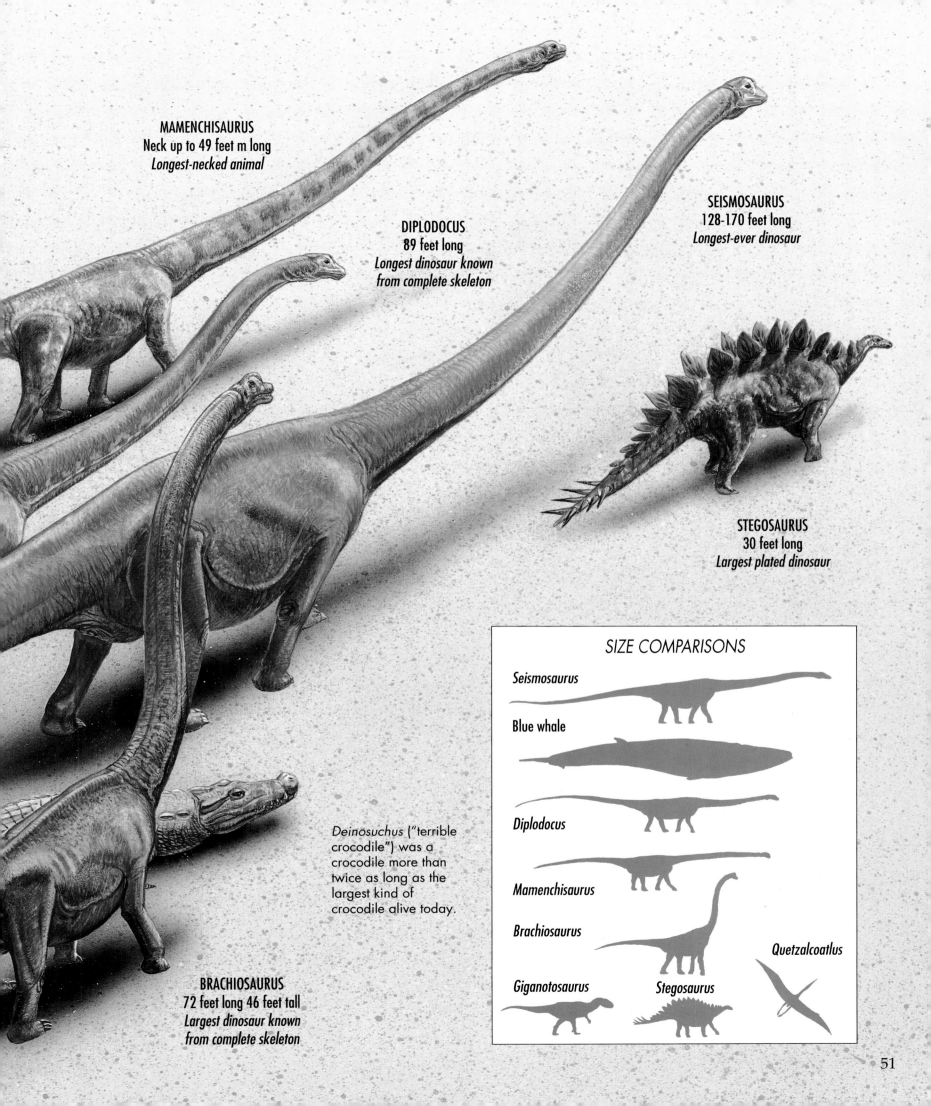

MAMENCHISAURUS
Neck up to 49 feet m long
Longest-necked animal

DIPLODOCUS
89 feet long
*Longest dinosaur known
from complete skeleton*

SEISMOSAURUS
128-170 feet long
Longest-ever dinosaur

STEGOSAURUS
30 feet long
Largest plated dinosaur

Deinosuchus ("terrible crocodile") was a crocodile more than twice as long as the largest kind of crocodile alive today.

BRACHIOSAURUS
72 feet long 46 feet tall
*Largest dinosaur known
from complete skeleton*

SIZE COMPARISONS

Seismosaurus

Blue whale

Diplodocus

Mamenchisaurus

Brachiosaurus

Quetzalcoatlus

Giganotosaurus

Stegosaurus

THE TALLEST ANIMALS THAT EVER LIVED

THE LONG-NECKED SAUROPODS

THE TALLEST ANIMAL in the world today is the giraffe. One hundred and fifty million years ago, it would have been dwarfed by the towering, long-necked sauropod dinosaurs, standing more than three times its height. A museum skeleton of *Brachiosaurus*, one of the tallest of all, shows that this high-shouldered sauropod could have peeped into a fifth-floor window if it were alive today.

Some sauropods had longer necks than *Brachiosaurus*. The longest-necked animal we know existed was *Mamenchisaurus*. One kind had a neck more than twice as long as a giraffe is tall. If a *Mamenchisaurus* reared up on its hind legs, it might have been able to reach up higher than *Brachiosaurus*.

Scientists once thought sauropods wallowed in lakes, using their necks to keep their heads above water. We now know that water pressing on their necks and chests would have suffocated them. Probably, sauropods lived on land, lowering their heads to crop ferns and lifting them to nibble leafy branches out of reach of other animals. *Mamenchisaurus* would have enjoyed the very highest leaves all to itself!

The heart of one of these skyscraper dinosaurs would have had to be immensely powerful to pump blood all the way up to its brain. Perhaps, some

HIGH BROWSERS

If the tallest creatures the world has ever seen came together, which animal could reach the highest? (Compare them with the human being and the giraffe, the tallest animal alive today.) *Indricotherium* (*see page 56*), an Asian rhinoceros, was the tallest prehistoric mammal. *Dinornis* ("terrible bird") may have been the tallest-ever bird. It died out in New Zealand only about 400 years ago. Both these animals, if they had lived in the age of the dinosaurs, would have walked in the shadows of the giant sauropods. *Seismosaurus* and *Brachiosaurus* lived in North America, *Mamenchisaurus* in Asia.

BRACHIOSAURUS 46 ft
Tallest animal known from a complete skeleton

SEISMOSAURUS 39 ft
Longest dinosaur

INDRICOTHERIUM 24 feet *Tallest-ever mammal*

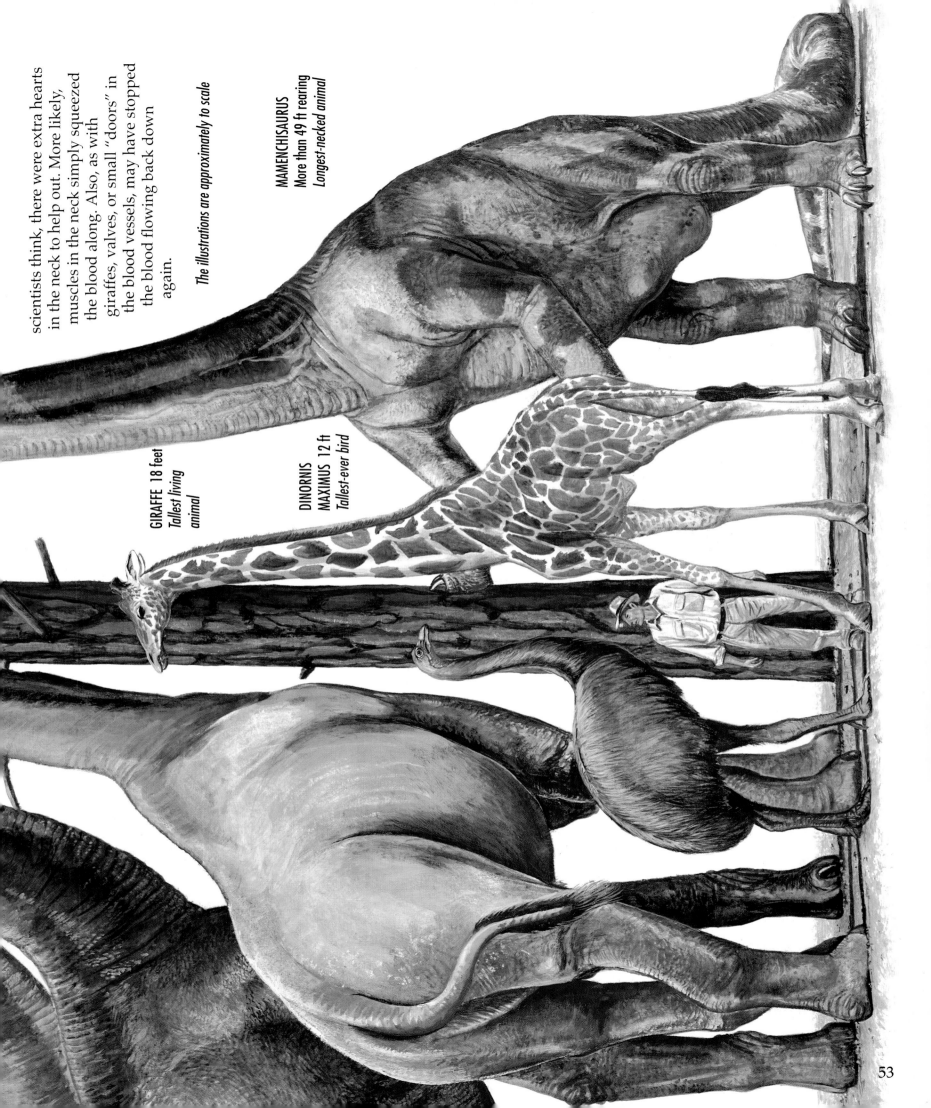

scientists think, there were extra hearts in the neck to help out. More likely, muscles in the neck simply squeezed the blood along. Also, as with giraffes, valves, or small "doors" in the blood vessels, may have stopped the blood flowing back down again.

The illustrations are approximately to scale

MAMENCHISAURUS
More than 49 ft rearing
Longest-necked animal

GIRAFFE 18 feet
Tallest living animal

DINORNIS MAXIMUS 12 ft
Tallest-ever bird

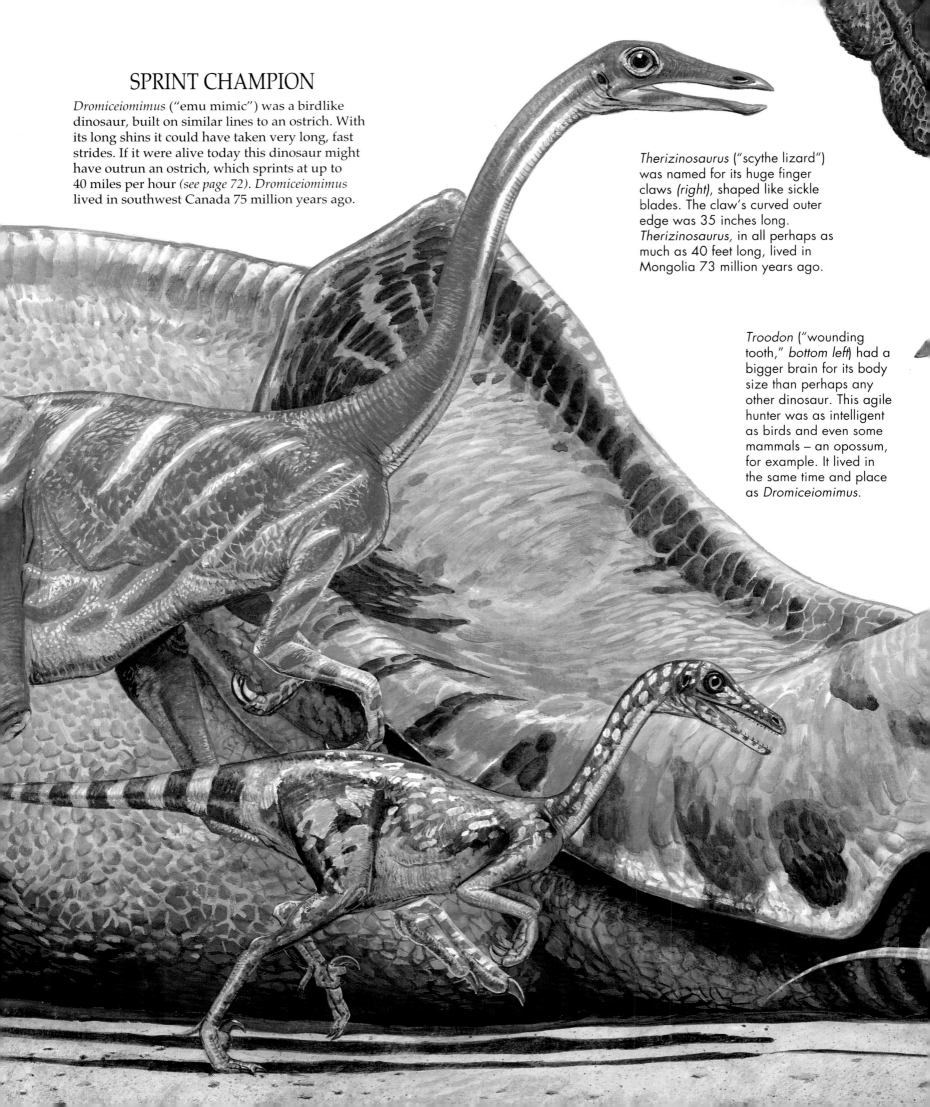

SPRINT CHAMPION

Dromiceiomimus ("emu mimic") was a birdlike dinosaur, built on similar lines to an ostrich. With its long shins it could have taken very long, fast strides. If it were alive today this dinosaur might have outrun an ostrich, which sprints at up to 40 miles per hour *(see page 72)*. *Dromiceiomimus* lived in southwest Canada 75 million years ago.

Therizinosaurus ("scythe lizard") was named for its huge finger claws *(right)*, shaped like sickle blades. The claw's curved outer edge was 35 inches long. *Therizinosaurus*, in all perhaps as much as 40 feet long, lived in Mongolia 73 million years ago.

Troodon ("wounding tooth," *bottom left*) had a bigger brain for its body size than perhaps any other dinosaur. This agile hunter was as intelligent as birds and even some mammals – an opossum, for example. It lived in the same time and place as *Dromiceiomimus*.

THE LARGEST SKULL
DINOSAUR RECORD HOLDERS

Horned *Torosaurus* ("bull lizard," *below*) had a massive skull, about the size of a small car. Measured from its beak to the back of its neck frill it was 8.5 feet long. This plant-eating dinosaur lived in North America 70 million years ago.

FROM FOSSIL BONES found in the rocks, scientists have worked out which dinosaurs were special in various ways. This illustration shows five kinds of dinosaurs that held a record of one kind or another. *Torosaurus* had the largest head of any animal that ever lived on land. The longest claws yet found belonged to *Therizinosaurus*. *Dromiceiomimus*, with its long, thin legs, might have been the fastest running dinosaur. The smallest-ever dinosaur was, many scientists believe, *Compsognathus*. *Troodon* and its relatives were probably the most intelligent of all the dinosaurs.

The illustrations are approximately to scale

This eight-year-old child *(right)* gives an idea of the sizes of the dinosaurs.

Compsognathus ("elegant jaw," *below left*) was a quick hunter. Just 30 inches long, it was little bigger than a chicken. *Compsognathus* lived in Europe, 150 million years ago.

THE LARGEST-EVER LAND MAMMAL
INDRICOTHERIUM, THE GIANT RHINOCEROS

THE FIRST MAMMALS were no bigger than shrews (see page 49), yet some of their descendants were prehistoric rhinoceroses, elephants, and other animals that weighed several tons. Being big gave these giant animals advantages. They could browse on leafy twigs too high for smaller creatures to reach, while their size and tough hides protected them from the teeth and claws of carnivores – although some of them (like *Andrewsarchus*) had grown massive, too.

The largest land mammal the world has ever seen was a giant prehistoric rhinoceros. Called *Indricotherium*, this mighty tree-browser roamed Asia about 30 million years ago. After studying its fossil bones, scientists at first believed that a living *Indricotherium* weighed as much as 33 tons. A closer look showed that *Indricotherium* normally weighed "only" about 12 tons. Even that would make it twice as heavy as an African elephant!

The very largest *Indricotherium* probably grew up to 22 tons. This monster would have been as heavy as 10 living rhinoceroses. From snout to tail, *Indricotherium* might have grown up to 36 feet – longer than a doubles tennis court is wide. It stood so tall that a giraffe's head would only reach up to its shoulders (see page 53). Besides being so much bigger than any living rhinoceros, *Indricotherium* was different in another way: There were no horns on its head.

This illustration compares an average-size human being with five giant prehistoric mammals of different kinds.

ANDREWSARCHUS
13 feet long
Largest-ever carnivorous mammal

INDRICOTHERIUM
Up to 18 feet high at
the shoulder
*Largest-ever land
mammal*

**MAMMUTHUS
TROGONTHERII**
Up to 14.8 feet high
at the shoulder
Largest-ever elephant

MAMMAL GIANTS

Each prehistoric land mammal shown here was the biggest or the heaviest of its kind. *Andrewsarchus* was the largest-known flesh-eating land mammal. Something like a cross between a bear and a hyena, this ferocious beast lived in east Asia about 40 million years ago.

The steppe mammoth, *Mammuthus trogontherii*, was the largest-ever member of the elephant family. Roaming Europe in the depths of the Ice Ages, its shaggy coat kept it warm in the bitterly cold winters.

Gigantopithecus, the greatest ape, lived in east and southeast Asia, also during Ice Age times. Standing about ten feet tall, it would have been as heavy as a large pony. Early humans might well have met this monster face to face but *Gigantopithecus*, a harmless plant-eater, would probably have left them alone. Some people think that *Gigantopithecus* never became extinct, but survives even to this day in the Himalayas, where it is known as the Yeti.

Glyptodon was a South American Ice Age mammal related to the little living armadillos. Its thick, bony armor probably made this tanklike creature the heaviest and best protected mammal of its kind. *Glyptodon* even had a bony "hat" protecting its head, and bony rings that ran around its tail.

*The illustrations are
approximately to scale*

GIGANTOPITHECUS
Up to 10 feet tall
Largest-ever primate

GLYPTODON
Shell 8.2 feet long
*Most heavily
armored mammal*

THE FIRST HUMANS
OUR EARLIEST ANCESTORS

IN 1856 miners found a strange skeleton in a limestone quarry in the Neander Thal (Neander Valley), Germany. The skull was quite apelike, the leg bones strong and curved. At the time, some people thought that this Neanderthal person had been a soldier who had died in a war about 50 years earlier. Scientists later realized they had discovered a prehistoric human who had died 50,000 years ago!

Since then, even older bones have turned up elsewhere. Scientists now believe that humans, apes, and monkeys (mammals of the group called primates) all share one ancestor. That ancestor may have been *Aegyptopithecus* ("Egyptian ape") which lived in Egypt 35 million years ago.

Thirteen million years later, the first apelike animals were climbing trees in East Africa. From their descendants came today's chimpanzee and gorilla – and the now extinct australopithecines ("southern apes"). A skeleton of an australopithecine was dug up in Africa in 1974. Called Lucy by the scientists who found her bones, she probably walked upright about five million years ago. She was the first known "humanlike" animal, a hominid.

By two million years ago, the first real humans, *Homo rudolfensis*, and the closely related *Homo habilis*, had appeared. *Homo habilis* ("handy man") could use tools and, perhaps, talk a little. By 200,000 years later, little *Homo habilis* had given rise to a bigger, brainier kind of prehistoric person: *Homo erectus* ("upright man").

Homo sapiens ("wise man"), the first modern human, appeared, it is thought, about 400,000 years ago. There were once two types of *Homo sapiens*: the Neanderthals, who died out about 30,000 years ago, and humans almost just like ourselves.

Aegyptopithecus (above) was the earliest-known primate mammal belonging to the Anthropoidea, a group which includes monkeys, apes, and humans. Weighing about the same as a human baby, tiny *Aegyptopithecus* climbed on all fours.

Australopithecus afarensis ("southern ape of Afar," left) was, perhaps, the first member of the human family of primates. Only about 4 feet tall, it walked on two legs, although it may have spent some of its life in the trees.

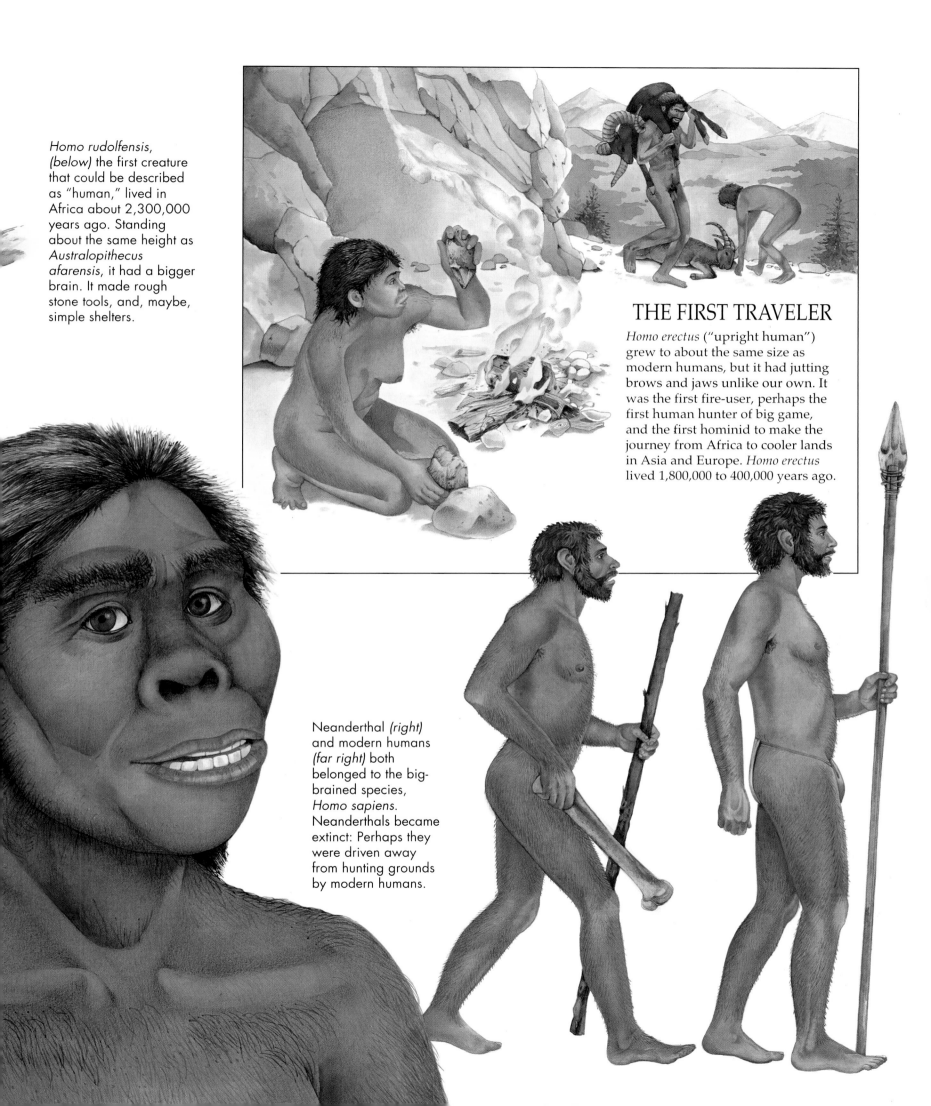

Homo rudolfensis, (below) the first creature that could be described as "human," lived in Africa about 2,300,000 years ago. Standing about the same height as *Australopithecus afarensis*, it had a bigger brain. It made rough stone tools, and, maybe, simple shelters.

THE FIRST TRAVELER

Homo erectus ("upright human") grew to about the same size as modern humans, but it had jutting brows and jaws unlike our own. It was the first fire-user, perhaps the first human hunter of big game, and the first hominid to make the journey from Africa to cooler lands in Asia and Europe. *Homo erectus* lived 1,800,000 to 400,000 years ago.

Neanderthal *(right)* and modern humans *(far right)* both belonged to the big-brained species, *Homo sapiens*. Neanderthals became extinct: Perhaps they were driven away from hunting grounds by modern humans.

THE HUMAN BODY
ANATOMICAL RECORD HOLDERS

Y OUR BODY is made of billions of invisibly tiny building-bricks, living cells so small that hundreds would fit inside one period. Different kinds of cell make up the different tissues that build the bones, the muscles, and organs (working parts) such as the heart, brain, liver, or skin. Organs that produce chemicals that help our bodies work are known as glands. This illustration, a diagram showing the inside of the body, shows some of the largest and smallest parts of the body.

Sometimes something goes wrong with the chemicals controlling how someone's body grows. It may grow scarcely at all or become extremely tall or fat. The shortest-known adult is a man less than 23 inches high, shorter than a penguin. The tallest man stood about 9 feet tall, about the height of an Asian elephant. The lightest woman weighed no more than a little dog. The heaviest-known man outweighed a horse.

Three tiny bones are found inside your ear, attached to the eardrum. They are called the hammer, the anvil, and, tiniest of all, the stirrup, or stapes. When your eardrum vibrates to sounds, these three bones pass the vibrations on to your inner ear, which sends signals to the brain.

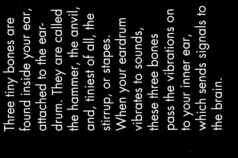

Inner ear

Eardrum

KEY

1 Tooth enamel *Hardest tissue*
2 Liver *Largest gland* Average weight 3 pounds
3 Skin *Largest organ* Average size 20 sq feet
4 Stapes in the middle ear *Smallest bone* 0.12 in
5 Femur (thigh bone) *Largest bone* More than a quarter of total body length
6 Stapedius (moves the stapes) *Smallest muscle*
7 Gluteus maximus (buttock muscle) *Largest muscle*

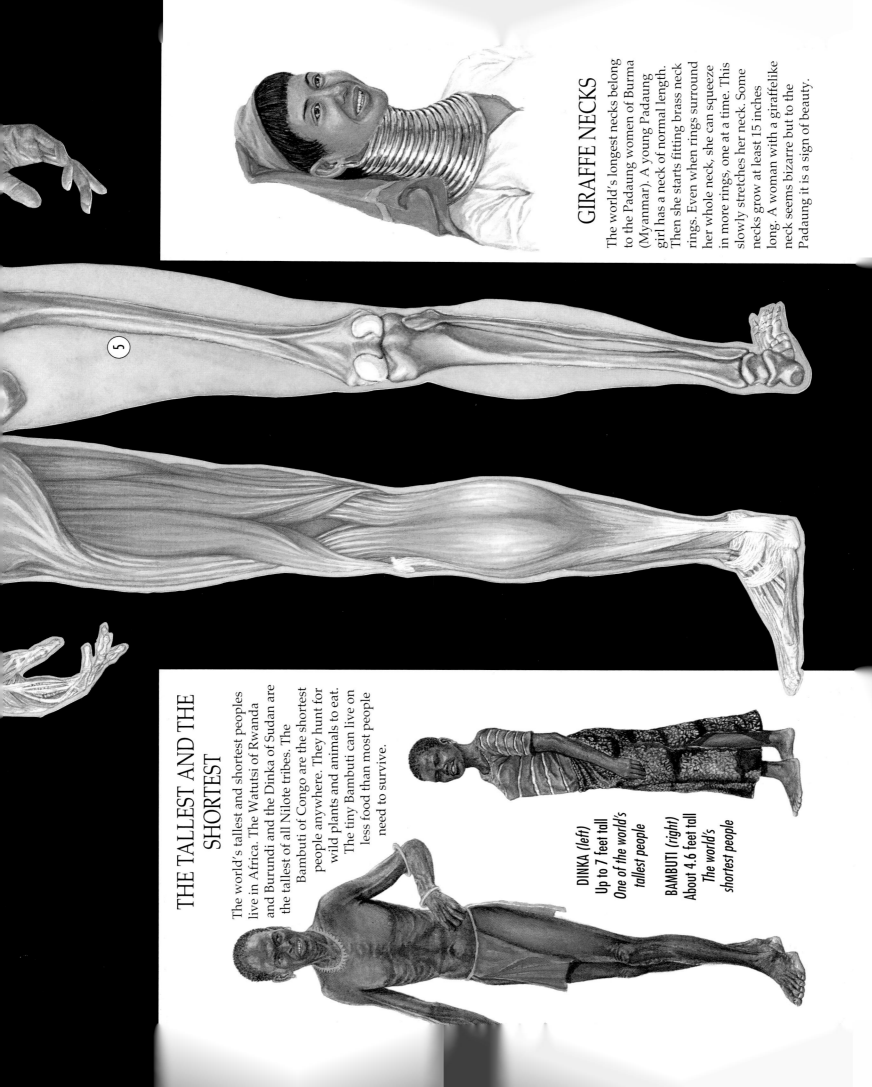

GIRAFFE NECKS

The world's longest necks belong to the Padaung women of Burma (Myanmar). A young Padaung girl has a neck of normal length. Then she starts fitting brass neck rings. Even when rings surround her whole neck, she can squeeze in more rings, one at a time. This slowly stretches her neck. Some necks grow at least 15 inches long. A woman with a giraffelike neck seems bizarre but to the Padaung it is a sign of beauty.

⑤

THE TALLEST AND THE SHORTEST

The world's tallest and shortest peoples live in Africa. The Watutsi of Rwanda and Burundi and the Dinka of Sudan are the tallest of all Nilote tribes. The Bambuti of Congo are the shortest people anywhere. They hunt for wild plants and animals to eat. The tiny Bambuti can live on less food than most people need to survive.

DINKA *(left)*
Up to 7 feet tall
One of the world's tallest people

BAMBUTI *(right)*
About 4.6 feet tall
The world's shortest people

THE LARGEST ANIMAL THAT EVER LIVED
THE INCREDIBLE BLUE WHALE

THE BLUE WHALE is probably the biggest creature of all time. The longest reliably recorded specimen measured more than 105 feet, nearly one-third the length of a football field (in this illustration, it runs over six pages!). The heaviest ever caught weighed more than 209 tons. Even an "ordinary" blue whale is as heavy as more than 1,800 people!

Blue whales can grow to this size because water supports their colossal bodies. On dry land they would collapse under their own weight, even if they had legs instead of flippers. But although blue whales can never leave the sea, they must come up to the surface to breathe in air like any other mammal.

The world's largest animal feeds on a tiny, shrimplike creature called krill. One blue whale eats about 4.4 tons of krill every day. It swims open-mouthed, trapping krill on the whalebone "comb" which hangs down inside its huge mouth instead of teeth.

While blue whales are the largest

whalebone, or baleen, whales, sperm whales are the biggest whales that have teeth. A sperm whale is shorter and lighter than a blue whale, with as much as one-third of its length taken up by its enormous head. The sperm whale has two other records to its name: It has the largest brain of any animal, and it is the champion mammalian diver *(see pages 76-77)*.

SPERM WHALE
Length: 69 feet
Weight: 77 tons
Largest toothed whale

62

A BLUE WHALE CALF

A newborn blue whale is as long
as a soccer goal and as heavy as a
large hippopotamus. Its length
doubles in seven months. By the
time it is a year old its weight has
multiplied eight times.

BLUE WHALE
Length: 105 feet
Weight: 209 tons
Largest animal

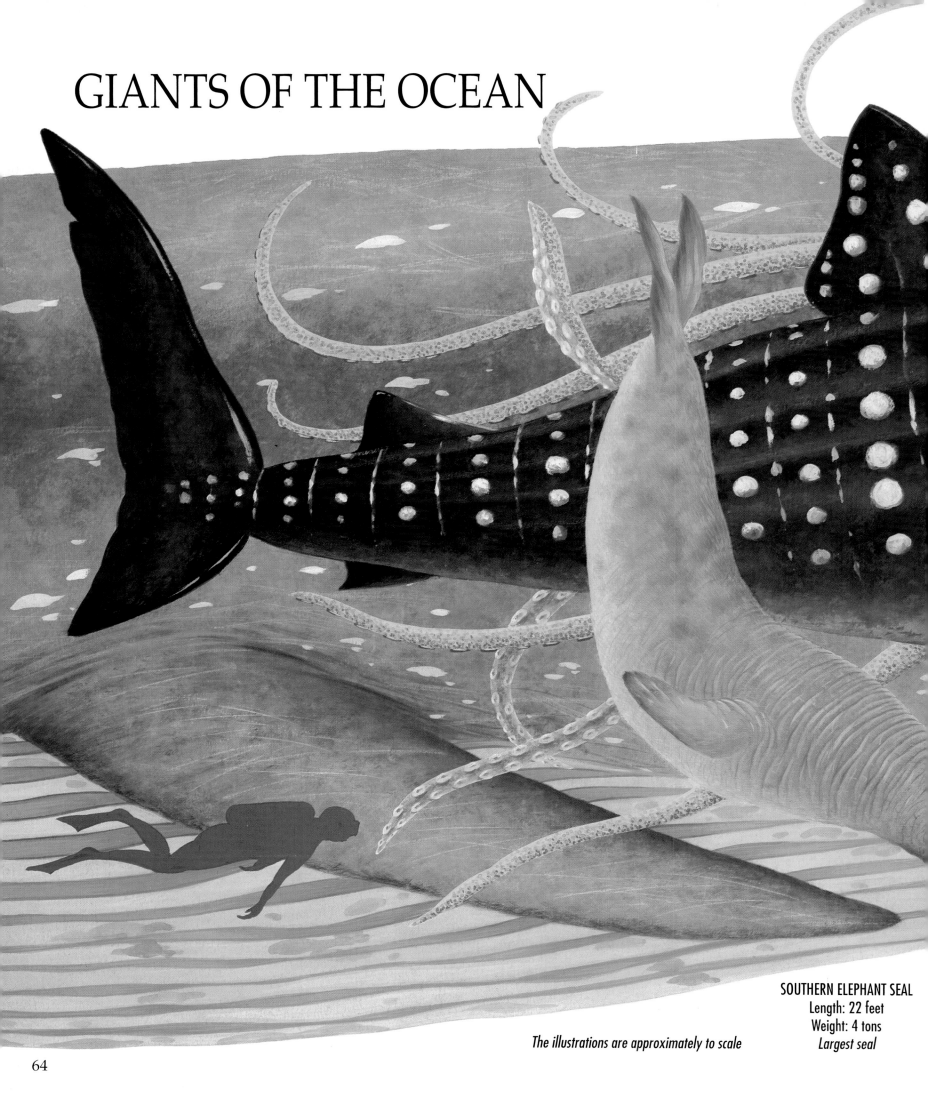

GIANTS OF THE OCEAN

SOUTHERN ELEPHANT SEAL
Length: 22 feet
Weight: 4 tons
Largest seal

The illustrations are approximately to scale

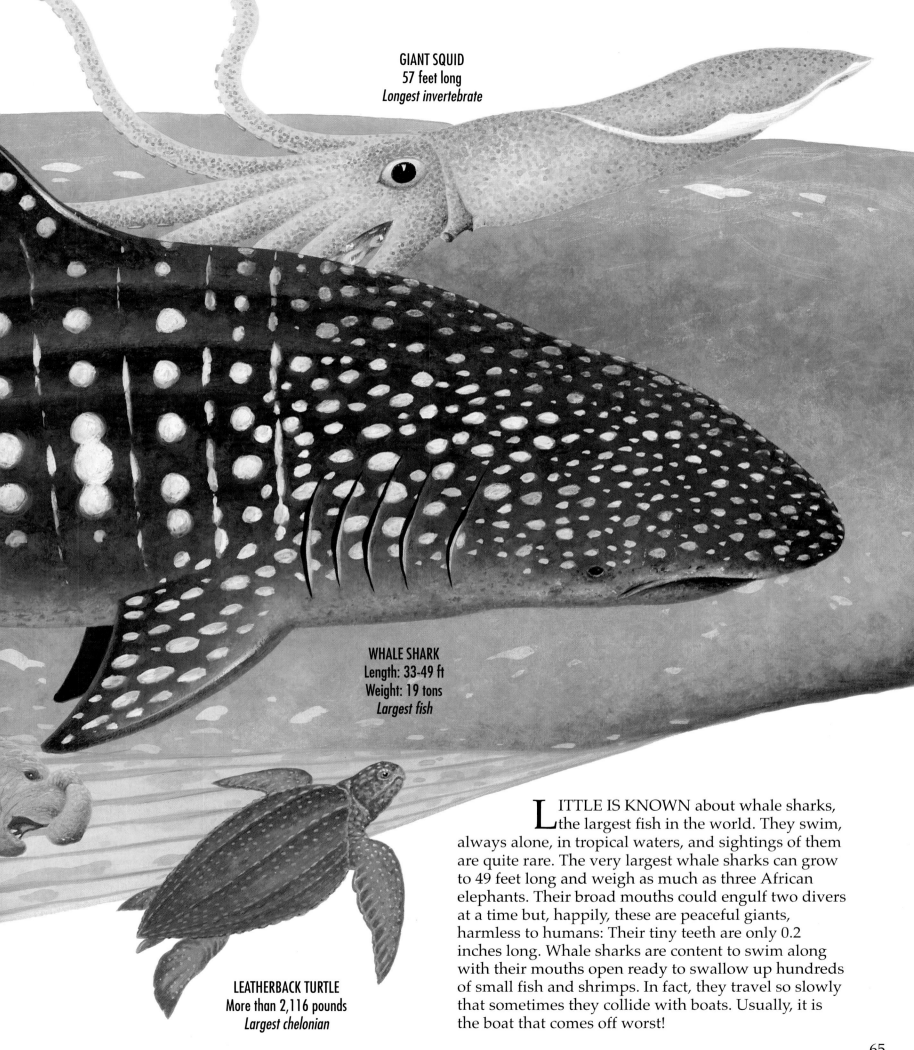

GIANT SQUID
57 feet long
Longest invertebrate

WHALE SHARK
Length: 33-49 ft
Weight: 19 tons
Largest fish

LEATHERBACK TURTLE
More than 2,116 pounds
Largest chelonian

LITTLE IS KNOWN about whale sharks, the largest fish in the world. They swim, always alone, in tropical waters, and sightings of them are quite rare. The very largest whale sharks can grow to 49 feet long and weigh as much as three African elephants. Their broad mouths could engulf two divers at a time but, happily, these are peaceful giants, harmless to humans: Their tiny teeth are only 0.2 inches long. Whale sharks are content to swim along with their mouths open ready to swallow up hundreds of small fish and shrimps. In fact, they travel so slowly that sometimes they collide with boats. Usually, it is the boat that comes off worst!

LARGEST ON LAND...

...AND IN THE AIR

GIRAFFE
19 feet tall
Tallest land animal

POLAR BEAR
2,200 pounds
Largest carnivore on land

KORI BUSTARD
42 pounds
Heaviest flying bird

ALDABRA GIANT TORTOISE
660 pounds
Heaviest land chelonian

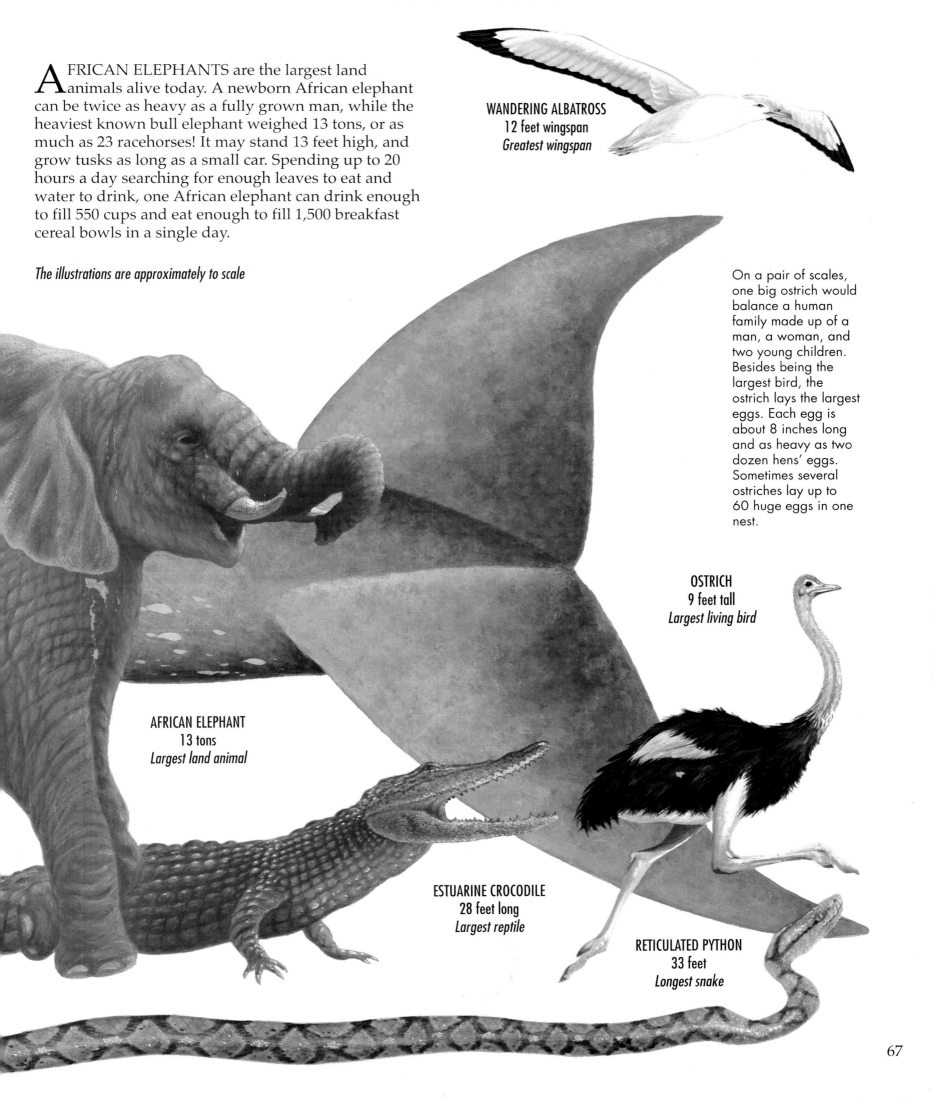

AFRICAN ELEPHANTS are the largest land animals alive today. A newborn African elephant can be twice as heavy as a fully grown man, while the heaviest known bull elephant weighed 13 tons, or as much as 23 racehorses! It may stand 13 feet high, and grow tusks as long as a small car. Spending up to 20 hours a day searching for enough leaves to eat and water to drink, one African elephant can drink enough to fill 550 cups and eat enough to fill 1,500 breakfast cereal bowls in a single day.

The illustrations are approximately to scale

WANDERING ALBATROSS
12 feet wingspan
Greatest wingspan

On a pair of scales, one big ostrich would balance a human family made up of a man, a woman, and two young children. Besides being the largest bird, the ostrich lays the largest eggs. Each egg is about 8 inches long and as heavy as two dozen hens' eggs. Sometimes several ostriches lay up to 60 huge eggs in one nest.

OSTRICH
9 feet tall
Largest living bird

AFRICAN ELEPHANT
13 tons
Largest land animal

ESTUARINE CROCODILE
28 feet long
Largest reptile

RETICULATED PYTHON
33 feet
Longest snake

THE SMALLEST ANIMALS
PICTURED AT ACTUAL SIZE

SMALL ANIMALS always live in danger of being gobbled up by larger ones, yet being small does have its advantages. The fairy fly can lay its invisibly tiny eggs on top of the eggs of little insects larger than itself. These become food for the fairy fly's grubs when they hatch out. A least weasel is slim enough to chase mice down their holes. The tiniest fishes, lizards, mice, and shrews can hide in holes or cracks too narrow for their enemies to enter. The lightweight pygmy mouse lemur can climb about on twigs that would not bear a monkey's weight. Agile flyers, tiny bats dart here and there in pursuit of small moths, while bee-sized hummingbirds can hover in midair to suck nectar from a flower.

Some animal-like creatures are so small they are invisible. You cannot see them even under a powerful magnifying glass. These mini-beasts are called protozoans, a name meaning "first animals." Most animals are made of millions of tiny building blocks called cells, but a protozoan consists of just a single cell. Some protozoans are so small that thousands could live on your thumbnail.

One organism, called a mycoplasma, is the smallest form of life capable of living by itself. You would have to magnify it 10,000 times for it to appear the size of a period on this page!

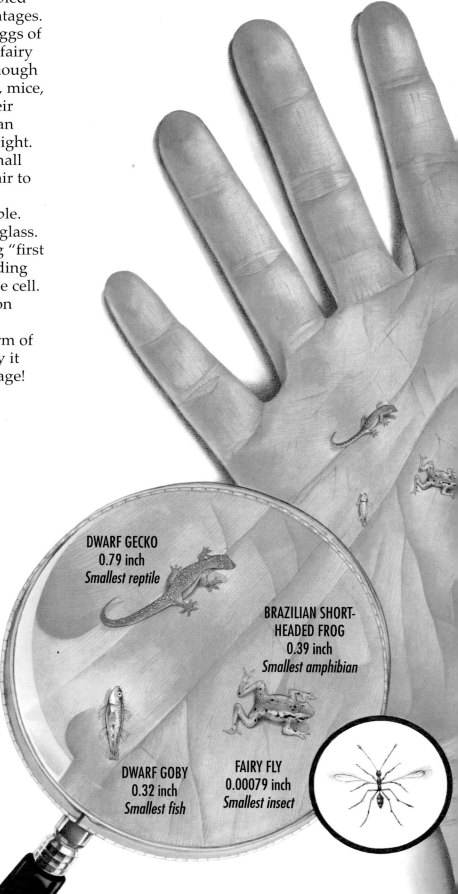

BEE HUMMINGBIRD
2.1 inches
Smallest bird

DWARF GECKO
0.79 inch
Smallest reptile

BRAZILIAN SHORT-HEADED FROG
0.39 inch
Smallest amphibian

DWARF GOBY
0.32 inch
Smallest fish

FAIRY FLY
0.00079 inch
Smallest insect

Even some moths grow larger than a male bee hummingbird, the smallest bird. In flight, its tiny whirring wings hum like a bee's. Bee hummingbirds live in Cuba and on the nearby Isle of Pines.

This magnifying glass reveals three tiny creatures magnified to twice actual size. Dwarf gobies are the lightest of all the backboned animals.

Fairy flies (magnified 1,400 times, *right*) are wasps so small they can walk through a needle's eye.

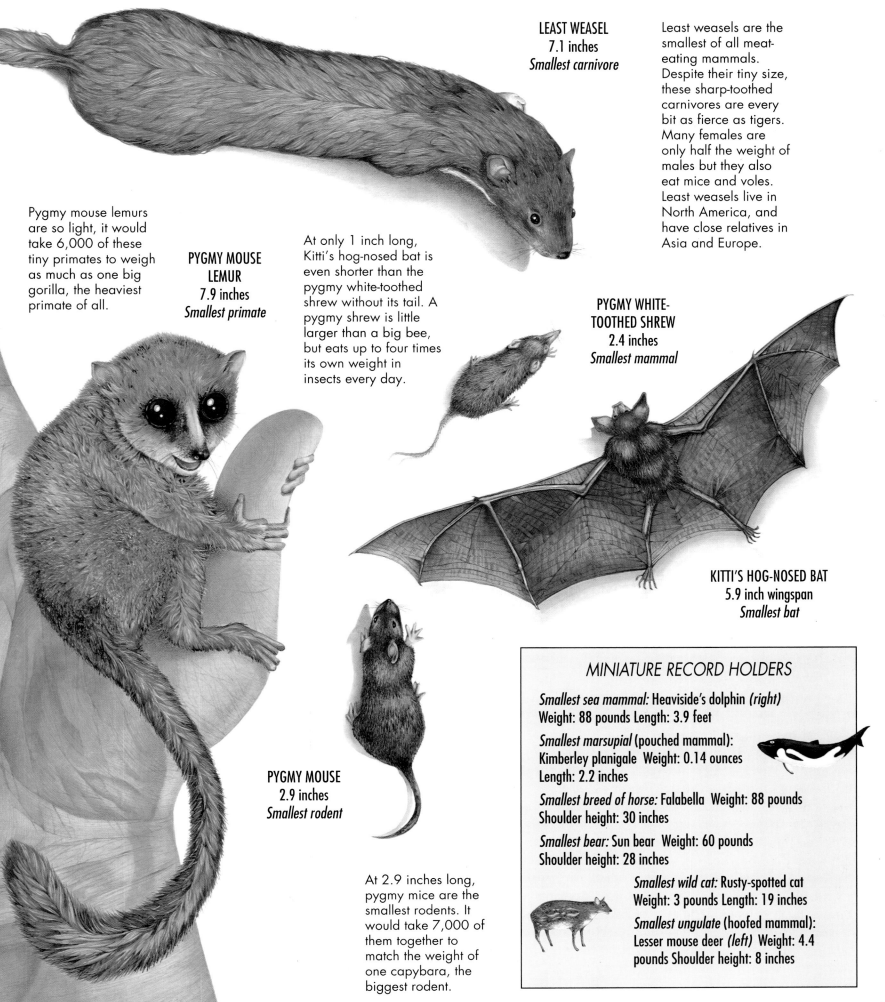

LEAST WEASEL
7.1 inches
Smallest carnivore

Least weasels are the smallest of all meat-eating mammals. Despite their tiny size, these sharp-toothed carnivores are every bit as fierce as tigers. Many females are only half the weight of males but they also eat mice and voles. Least weasels live in North America, and have close relatives in Asia and Europe.

Pygmy mouse lemurs are so light, it would take 6,000 of these tiny primates to weigh as much as one big gorilla, the heaviest primate of all.

PYGMY MOUSE LEMUR
7.9 inches
Smallest primate

At only 1 inch long, Kitti's hog-nosed bat is even shorter than the pygmy white-toothed shrew without its tail. A pygmy shrew is little larger than a big bee, but eats up to four times its own weight in insects every day.

PYGMY WHITE-TOOTHED SHREW
2.4 inches
Smallest mammal

KITTI'S HOG-NOSED BAT
5.9 inch wingspan
Smallest bat

PYGMY MOUSE
2.9 inches
Smallest rodent

At 2.9 inches long, pygmy mice are the smallest rodents. It would take 7,000 of them together to match the weight of one capybara, the biggest rodent.

MINIATURE RECORD HOLDERS

Smallest sea mammal: Heaviside's dolphin *(right)*
Weight: 88 pounds Length: 3.9 feet

Smallest marsupial (pouched mammal):
Kimberley planigale Weight: 0.14 ounces
Length: 2.2 inches

Smallest breed of horse: Falabella Weight: 88 pounds
Shoulder height: 30 inches

Smallest bear: Sun bear Weight: 60 pounds
Shoulder height: 28 inches

Smallest wild cat: Rusty-spotted cat
Weight: 3 pounds Length: 19 inches

Smallest ungulate (hoofed mammal):
Lesser mouse deer *(left)* Weight: 4.4
pounds Shoulder height: 8 inches

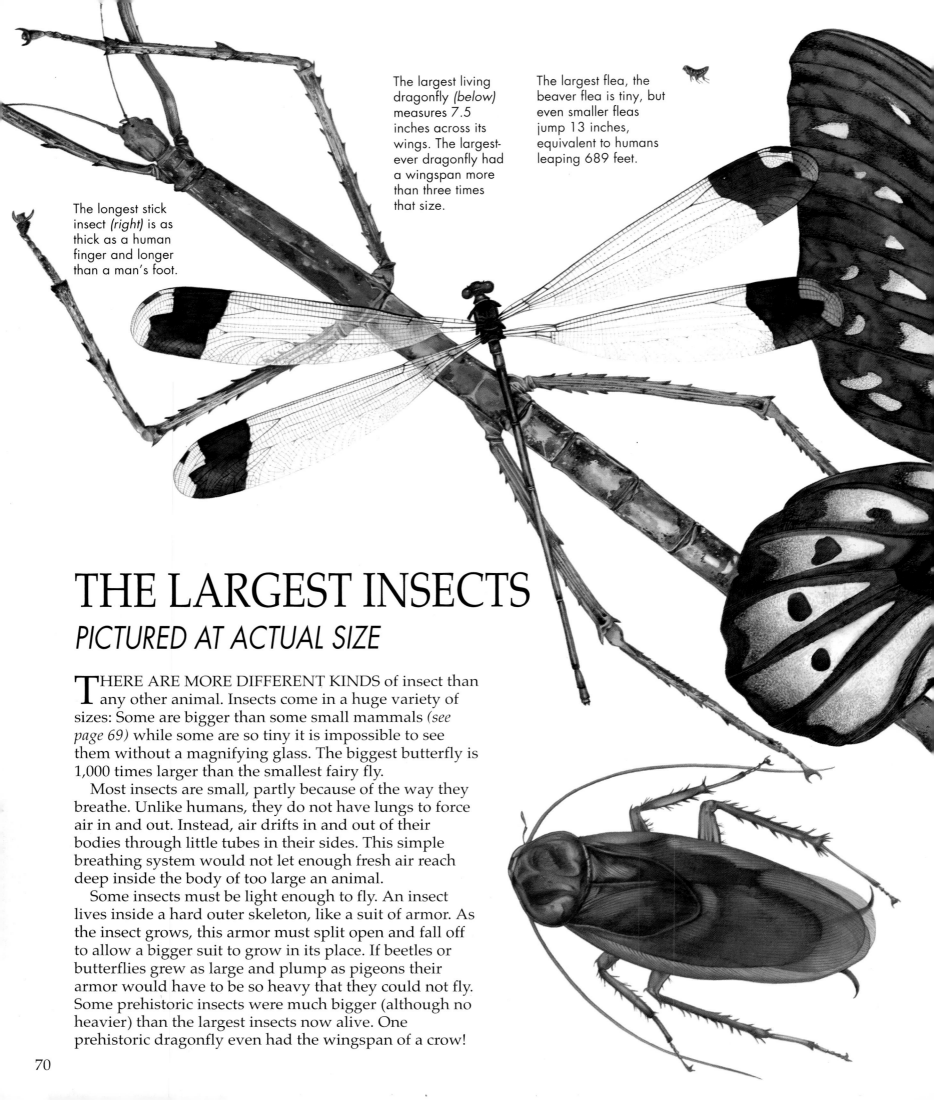

The longest stick insect *(right)* is as thick as a human finger and longer than a man's foot.

The largest living dragonfly *(below)* measures 7.5 inches across its wings. The largest-ever dragonfly had a wingspan more than three times that size.

The largest flea, the beaver flea is tiny, but even smaller fleas jump 13 inches, equivalent to humans leaping 689 feet.

THE LARGEST INSECTS
PICTURED AT ACTUAL SIZE

THERE ARE MORE DIFFERENT KINDS of insect than any other animal. Insects come in a huge variety of sizes: Some are bigger than some small mammals *(see page 69)* while some are so tiny it is impossible to see them without a magnifying glass. The biggest butterfly is 1,000 times larger than the smallest fairy fly.

Most insects are small, partly because of the way they breathe. Unlike humans, they do not have lungs to force air in and out. Instead, air drifts in and out of their bodies through little tubes in their sides. This simple breathing system would not let enough fresh air reach deep inside the body of too large an animal.

Some insects must be light enough to fly. An insect lives inside a hard outer skeleton, like a suit of armor. As the insect grows, this armor must split open and fall off to allow a bigger suit to grow in its place. If beetles or butterflies grew as large and plump as pigeons their armor would have to be so heavy that they could not fly. Some prehistoric insects were much bigger (although no heavier) than the largest insects now alive. One prehistoric dragonfly even had the wingspan of a crow!

The world's heaviest insects are the goliath beetles from West Africa *(right)*. One big male goliath beetle is as heavy as 50 pygmy shrews, the lightest land mammals *(see page 69)*. Elephant beetles from Central America are bigger than goliaths but weigh less.

The male Queen Alexandra's birdwing *(below)* is smaller than the female. His bright colors warn hungry birds that he is poisonous to eat.

The world's largest butterfly, the Queen Alexandra's birdwing, is also probably the rarest. Females *(above)* can grow to 11 inches across the wings. They fly so high they are difficult to net. The first specimen collected was shot down instead!

The largest cockroach *(left)* has a body nearly 4 inches long. Its antennae (feelers) are even longer.

71

THE FASTEST...

IF ALL THE FASTEST ANIMALS came together to run a race, who would win? First, of course, would be a bird. Birds can swoop and glide unhindered through the air in search of their prey, escaping from their predators, or simply to cover the long distances over which they migrate each year.

Following – some distance behind – is a fish. Although their speeds are difficult to measure, speeds of over 60 miles per hour have been recorded for the sailfish. The fastest runner on land is the cheetah, which chases its prey at up to 62 miles per hour, although it cannot keep this up for more than a minute or so. Racehorses are also very fast sprinters, but the fastest land animal over distance is the pronghorn. The hare, with its reputation for speed, is, however, easily outsprinted by the fastest human over short distances. Athletes recording times of under ten seconds for a race of 100 meters reach peak speeds of around 27 miles per hour during the course of their sprint.

Speed records for spiders and insects are very difficult to time. Dragonflies may be the fastest flying insects over short bursts, while tropical cockroaches are probably the fastest-moving insects on land.

The illustrations are not drawn to scale

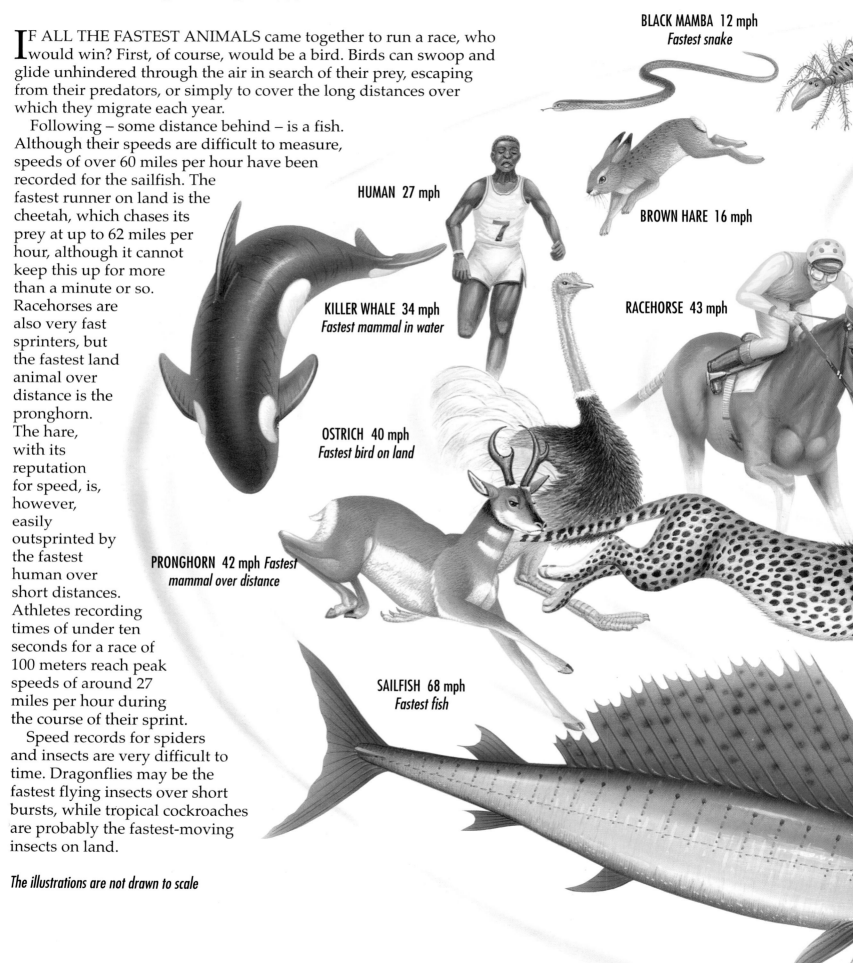

BLACK MAMBA 12 mph
Fastest snake

HUMAN 27 mph

BROWN HARE 16 mph

KILLER WHALE 34 mph
Fastest mammal in water

RACEHORSE 43 mph

OSTRICH 40 mph
Fastest bird on land

PRONGHORN 42 mph *Fastest mammal over distance*

SAILFISH 68 mph
Fastest fish

GIANT TORTOISE

SLOTH

SNAIL

COCKROACH 2.9 mph
Fastest insect on land

LONG-LEGGED SUN SPIDER 10 mph
Fastest arachnid

DRAGONFLY 36 mph
Fastest insect

...AND THE SLOWEST

Bringing up the rear are three animals well-known for lacking fleetness of foot. The largest living tortoise, the Aldabra giant tortoise of the Seychelles and Mauritius, is capable of covering 1,214 feet an hour (over 19 feet a minute). Spending most of its life asleep, the three-toed sloth, can, in a burst of speed through the trees, make sixteen feet in a minute. The snail, however, easily wins the wooden spoon. Even the world record holder travels no further than six inches in a one-minute "dash."

STOOPING TO CONQUER

The peregrine falcon is the fastest living creature on Earth. A bird of prey, it climbs high in the sky, before folding its wings and diving or "stooping" at speeds of more than 120 miles per hour to catch other birds in mid-flight. Smaller birds may be killed with a single blow from the falcon's talons; The necks of larger birds are broken by a stab from its powerful beak.

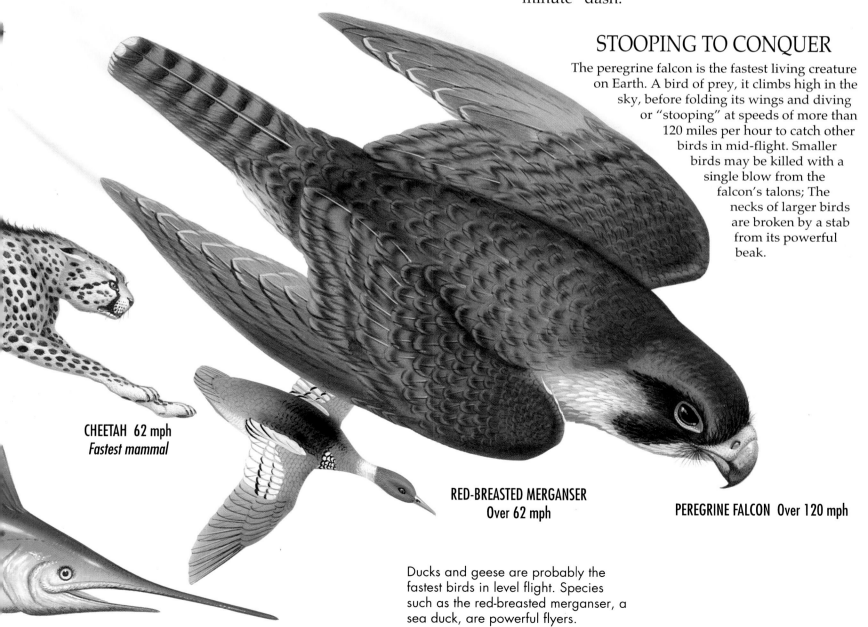

CHEETAH 62 mph
Fastest mammal

RED-BREASTED MERGANSER
Over 62 mph

PEREGRINE FALCON Over 120 mph

Ducks and geese are probably the fastest birds in level flight. Species such as the red-breasted merganser, a sea duck, are powerful flyers.

JEWEL BEETLE
More than 30 years
Longest-lived insect

JAPANESE GIANT SALAMANDER
More than 50 years
Longest-lived amphibian

WANDERING ALBATROSS
More than 70 years
Longest-lived bird

LAKE STURGEON
More than 80 years
Longest-lived fish

KILLER WHALE
Up to 80 years
*Longest-lived
marine mammal*

In some countries, the life expectancy of women exceeds 80 years. A few people have even reached ages of 120 years and above.

Killer whales move around in family "pods," ranging from 5 to 50 members. The females, or cows, are the dominant animals. In the wild, male killer whales can live to about 50, females up to 80 years.

THE LONGEST-LIVED ANIMALS
NATURE'S SENIOR CITIZENS

NO ANIMAL lives for ever. Accidents, diseases, or enemies kill many of them while they are still young. Only one Atlantic mackerel in every 100,000 is likely to survive more than 90 days. But creatures that escape an early end may live on until their bodies wear out. Animals that live protected lives in zoos often live to greater ages than they would do in the wild.

Tiny animals tend to have the shortest lives. A mayfly, for example, once it gets its wings, usually lives no more than a single day. An albatross or an elephant, on the other hand, can go on for many years. After an elephant turns 60, however, its teeth begin to wear out; it cannot chew so eventually it starves to death.

In prehistoric times, few human beings lasted even 40 years. Most died young of hunger, injury, or illness. Now, many people live to 80 and beyond, while some have even survived for over 120 years!

The illustrations are not drawn to scale

ASIAN ELEPHANT
More than 60 years
*Longest-lived land mammal
(after humans)*

LONG-LIVED REPTILES

Tuataras and tortoises live longer than any other land animals. Tuataras *(above)* are lizardlike creatures found only on small islands off New Zealand. In chilly weather, a tuatara breathes no more than once an hour. Scientists think that creatures which lead such slow-motion lives are capable of living 120 years or more.

Several kinds of tortoises normally live for more than 100 years. One giant tortoise, collected by the French explorer Marion de Fresne from the Seychelles in 1766, died (from a fall) in 1918, 152 years later. Known as "Marion's" tortoise, it was probably an adult when captured and so could have been more than 200 years old when it died!

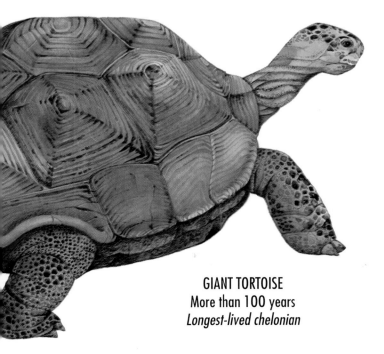

GIANT TORTOISE
More than 100 years
Longest-lived chelonian

REALM OF THE DEEP
THE DEEPEST-LIVING OCEAN ANIMALS

BENEATH THE OCEANS, beyond the shallow waters that fringe the continents, lie vast undersea plains. Towering mountain ranges rise from them while great trenches plunge even deeper. The Marianas Trench in the Pacific Ocean reaches down more than 36,000 feet (see page 29).

Most animal life is found in sunlit shallow waters, down to around 330 feet. There are some animals that live at greater depths, eating the remains of animals and plants that have fallen from the surface. And other animals feed on these, some diving thousands of feet down in search of their prey.

Sperm whales are the champion divers. Some males are known to dive to more than 9,800 feet to prey on giant squid. They can stay underwater for more than one hour (as mammals they need to breathe air), diving from and rising to the same point at the surface at great speed.

Fish and other types of animals live at still greater depths. Brotulid fish have been caught in deep ocean trenches. They are the deepest-living vertebrates (animals with backbones). The deepest-living creature of all is the amphipod, a kind of crustacean, which has been found in the Marianas Trench at depths of more than 32,800 feet.

The illustrations are not drawn to scale

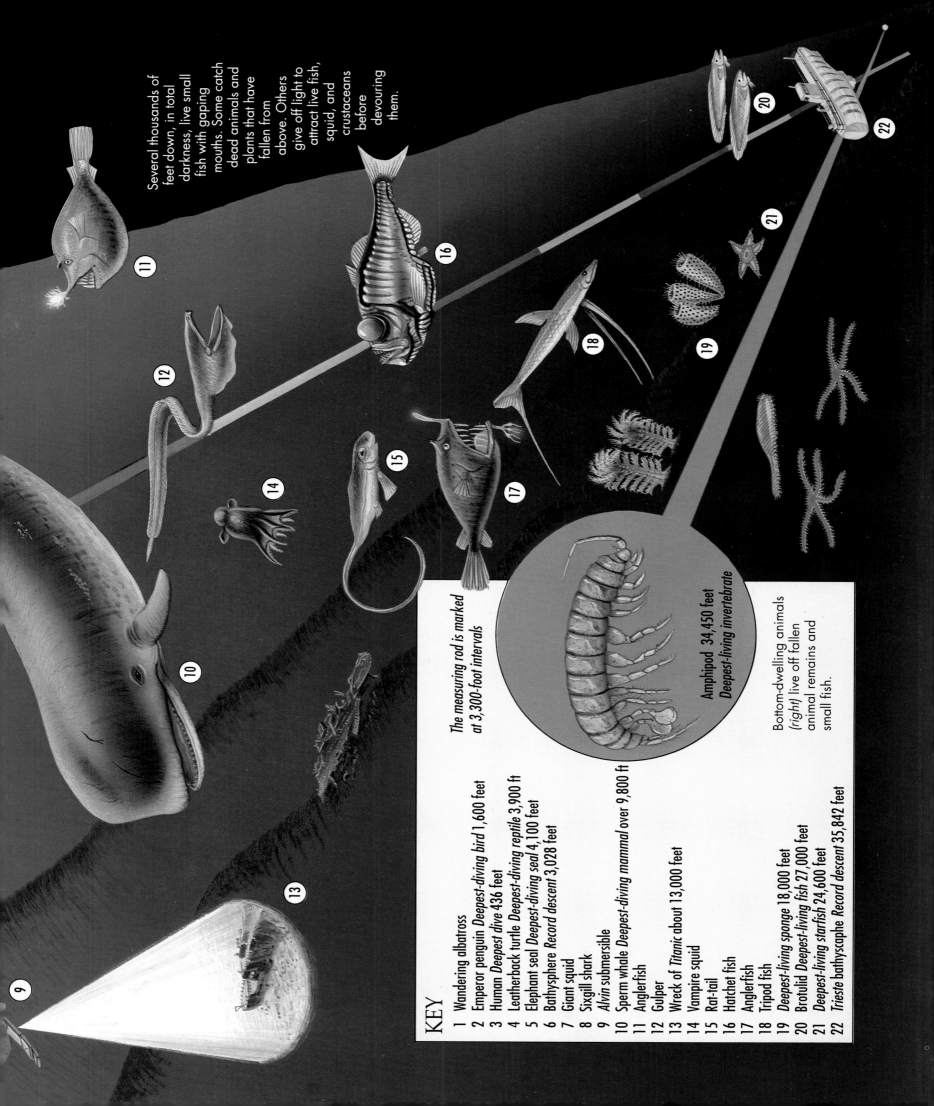

Several thousands of feet down, in total darkness, live small fish with gaping mouths. Some catch dead animals and plants that have fallen from above. Others give off light to attract live fish, squid, and crustaceans before devouring them.

The measuring rod is marked at 3,300-foot intervals

Amphipod 34,450 feet
Deepest-living invertebrate

Bottom-dwelling animals (*right*) live off fallen animal remains and small fish.

KEY

1   Wandering albatross
2   Emperor penguin *Deepest-diving bird* 1,600 feet
3   Human *Deepest dive* 436 feet
4   Leatherback turtle *Deepest-diving reptile* 3,900 ft
5   Elephant seal *Deepest-diving seal* 4,100 feet
6   Bathysphere *Record descent* 3,028 feet
7   Giant squid
8   Sixgill shark
9   *Alvin* submersible
10 Sperm whale *Deepest-diving mammal* over 9,800 ft
11 Anglerfish
12 Gulper
13 Wreck of *Titanic* about 13,000 feet
14 Vampire squid
15 Rat-tail
16 Hatchet fish
17 Anglerfish
18 Tripod fish
19 *Deepest-living sponge* 18,000 feet
20 Brotulid *Deepest-living fish* 27,000 feet
21 *Deepest-living starfish* 24,600 feet
22 *Trieste* bathyscaphe *Record descent* 35,842 feet

OCEAN TRAVELERS
THE LONGEST JOURNEYS

ANIMALS ARE ALWAYS ON THE MOVE in search of fresh sources of food. Some travel at the same time each year to places where the new season brings a more favorable climate for feeding or breeding. Called migration, these journeys are sometimes made to distant parts of the world. The most ambitious travelers fly or swim incredible distances across oceans and back again to the same places each year.

The champion long-distance specialist is the Arctic tern. In one year, this small bird flies from the Arctic to the Antarctic and back again – almost all the way around the world. The wandering albatross does circle the world, but near the South Pole where the distance is shorter.

Animal swimmers can also make amazingly long sea trips. Green turtles feed off Brazil but swim far out into the Atlantic Ocean to breed on lonely Ascension Island. Gray whales make the longest journeys of any mammal. They feed in Arctic waters in summer, before swimming south in winter to breed off Mexico.

European eel

Arctic tern

ATLANTIC

OCEAN

Green turtle

The young of the European eel *(right)* are born in the Sargasso Sea east of Florida. They spend the next few years drifting 6,000 miles across to Europe. They swim up rivers to grow into adults.

The wandering albatross *(below)* travels round the world near Antarctica.

The albacore *(bottom)* may make two journeys across the Pacific totaling 9,800 miles.

Probably the farthest-traveled reptile, the green turtle *(above)* swims up to 1,400 miles to its breeding grounds on Ascension Island then back again.

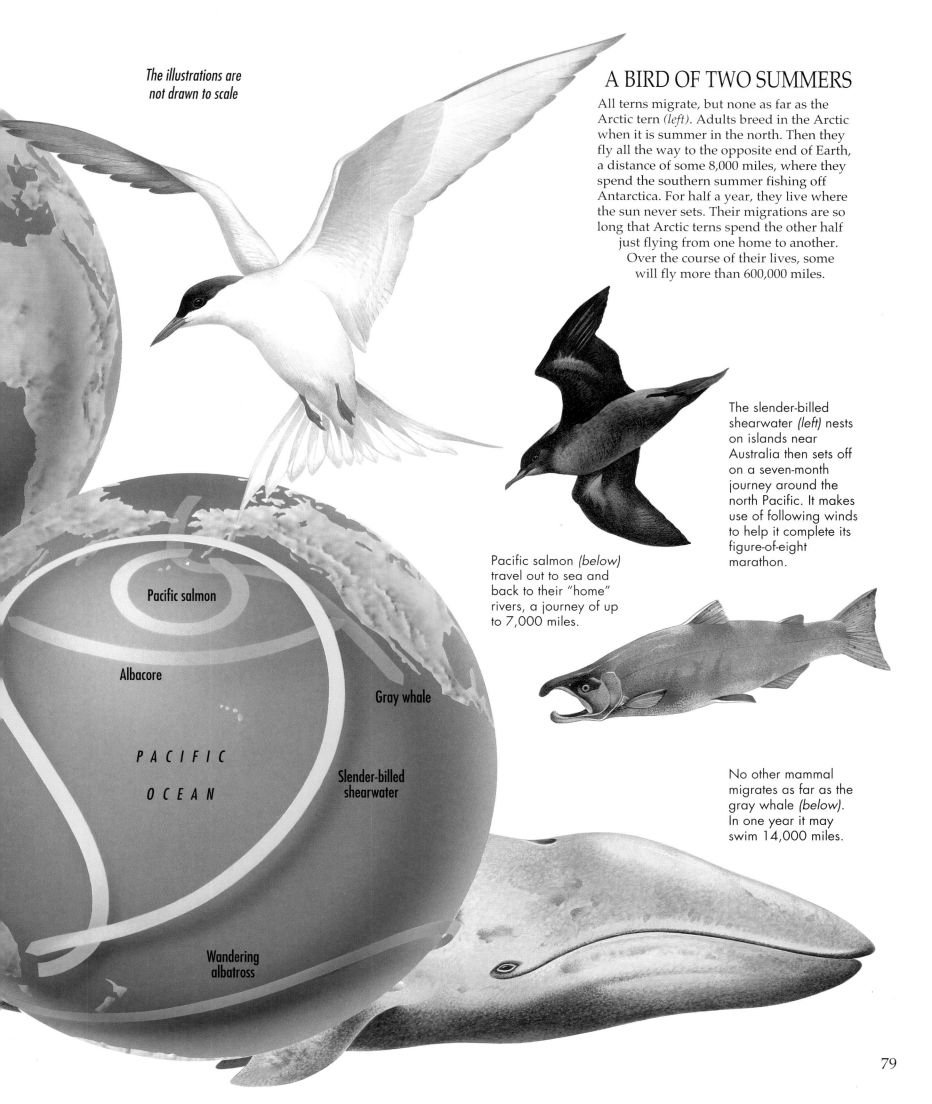

The illustrations are not drawn to scale

A BIRD OF TWO SUMMERS

All terns migrate, but none as far as the Arctic tern *(left)*. Adults breed in the Arctic when it is summer in the north. Then they fly all the way to the opposite end of Earth, a distance of some 8,000 miles, where they spend the southern summer fishing off Antarctica. For half a year, they live where the sun never sets. Their migrations are so long that Arctic terns spend the other half just flying from one home to another. Over the course of their lives, some will fly more than 600,000 miles.

The slender-billed shearwater *(left)* nests on islands near Australia then sets off on a seven-month journey around the north Pacific. It makes use of following winds to help it complete its figure-of-eight marathon.

Pacific salmon *(below)* travel out to sea and back to their "home" rivers, a journey of up to 7,000 miles.

No other mammal migrates as far as the gray whale *(below)*. In one year it may swim 14,000 miles.

Pacific salmon

Albacore

Gray whale

PACIFIC

OCEAN

Slender-billed shearwater

Wandering albatross

OVERLAND TRAVELERS
LONG-DISTANCE SPECIALISTS

MANY ANIMAL MIGRANTS that go by air – birds, bats, and insects – prefer to avoid traveling over the sea. They may be unable to find their usual sources of food, or to rest from long periods of flight. If they do need to cross the sea on their journey, they will cross where there are narrow straits or island "stepping-stones."

In the Northern Hemisphere spring, millions of birds flock thousands of miles northward. Warblers, plovers, and others will rear their young during the long northern summer days when food is plentiful. Bats and butterflies join in the great airborne migration. There are even some animals that go by foot: Herds of caribou, a kind of deer, wander hundreds of miles across the far north of Canada.

Sometimes, the travelers must cross deserts. To many, these are just as forbidding as the open seas. Warblers feed well before they overfly a desert. A plump willow warbler's body holds enough energy to enable it to fly 60 hours nonstop.

As summer ends, the long-distance travelers, or their young, head back south to spend winter in warmer climates.

Probably the farthest-traveled bat, the noctule flies up to 1,000 miles north across eastern Europe in the spring.

Golden plovers fly overland from Brazil to northern Canada, then back across the Atlantic Ocean, a flight of 12,000 miles each year.

Every autumn, clouds of monarch butterflies flutter a record 2,000 miles south from Canada to Mexico. Billions of these insects spend winter clustered together on tall evergreen trees. In spring they fly back north, laying eggs as they go. Most adults die, but their young complete the journey begun by their parents.

Caribou

NORTH AMERICA

Monarch butterfly

Golden plover

SOUTH AMERICA

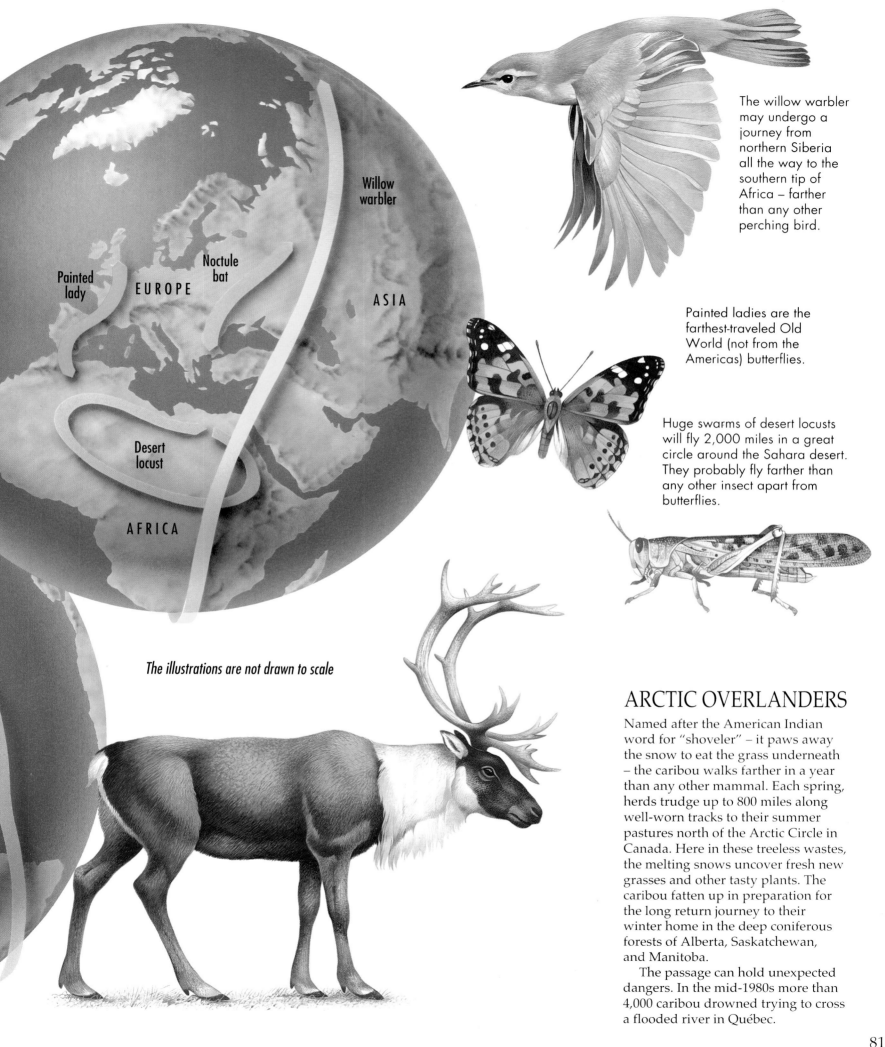

The willow warbler may undergo a journey from northern Siberia all the way to the southern tip of Africa – farther than any other perching bird.

Painted ladies are the farthest-traveled Old World (not from the Americas) butterflies.

Huge swarms of desert locusts will fly 2,000 miles in a great circle around the Sahara desert. They probably fly farther than any other insect apart from butterflies.

Willow warbler

Painted lady

EUROPE

Noctule bat

ASIA

Desert locust

AFRICA

The illustrations are not drawn to scale

ARCTIC OVERLANDERS

Named after the American Indian word for "shoveler" – it paws away the snow to eat the grass underneath – the caribou walks farther in a year than any other mammal. Each spring, herds trudge up to 800 miles along well-worn tracks to their summer pastures north of the Arctic Circle in Canada. Here in these treeless wastes, the melting snows uncover fresh new grasses and other tasty plants. The caribou fatten up in preparation for the long return journey to their winter home in the deep coniferous forests of Alberta, Saskatchewan, and Manitoba.

The passage can hold unexpected dangers. In the mid-1980s more than 4,000 caribou drowned trying to cross a flooded river in Québec.

THE RAREST ANIMALS
CREATURES CLOSE TO EXTINCTION

Fewer than 300 Tonkin snub-nosed monkeys live in the wild, in four small patches of bamboo forest in Vietnam.

SOME ANIMALS ARE VERY RARE, numbering perhaps only a few hundred in the wild. They include some very well-known animals, like the giant panda or the blue whale. Some are getting even scarcer and could soon disappear.

In the course of evolution *(see page 49)*, every kind of animal eventually dies out, but we humans are speeding up the rate at which many become extinct. In the past, hunters were the worst culprits, wiping out some animals for food or sport, and others because they threatened people or livestock. Now wild creatures die out when farms and cities gobble up the forests, prairies, and marshes where they live.

In 1990 scientists counted 5,000 kinds of animals known to be at risk of extinction. More than 2,000 were invertebrates (animals without a backbone), more than 1,000 were birds, about 760 were fishes, about 700 were mammals, nearly 200 were reptiles, and 63 were amphibians (frogs, toads, and salamanders). Besides all these, millions of unknown kinds of insects could vanish for ever even before we have discovered them!

By 1990 only one Spix's macaw remained wild in Brazil. Thirty more were kept as pets. Breeding these captive birds seems the only hope of keeping this species alive.

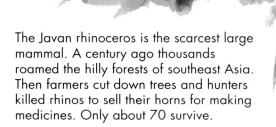

The Javan rhinoceros is the scarcest large mammal. A century ago thousands roamed the hilly forests of southeast Asia. Then farmers cut down trees and hunters killed rhinos to sell their horns for making medicines. Only about 70 survive.

The vaquita lives only in the Gulf of California. The victims of nets set for sharks and rays, only 200 of these tiny whales, each no longer than a human being, may still survive.

The illustrations are not drawn to scale

A SUCCESS STORY?

Of the animals pictured here, only the black-footed ferret, which is enjoying the special care of people determined to save it, has a good chance of survival. By the mid-1980s, there were just 18 ferrets left, all living in Wyoming. Scientists caught and bred them, and in 1991 the first ferrets were returned to the wild.

Kemp's ridley sea turtle breeds mainly on one beach in Mexico. Once tens of thousands came; now only a few hundred arrive. Many have drowned in fishing nets or died in oil-polluted waters.

PRECARIOUS POND-DWELLERS

Changes in the weather can put some animals at risk. Golden toads live only in Costa Rica's moist, misty mountain forests. In 1988 little rain fell and the toads' breeding ponds dried up. By 1990 no toads could be found at all.

The Devil's Hole pupfish lives only in a flooded Californian cave. If its pool dried up the little fish could disappear for good.

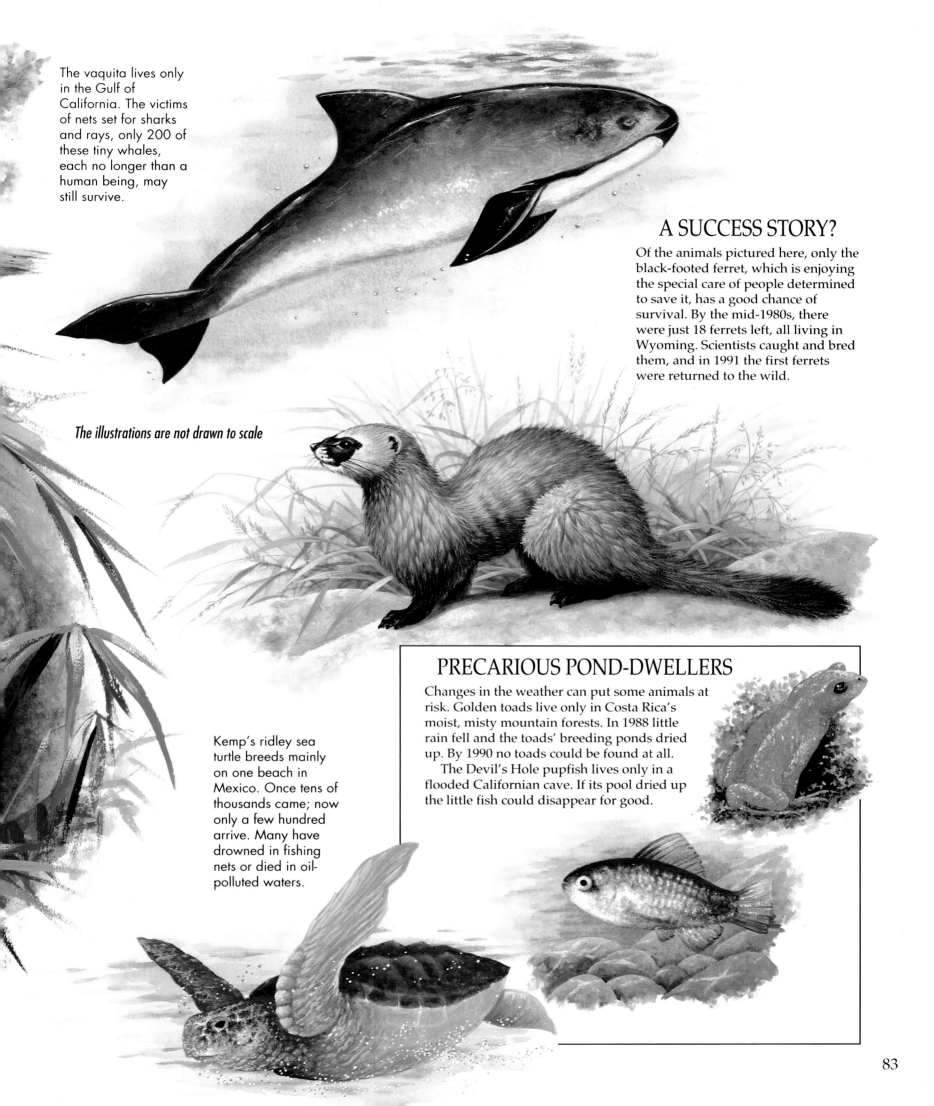

83

THE TALLEST TREES
NATURE'S SKYSCRAPERS

TREES CAN GROW far higher and heavier than any other living thing. The tallest known tree was a Douglas Fir: One felled on Vancouver Island, British Columbia 100 years ago was 420 feet tall! The tallest trees alive today are coast redwoods growing on the slopes of north California's Coast Ranges.

The heaviest living tree and the most massive living thing of all is one of another kind of redwood from California. Called "General Sherman," this giant sequoia, perhaps more than 3,000 years old, is thirteen times heavier than a blue whale, the largest animal. Its trunk is 82 feet wide just above the ground. You can punch its thick, spongy bark without hurting your hand!

Trees can live longer than almost any other kind of plant. One of the longest-living trees in the world, the bristlecone pine can live to be more than 5,000 years old. The oldest bristlecone pines would have begun life around the same time as the dawn of the ancient Egyptian civilization. Probably the oldest *kind* of living tree is the maidenhair, or ginkgo. Its fan-shaped leaves look almost exactly like fossil leaves preserved in rocks known to be more than 160 million years old.

GIANT SEQUOIA
2,755 tons
Heaviest living tree

EUCALYPTUS (MOUNTAIN ASH)
348 feet tall
Tallest broadleaf tree

COAST REDWOOD
367 feet tall
Tallest living tree

DOUGLAS FIR
420 feet tall
Tallest known tree

The banyan tree, a kind of fig, is a holy tree in India. Its roots grow downward from its branches and support them like pillars. This allows the tree to keep growing outward.

A fat baobab tree (below) can measure more than 164 feet around its trunk. Its huge, bottle-shaped trunk is for storing water during the dry season in Africa. In long droughts, some baobabs may actually shrink in size.

BANYAN TREE
1,970 feet around
Greatest canopy
(spread of branches)

One of the oldest-living trees is the bristlecone pine (below). Bristlecones grow very slowly on the high, windswept slopes of the Rocky Mountains.

The ginkgo (below) is a living fossil, probably the oldest kind of tree alive today. Ginkgoes existed in the age of the dinosaurs.

GIRAFFE
18 feet
Tallest animal

The illustrations are approximately to scale

85

THE LARGEST FLOWER
THE MYSTERIOUS RAFFLESIA

WALKING THROUGH a southeast Asian forest, you might sniff a disgusting smell like rotting meat. This stench would lead you to one of the strangest plants on Earth. A scientist named it *Rafflesia* for Sir Thomas Stamford Raffles, the British colonial governor who founded Singapore. People also call it the stinking corpse lily. But *Rafflesia* is not a lily, nor is it like any other ordinary flowering plant.

You will see no stem, and there are no leaves or roots. The whole plant consists of long, thin threads hidden from sight – and one huge flower up to 3 feet across, the largest flower in the world. With five reddish "petals" resembling slices of raw meat, the flower is very heavy, too. A large specimen may weigh more than a one-year-old child.

THE SMALLEST FLOWER

This picture shows *Wolffia*, the world's tiniest flowering plant, hugely magnified and cut open from one side. Its flowers grow inside a special hollow. About the size of a comma on this page, *Wolffia* is so small that you cannot see it properly without a magnifying glass. Millions of these floating plants mass together to form green scum on ponds. There are about a dozen sorts of *Wolffia* in different parts of the world. The smallest kind, *Wolffia arrhiza*, lives in Australia.

Rafflesia has a flower almost as big as a bus wheel but no roots, stem, or leaves for making food. This parasite steals ready-made nourishment from another plant.

From the sticky seeds produced by female flowers sprout the threads that form a new *Rafflesia* plant. The threads burrow through the rough bark of a jungle vine. Nine months later, a new flower bud bursts open.

THE FIRST FLOWER

No one knows when the world's first flowering plant bloomed, or what it was. But fossil leaves and pollen found in rocks do show that flowering plants existed more than 125 million years ago. The earliest kinds *(left)* may have looked like today's magnolias. Scientists believe that the magnolias' ancestors were related to cone-bearing pines and fir trees. Unlike these kinds of plants, flowering plants carry seeds covered with a special outer coat. These well-protected seeds helped flowering plants to multiply and spread around the world.

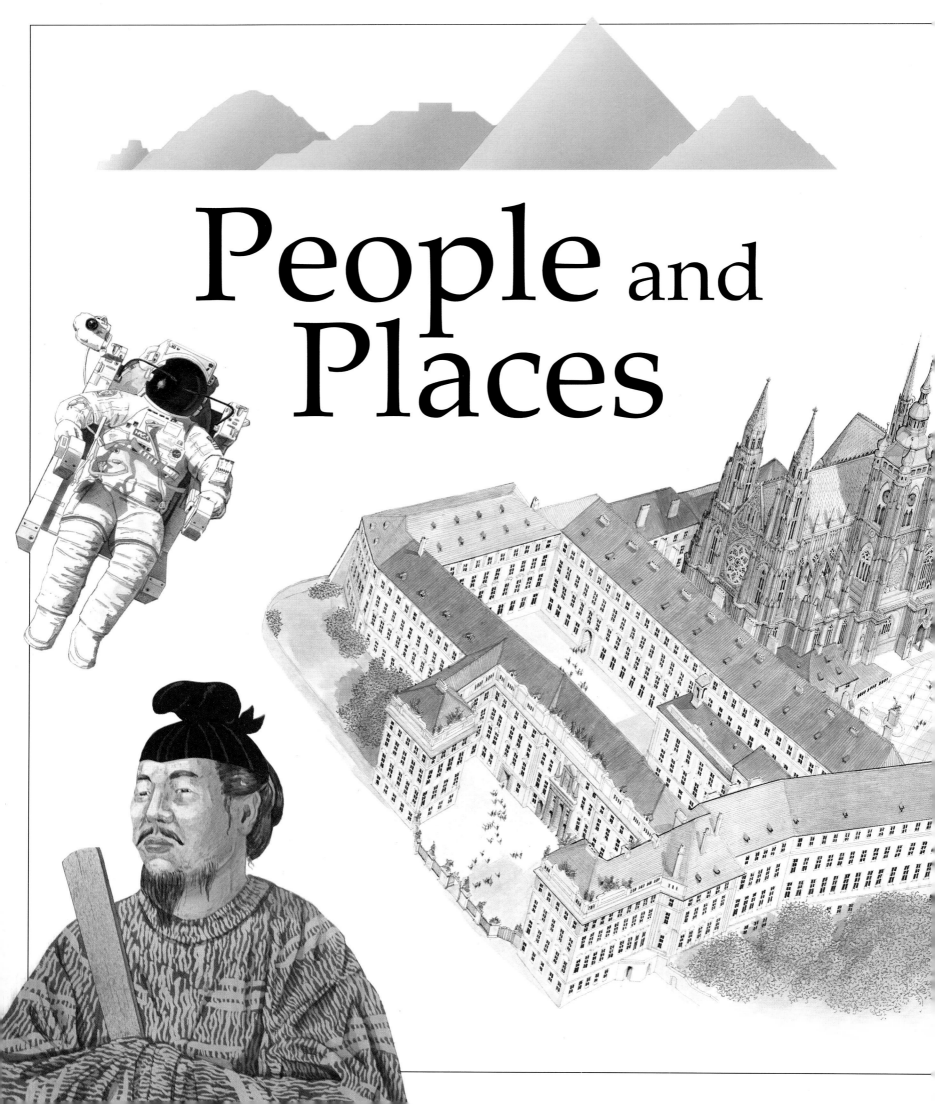

People and Places

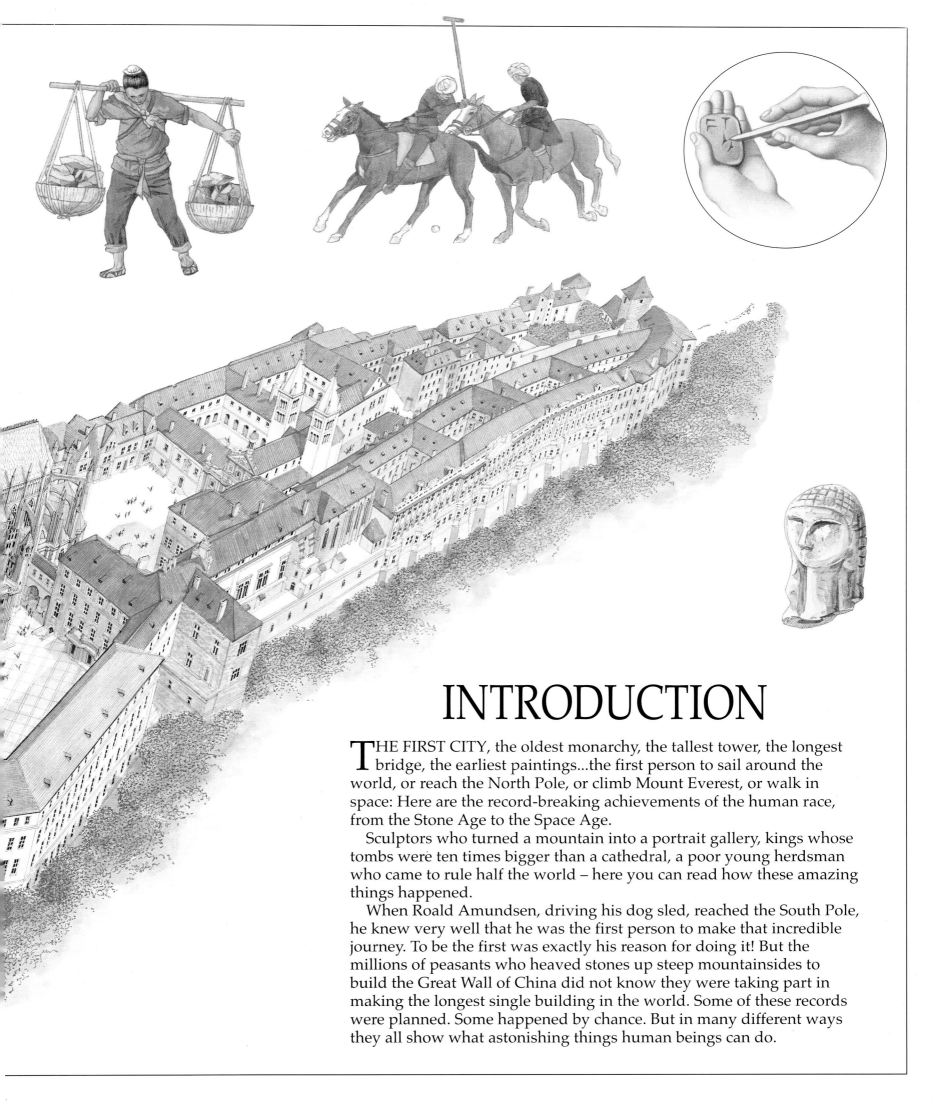

INTRODUCTION

THE FIRST CITY, the oldest monarchy, the tallest tower, the longest bridge, the earliest paintings...the first person to sail around the world, or reach the North Pole, or climb Mount Everest, or walk in space: Here are the record-breaking achievements of the human race, from the Stone Age to the Space Age.

Sculptors who turned a mountain into a portrait gallery, kings whose tombs were ten times bigger than a cathedral, a poor young herdsman who came to rule half the world – here you can read how these amazing things happened.

When Roald Amundsen, driving his dog sled, reached the South Pole, he knew very well that he was the first person to make that incredible journey. To be the first was exactly his reason for doing it! But the millions of peasants who heaved stones up steep mountainsides to build the Great Wall of China did not know they were taking part in making the longest single building in the world. Some of these records were planned. Some happened by chance. But in many different ways they all show what astonishing things human beings can do.

WORLD RECORD HOLDERS
FIRST AND FOREMOST FROM EVERY CONTINENT

KEY

1 Gateway Arch, St. Louis *Tallest monument* 630 feet
2 Mount Rushmore, South Dakota *Largest sculpture*
3 CN Tower, Toronto, Canada *Tallest self-supporting structure* 1,814 feet
4 Grand Central, New York *Largest railroad station* 47 acres
5 St. John the Divine, New York *Largest cathedral (by volume)* 16,820,000 cu feet
6 Louisiana Superdome, New Orleans *Largest indoor stadium* 13 acres
7 Cholula, Mexico (now built over by a church) *Largest pyramid* 44.5 acres
8 Mexico City *Second largest city* 23,913,000 people
9 Morococha, Peru *Highest railroad line* More than 15,700 feet above sea level
10 La Paz, Bolivia *Highest capital city* 11,910 feet above sea level
11 Maracana Stadium, Rio de Janeiro, Brazil *Largest soccer stadium* 205,000 capacity
12 Ushuaia, Argentina *Southernmost town*
13 Greenland *Least densely-populated country* 0.07 people per sq mile
14 Ny Ålesund, Svalbard *Northernmost village*
15 Rotterdam, Netherlands *Busiest port* 330 million tons of cargo handled annually
16 Hradcany, Prague, Czechoslovakia *Largest ancient castle* 877,600 sq feet
17 Heathrow Airport, London, UK *Most international traffic* About 47,000,000 passengers annually
18 Ulm Cathedral, Germany *Tallest steeple* 528 feet
19 Seville Cathedral, Spain *Largest cathedral (by area)* 381 feet long, 249 feet wide
20 Vatican City State *Smallest country* 0.17 sq miles
21 Jericho, West Bank, Israel *Oldest city* Built about 10,000 years ago
22 Saqqara, Egypt *Oldest pyramid* Built 2700 BC
23 Lake Volta, Ghana *Largest reservoir (by area)* 3,274 sq miles
24 Liberia *Fastest growing population* 8.6% since 1995
25 Dinka people, Sudan *Tallest people* Average 6.9 feet tall
26 Bambuti people, Congo *Shortest people* Average 4.6 feet tall
27 Russia *Largest country* 6,592,800 sq miles
28 Forbidden City, Beijing, China *Largest palace* About 0.4 sq miles
29 Seikan rail tunnel, Japan *Longest rail tunnel* 33.6 miles
30 Tokyo-Yokohama, Japan *Largest city* 28,447,000 people
31 Amida Buddha, Ushiku City, Japan *Tallest statue* 394 feet
32 Akashi-Kaikyo Bridge, Japan *Longest suspension bridge* 6,530 feet
33 China *Largest population* 1,243,738,000 people
34 Shah Faisal, Islamabad, Pakistan *Largest mosque* 47 acres
35 Angkor, Cambodia *Largest temple complex* More than 95 sq miles
36 Sultan's Palace, Brunei *Largest residential palace*
37 Petronas Twin Towers, Kuala Lumpur, Malaysia *Tallest office building* 1,483 feet
38 Borobudur, Indonesia *Largest Buddhist temple* 161,400 sq feet
39 Sydney Harbor Bridge, Australia *Widest long-span bridge* 161 feet wide
40 Trans-Australia line, Nullarbor Plain *Longest straight railroad track* 297 miles

THE LARGEST CITIES

		approximate population
1	Tokyo, Japan	28,447,000
2	Mexico City, Mexico	23,913,000
3	São Paulo, Brazil	21,539,000
4	Seoul, South Korea	19,065,000
5	New York, USA	16,332,000
6	Bombay, India	15,138,000
7	Osaka, Japan	14,060,000
8	Shanghai, China	13,584,000
9	Calcutta, India	12,885,000
10	Rio de Janeiro, Brazil	12,788,000

figures are for the entire built-up area

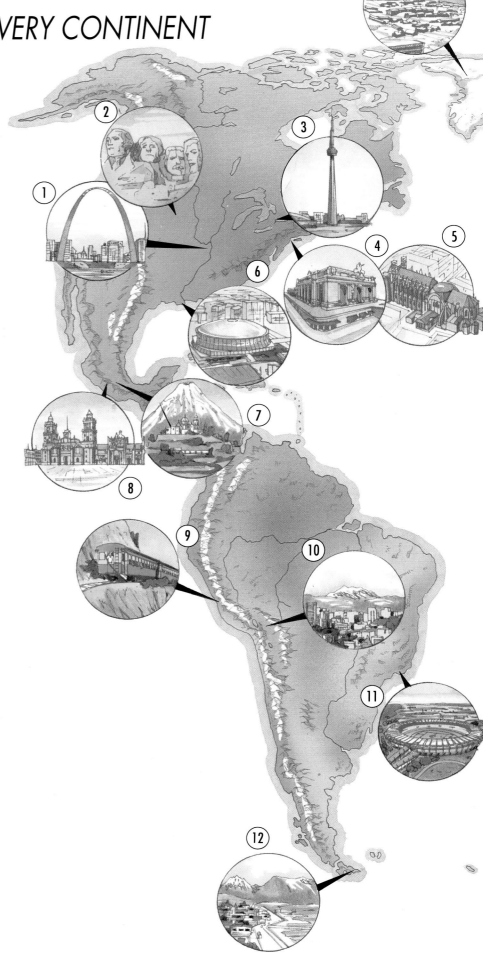

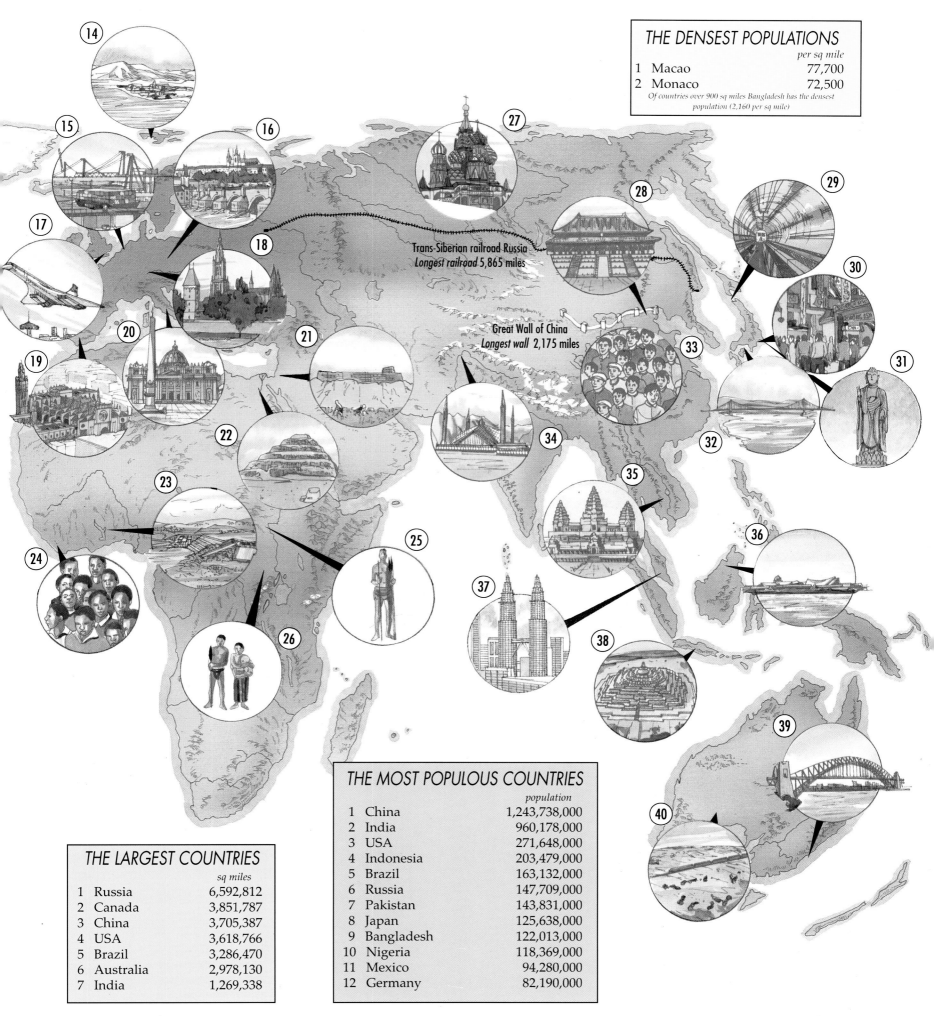

THE DENSEST POPULATIONS

		per sq mile
1	Macao	77,700
2	Monaco	72,500

Of countries over 900 sq miles Bangladesh has the densest population (2,160 per sq mile)

Trans-Siberian railroad Russia
Longest railroad 5,865 miles

Great Wall of China
Longest wall 2,175 miles

THE MOST POPULOUS COUNTRIES

		population
1	China	1,243,738,000
2	India	960,178,000
3	USA	271,648,000
4	Indonesia	203,479,000
5	Brazil	163,132,000
6	Russia	147,709,000
7	Pakistan	143,831,000
8	Japan	125,638,000
9	Bangladesh	122,013,000
10	Nigeria	118,369,000
11	Mexico	94,280,000
12	Germany	82,190,000

THE LARGEST COUNTRIES

		sq miles
1	Russia	6,592,812
2	Canada	3,851,787
3	China	3,705,387
4	USA	3,618,766
5	Brazil	3,286,470
6	Australia	2,978,130
7	India	1,269,338

THE FIRST ARTISTS
SCULPTURE AND PAINTING OF THE STONE AGE

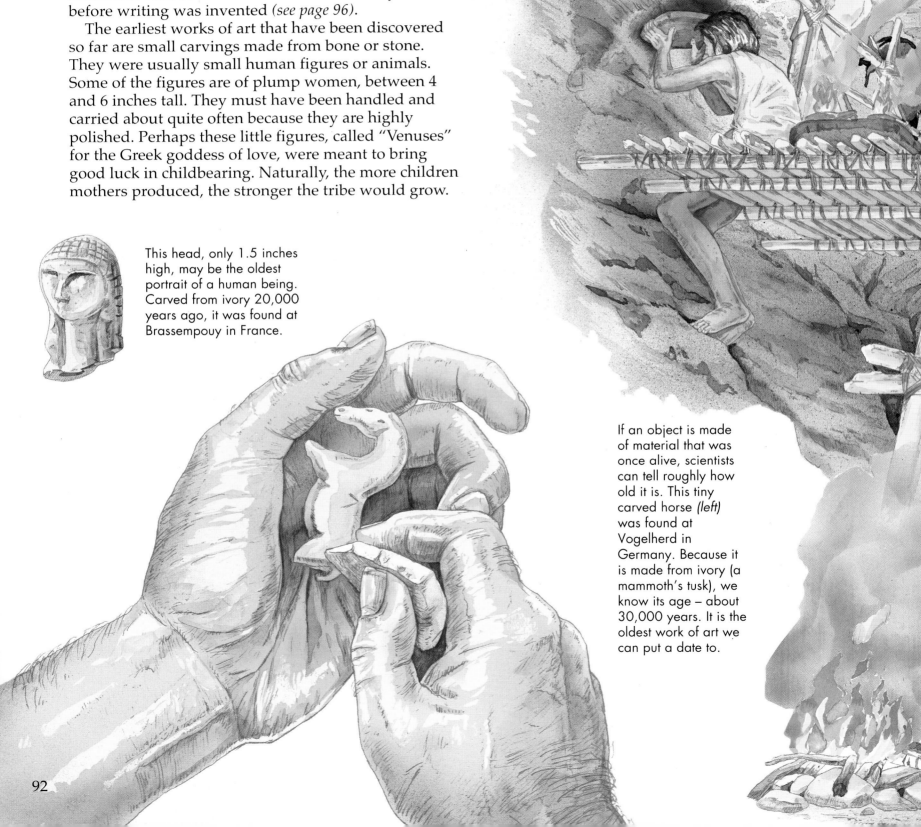

IF YOU GIVE a piece of paper and a pencil to a small child, he or she will probably draw a picture (usually a face). Human beings also made pictures before they learned to read or write – some thousands of years before writing was invented *(see page 96)*.

The earliest works of art that have been discovered so far are small carvings made from bone or stone. They were usually small human figures or animals. Some of the figures are of plump women, between 4 and 6 inches tall. They must have been handled and carried about quite often because they are highly polished. Perhaps these little figures, called "Venuses" for the Greek goddess of love, were meant to bring good luck in childbearing. Naturally, the more children mothers produced, the stronger the tribe would grow.

This head, only 1.5 inches high, may be the oldest portrait of a human being. Carved from ivory 20,000 years ago, it was found at Brassempouy in France.

If an object is made of material that was once alive, scientists can tell roughly how old it is. This tiny carved horse *(left)* was found at Vogelherd in Germany. Because it is made from ivory (a mammoth's tusk), we know its age – about 30,000 years. It is the oldest work of art we can put a date to.

THE CAVE PAINTERS OF LASCAUX

In 1940 four boys discovered a hole in the ground near Lascaux in France. They climbed down and found themselves in a system of caves. By the light of their lamp they saw, to their amazement, that the walls were covered with lifelike paintings of animals. This underground art gallery is now one of the most precious treasures in Europe.

The paintings on the walls, some of the earliest known, were made between 10,000 and 18,000 years ago. They were painted by hunters sheltering in the caves, who worked by the light of burning pine branches. These prehistoric painters, using colors made from powdered rock or plants, were as skilful as any modern painter. But why did they spend so much time making paintings that no-one could see? No one knows for sure, but the most common animals they painted were large grazing animals such as deer, wild cattle, and horses. These were the animals they hunted. The paintings may have been meant as offerings to the gods, urging them to bring success to the huntsmen.

Vogelherd

Lascaux

Brassempouy

THE FIRST MUSIC

Music-making of some kind may have come before carving or painting. The bone whistle that this girl is playing, which was found in North Africa, is thousands of years older than the earliest carvings. But the first musical instruments were probably percussion – drums and rattles – which are good for dancing to. Some very ancient instruments, like the didgeridoo (a long, hollow pipe) of the Australian Aborigines, are still played today.

93

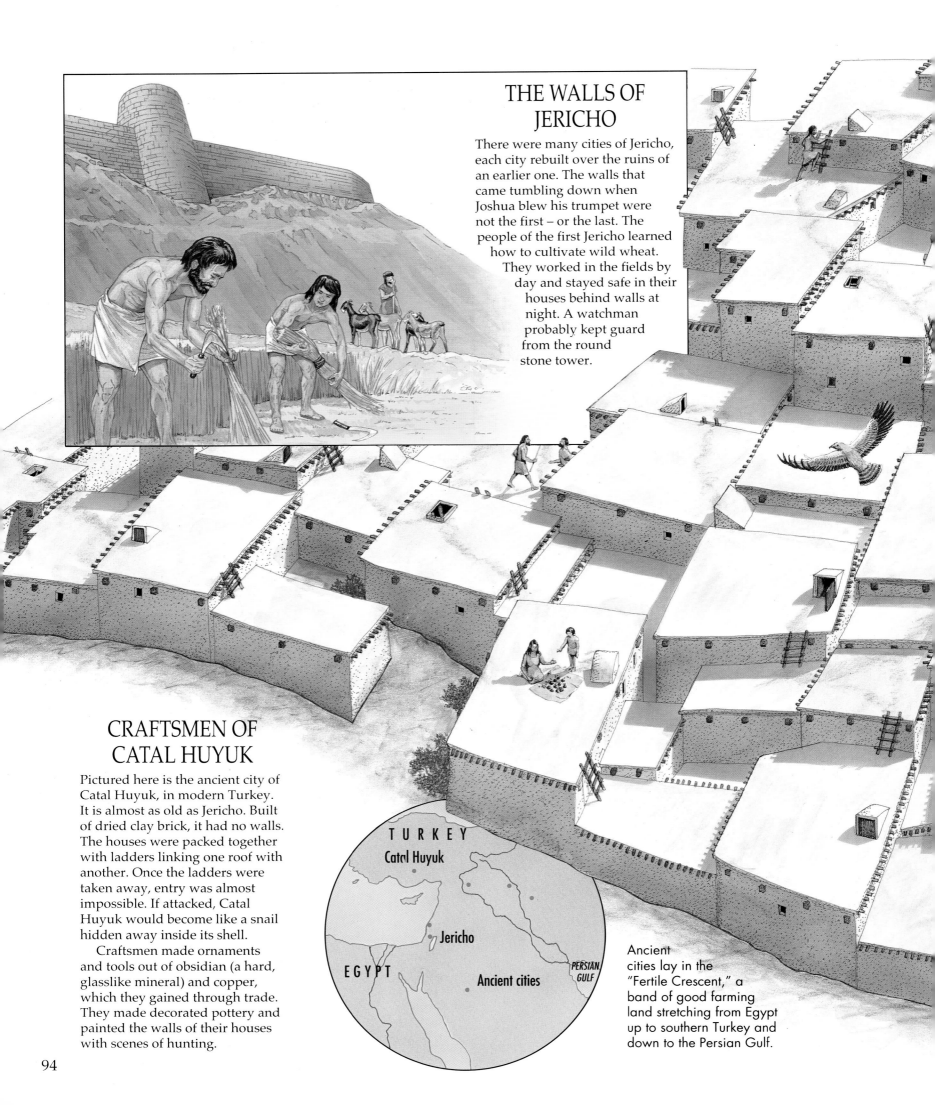

THE WALLS OF JERICHO

There were many cities of Jericho, each city rebuilt over the ruins of an earlier one. The walls that came tumbling down when Joshua blew his trumpet were not the first – or the last. The people of the first Jericho learned how to cultivate wild wheat. They worked in the fields by day and stayed safe in their houses behind walls at night. A watchman probably kept guard from the round stone tower.

CRAFTSMEN OF CATAL HUYUK

Pictured here is the ancient city of Catal Huyuk, in modern Turkey. It is almost as old as Jericho. Built of dried clay brick, it had no walls. The houses were packed together with ladders linking one roof with another. Once the ladders were taken away, entry was almost impossible. If attacked, Catal Huyuk would become like a snail hidden away inside its shell.

Craftsmen made ornaments and tools out of obsidian (a hard, glasslike mineral) and copper, which they gained through trade. They made decorated pottery and painted the walls of their houses with scenes of hunting.

TURKEY
Catal Huyuk

Jericho

EGYPT

Ancient cities

PERSIAN GULF

Ancient cities lay in the "Fertile Crescent," a band of good farming land stretching from Egypt up to southern Turkey and down to the Persian Gulf.

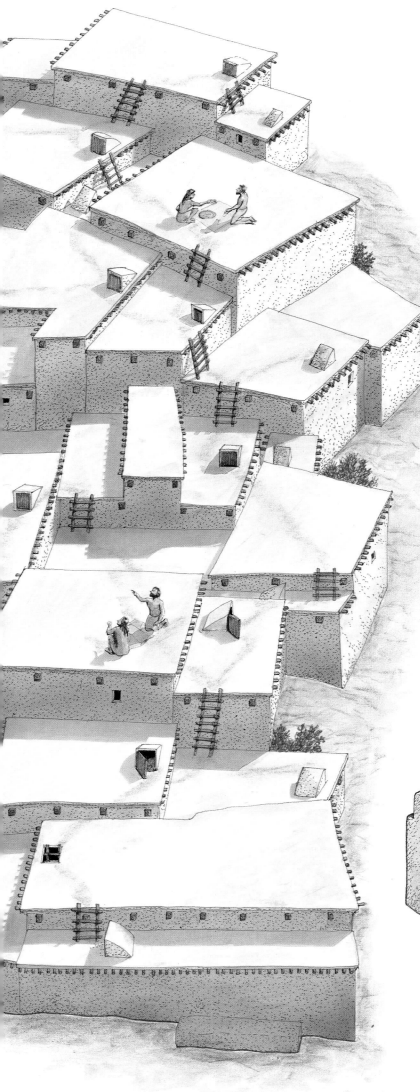

THE FIRST CITIES
TOWN LIFE 10,000 YEARS AGO

AT JERICHO, west of the Jordan River in Palestine, there is a spring that provides water for growing crops. That spring was there 10,000 years ago. It may be the reason why people first settled at Jericho, the oldest-known city in the world.

The earliest human beings were nomads who never lived in one place for long. They ate wild plants and hunted animals for food. When the food supply ran short, they moved on. About 12,000 years ago they discovered how to grow crops. They became farmers, living all year round in one place, sowing and harvesting grain, and keeping herds of animals.

Once people settled down in villages, many things became possible. It was not necessary for everyone to spend their time getting food. Farmers provided the food while some people did other work. They became builders and craftsmen, merchants and soldiers, teachers and priests. Civilization had arrived.

Town life first began in the Middle East, the countries around the eastern end of the Mediterranean Sea. The very first villages were near the mountain slopes where wild cereals grew. Most of them were also near rivers, like the Tigris and Euphrates, and the Nile, where the yearly floods gave rich, damp soil. Small hills, called *tell* in Arabic and *huyuk* in Turkish, mark the remains of ancient villages.

Some grew larger, with walls, towers, and homes made of mud-bricks. They were the first cities.

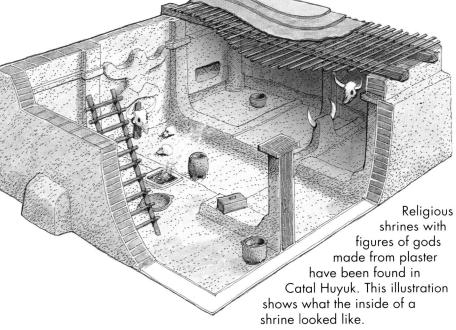

Religious shrines with figures of gods made from plaster have been found in Catal Huyuk. This illustration shows what the inside of a shrine looked like.

THE FIRST WRITING
THE BEGINNING OF HISTORY

IMAGINE WHAT the world would be like if no one could read or write! There would be no way of sending messages, keeping records, or learning new facts, except by speech.

Writing is a way of recording language by symbols. In languages like English or Russian these symbols are the letters of the alphabet. English has thousands of words, yet we can write them all using just 26 letters. But making words out of letters is not the only way of writing. People used a form of written language long before an alphabet existed.

The development of writing as we know it was a very long process, taking thousands of years. It started where civilization began, in the ancient land of Mesopotamia (roughly, modern Iraq). The first things people wanted to record were lists, say, of the animals owned by a farmer. The symbols that stood for these things were, simply, pictures. The symbol for a cow, for example, was a picture of a cow's head. You could make a new word by putting two signs together. The sign for "woman" and the sign for "mountains" written together, meant "foreign woman" ("woman from beyond the mountains").

WRITING WITH PICTURES

The first writing in picture symbols, or pictograms, that has been discovered so far comes from Uruk, a city of the Sumerians in Mesopotamia. It consists of records of goods and food supplies for a temple, written on slabs of clay with a pointed stick or reed. The clay slabs *(above)* have lasted very well. We can still read them although they were written 5,300 years ago.

Writing cuneiform with a reed pen *(below)*

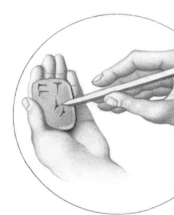

CHINESE WRITING

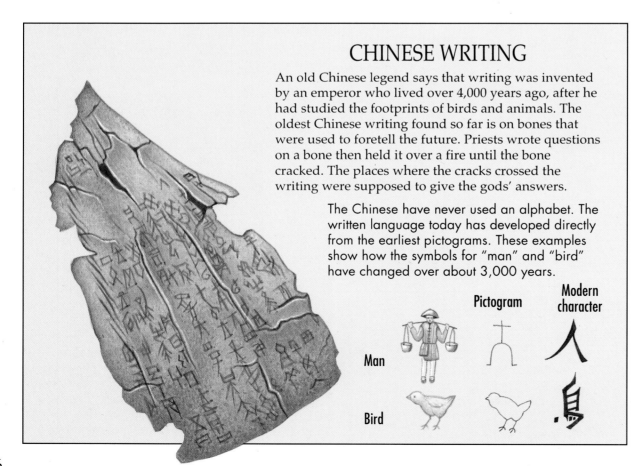

An old Chinese legend says that writing was invented by an emperor who lived over 4,000 years ago, after he had studied the footprints of birds and animals. The oldest Chinese writing found so far is on bones that were used to foretell the future. Priests wrote questions on a bone then held it over a fire until the bone cracked. The places where the cracks crossed the writing were supposed to give the gods' answers.

The Chinese have never used an alphabet. The written language today has developed directly from the earliest pictograms. These examples show how the symbols for "man" and "bird" have changed over about 3,000 years.

		Pictogram	Modern character
Man			
Bird			

Bull's head

Fish

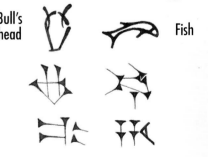

About 2900 BC, Sumerian writing changed. Curves disappeared. The symbols were drawn with straight lines, which were easier to write with a reed pen cut to a triangular point. This writing *(above)* is called cuneiform, meaning "wedgelike."

ANCIENT EGYPTIAN HIEROGLYPHS

A kind of picture-writing was invented in Egypt in about 3000 BC. Symbols called hieroglyphs ("holy writing," *top*) could record thoughts as well as things. With hieroglyphs, unlike cuneiform, it was possible to write poems, stories, and works on law or medicine. Writing hieroglyphs was, however, very slow. So the busy Egyptians developed another, quicker form of writing, called hieratic (*above*). The characters, or symbols, were based on hieroglyphs, but in a simpler form. It was not as beautiful, but much more practical!

The Egyptians were the first to use paper. They cut papyrus reed into strips and laid the strips side by side to make a square. Another layer went on top, with the strips at right angles to the first layer. The papermakers then pressed the sheet flat and polished it smooth.

The first people to use an alphabet were the Canaanites, who lived in Palestine over 3,000 years ago. Instead of having to learn hundreds of different word symbols, a person had only to learn 20 or 30 signs (letters), that stood for sounds. Learning to read and write was much easier. Our own alphabet has descended from the Canaanites' although it has changed a great deal in the past 30 centuries.

Canaanite	Modern
↶	A
⊓	B
∟	C
⋈	D
⚲	E
⚲	F
Ⅲ	H
⟨	I
⟨⟨⟨	K
⌇	L
⌇⌇	M
⌇⌇	N
◉	O
⊏	P
8	Q
⟨ⁿ	R
⌇⌇	S
✕	T

A young Egyptian learns to write on a piece of pottery using a reed pen. Hieroglyphs were "painted" with a thin brush. Ink was made by mixing powder with water.

THE GREATEST PYRAMIDS
MONUMENTS OF THE ANCIENT WORLD

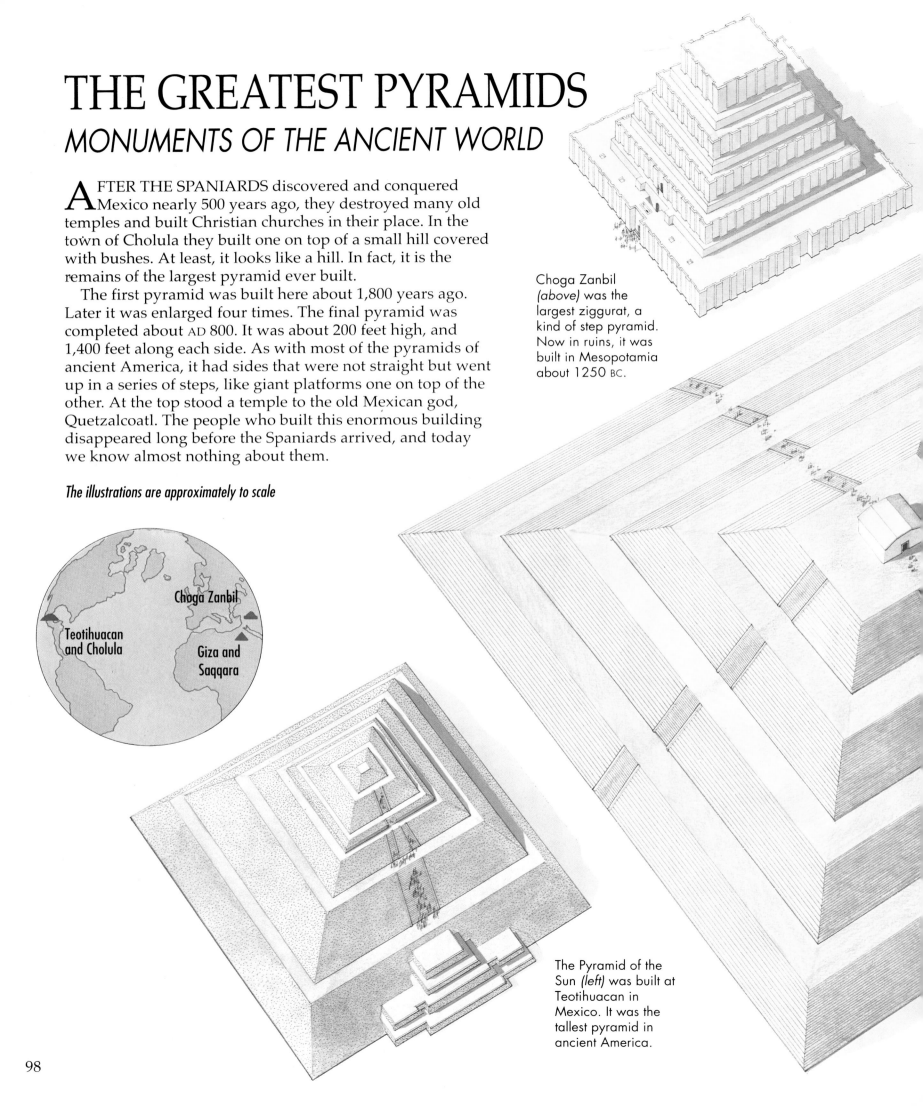

AFTER THE SPANIARDS discovered and conquered Mexico nearly 500 years ago, they destroyed many old temples and built Christian churches in their place. In the town of Cholula they built one on top of a small hill covered with bushes. At least, it looks like a hill. In fact, it is the remains of the largest pyramid ever built.

The first pyramid was built here about 1,800 years ago. Later it was enlarged four times. The final pyramid was completed about AD 800. It was about 200 feet high, and 1,400 feet along each side. As with most of the pyramids of ancient America, it had sides that were not straight but went up in a series of steps, like giant platforms one on top of the other. At the top stood a temple to the old Mexican god, Quetzalcoatl. The people who built this enormous building disappeared long before the Spaniards arrived, and today we know almost nothing about them.

The illustrations are approximately to scale

Choga Zanbil *(above)* was the largest ziggurat, a kind of step pyramid. Now in ruins, it was built in Mesopotamia about 1250 BC.

Choga Zanbil

Teotihuacan and Cholula

Giza and Saqqara

The Pyramid of the Sun *(left)* was built at Teotihuacan in Mexico. It was the tallest pyramid in ancient America.

THE GREAT PYRAMID

The most famous pyramids are in Egypt. This is the largest, the Great Pyramid at Giza *(right)*. It was built by King Khufu in about 2580 BC. There are more than 2,500,000 blocks of limestone, some weighing more than 16 tons. All were maneuvered carefully into position by ramps, levers, rollers, and sleds. The people who were in charge of building it were clearly sticklers for accuracy! Its base is almost a perfect square, each face pointing exactly north, south, east, and west. Why? No one knows for sure. *(See also pages 117 and 119.)*

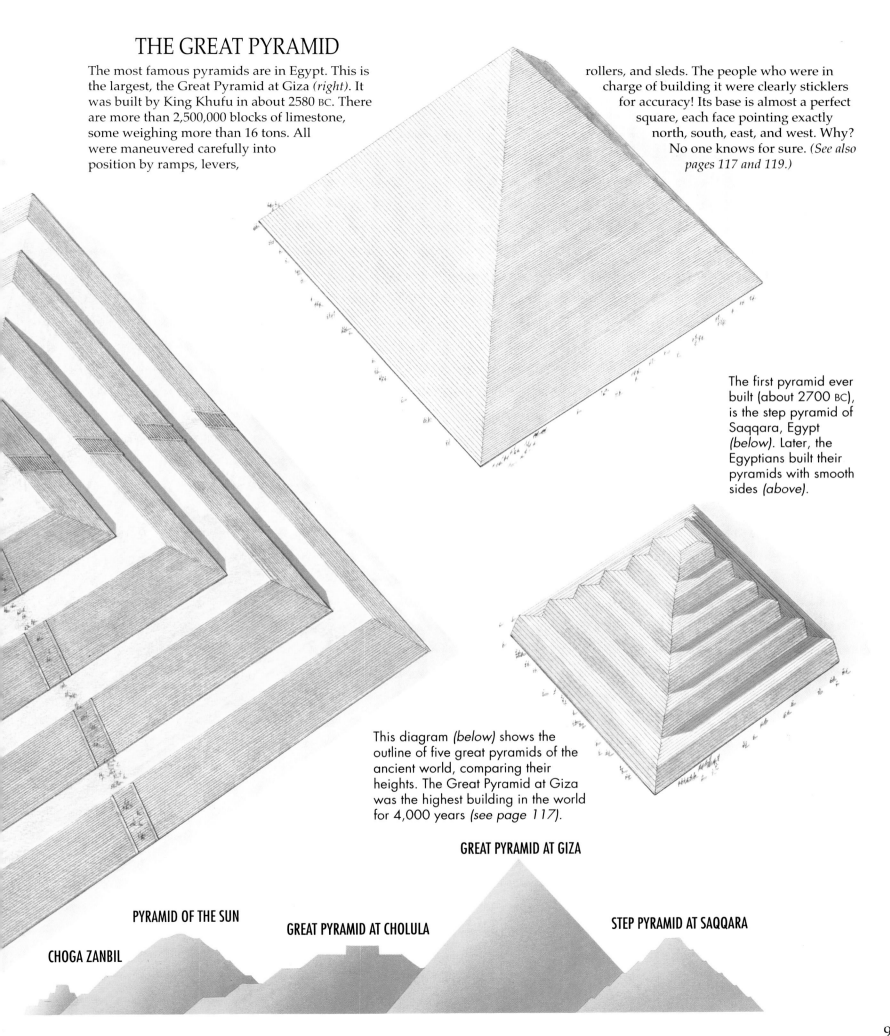

The first pyramid ever built (about 2700 BC), is the step pyramid of Saqqara, Egypt *(below)*. Later, the Egyptians built their pyramids with smooth sides *(above)*.

This diagram *(below)* shows the outline of five great pyramids of the ancient world, comparing their heights. The Great Pyramid at Giza was the highest building in the world for 4,000 years *(see page 117)*.

GREAT PYRAMID AT GIZA

PYRAMID OF THE SUN

GREAT PYRAMID AT CHOLULA

STEP PYRAMID AT SAQQARA

CHOGA ZANBIL

THE GREATEST TEMPLES
THE WORLD'S LARGEST RELIGIOUS BUILDINGS

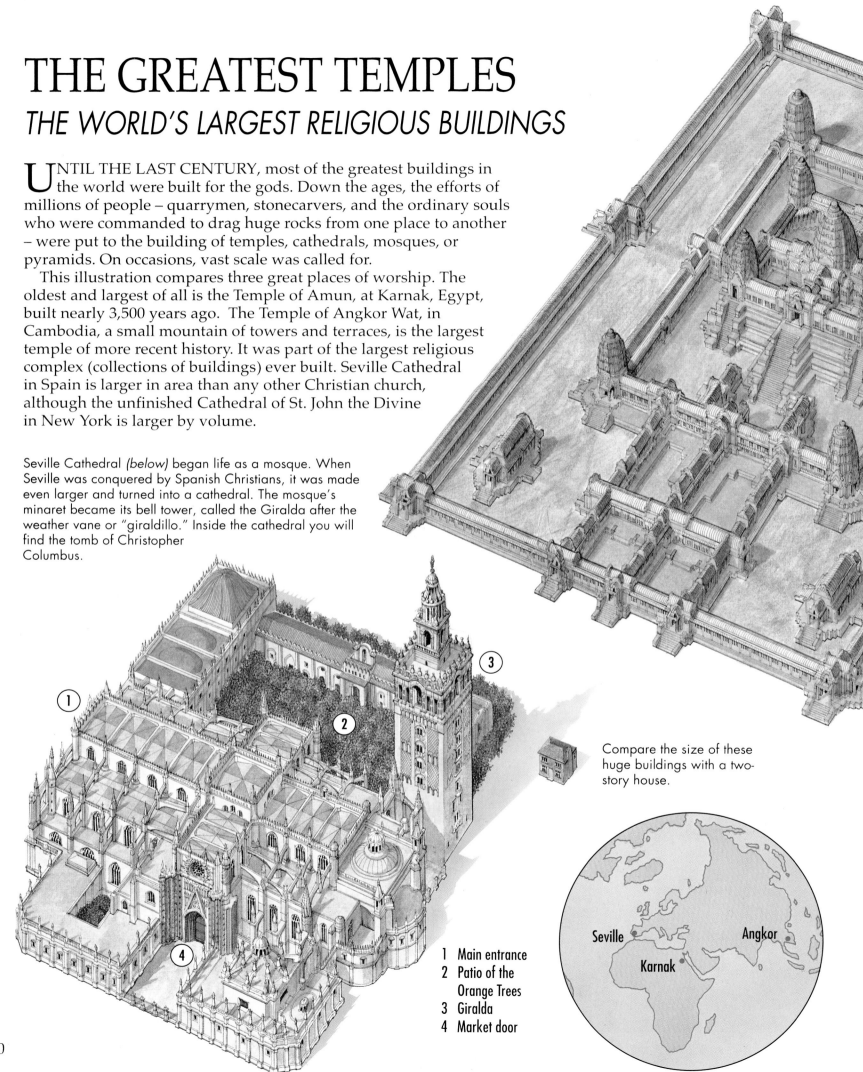

UNTIL THE LAST CENTURY, most of the greatest buildings in the world were built for the gods. Down the ages, the efforts of millions of people – quarrymen, stonecarvers, and the ordinary souls who were commanded to drag huge rocks from one place to another – were put to the building of temples, cathedrals, mosques, or pyramids. On occasions, vast scale was called for.

This illustration compares three great places of worship. The oldest and largest of all is the Temple of Amun, at Karnak, Egypt, built nearly 3,500 years ago. The Temple of Angkor Wat, in Cambodia, a small mountain of towers and terraces, is the largest temple of more recent history. It was part of the largest religious complex (collections of buildings) ever built. Seville Cathedral in Spain is larger in area than any other Christian church, although the unfinished Cathedral of St. John the Divine in New York is larger by volume.

Seville Cathedral *(below)* began life as a mosque. When Seville was conquered by Spanish Christians, it was made even larger and turned into a cathedral. The mosque's minaret became its bell tower, called the Giralda after the weather vane or "giraldillo." Inside the cathedral you will find the tomb of Christopher Columbus.

Compare the size of these huge buildings with a two-story house.

1 Main entrance
2 Patio of the Orange Trees
3 Giralda
4 Market door

Seville

Karnak

Angkor

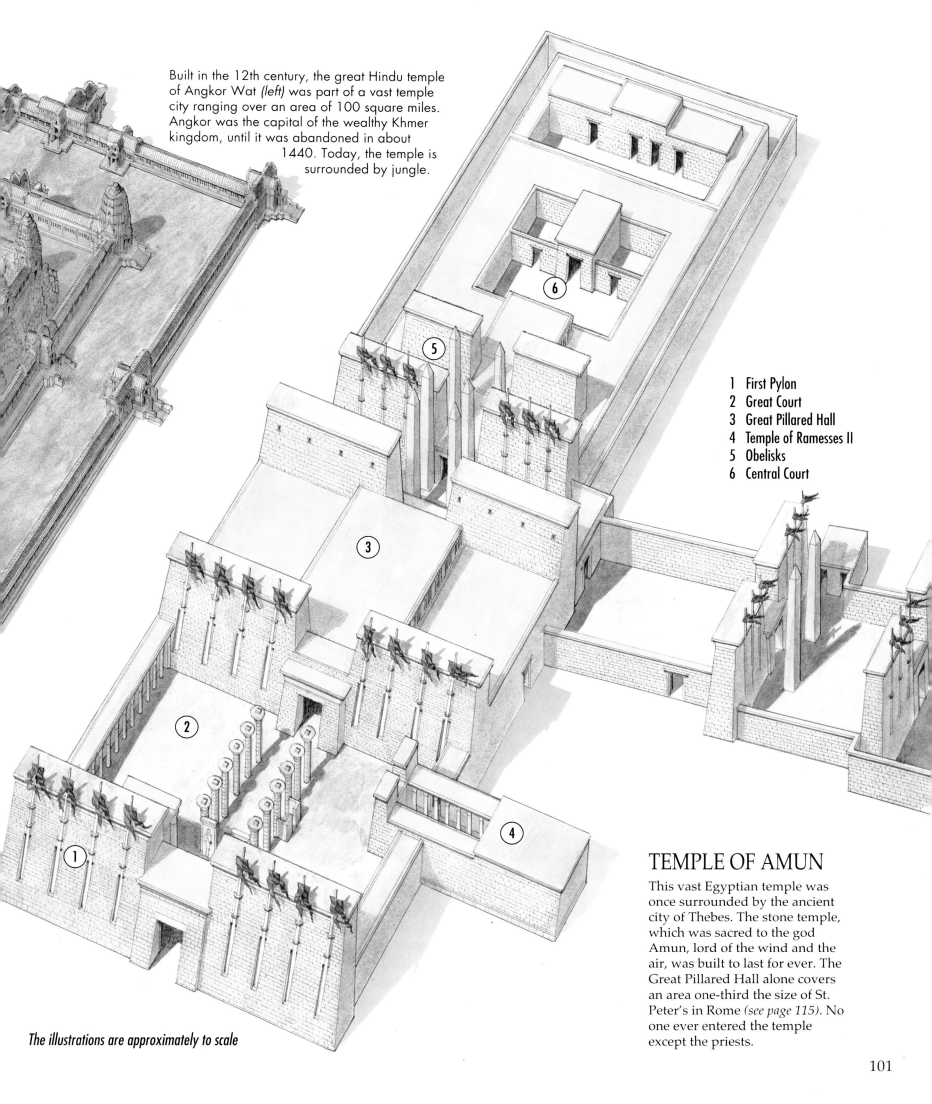

Built in the 12th century, the great Hindu temple of Angkor Wat *(left)* was part of a vast temple city ranging over an area of 100 square miles. Angkor was the capital of the wealthy Khmer kingdom, until it was abandoned in about 1440. Today, the temple is surrounded by jungle.

1 First Pylon
2 Great Court
3 Great Pillared Hall
4 Temple of Ramesses II
5 Obelisks
6 Central Court

The illustrations are approximately to scale

TEMPLE OF AMUN

This vast Egyptian temple was once surrounded by the ancient city of Thebes. The stone temple, which was sacred to the god Amun, lord of the wind and the air, was built to last for ever. The Great Pillared Hall alone covers an area one-third the size of St. Peter's in Rome *(see page 115)*. No one ever entered the temple except the priests.

101

THE EARLIEST SPORTS
MARTIAL ARTS IN ANCIENT EGYPT

OUR EARLIEST ANCESTORS were hunters, but they hunted for food, not for sport. Probably they played games of some kind, because all human beings do. True sports did not begin until civilization *(see page 95)* was established, when kings and noblemen hunted wild animals with spears. They hunted because they enjoyed it, not because they needed food.

Many of the earliest sports, the "martial arts" such as wrestling, archery, and fencing, were based on fighting. Young men had to be trained for battle by practicing combat with their hands or with weapons. That was how most sports began.

Egypt was one of the first civilizations. We know a great deal about it because the ancient Egyptians left records of nearly everything they did, in both words and pictures. We can still see paintings of young men wrestling or fencing and read descriptions of swimming contests and rowing matches held on the Nile River.

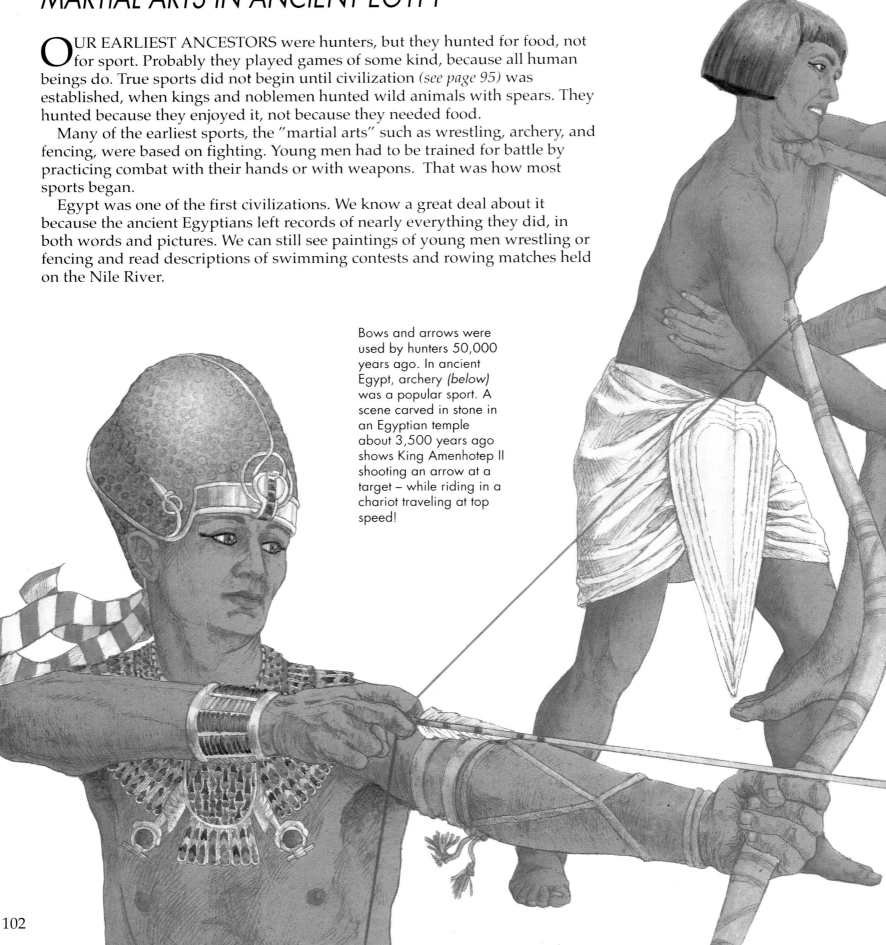

Bows and arrows were used by hunters 50,000 years ago. In ancient Egypt, archery *(below)* was a popular sport. A scene carved in stone in an Egyptian temple about 3,500 years ago shows King Amenhotep II shooting an arrow at a target – while riding in a chariot traveling at top speed!

STICK FIGHTING

Swords were used for fighting as soon as human beings learned how to make metal weapons. Sword fighting later became a sport called fencing, played with wooden swords. The first match of which we have a record was held in Egypt about 3,200 years ago. From this illustration you can tell it is a sporting contest and not a duel between enemies. The swords have blunted points and the fencers wear protection against accidental injury. Narrow shields cover their free arms, which they used to fend off a thrust from their opponent's sword. Crowds of spectators would turn up to watch the duelers perform.

THE FIRST OLYMPICS

All early civilizations practiced the martial arts, but we do not know when other sports began. The ancient Greeks were fond of athletics. They held the first Olympic Games, probably in 776 BC, then every four years after that. The Games included running races and events like long jump, discus, and javelin.

The oldest team game may have been polo, a game similar to hockey but played on horseback (below). It was played in Persia (Iran) at least 2,500 years ago.

The Minoan civilization existed in the Mediterranean island of Crete between about 2000 and 1400 BC. Here are two Minoan boys boxing (above).

Wrestling matches were popular in Egypt. They may have been the first organized sport. Championships were held in the presence of the king. The fight was over when one man had both shoulders pressed to the ground – just as in modern forms of wrestling. There were referees to ensure that rules were obeyed.

THE LARGEST PALACE
INSIDE THE FORBIDDEN CITY

IMAGINE A BOX. Open it and inside is another smaller box, inside that another, and so on. Beijing, the capital of China, is rather like that. It has an Inner City, the oldest part, and an Outer City in the form of a huge square. Inside the Inner City was the Imperial City, also square. Inside the Imperial City was yet another square, containing the Forbidden City.

Within its walls were the palace buildings where the emperors lived until 1912. The last emperor, Puyi, a boy of six, abdicated but lived on in the palace until 1924. It was called the Forbidden City because ordinary people were not allowed inside. If they disobeyed, they were executed. Today, the largest palace in the world is now a museum. You can go in with no danger of having your head chopped off!

Forbidden City marked in red

Beijing

CHINA

1 Meridian Gate
2 Gate of Supreme Harmony
3 Dragon Pavement
4 Hall of Supreme Harmony
5 Hall of Protecting Harmony
6 Palace of Heavenly Purity

The Ming Emperor Yong Le *(left)* began the building of the palace of the Forbidden City in 1404.

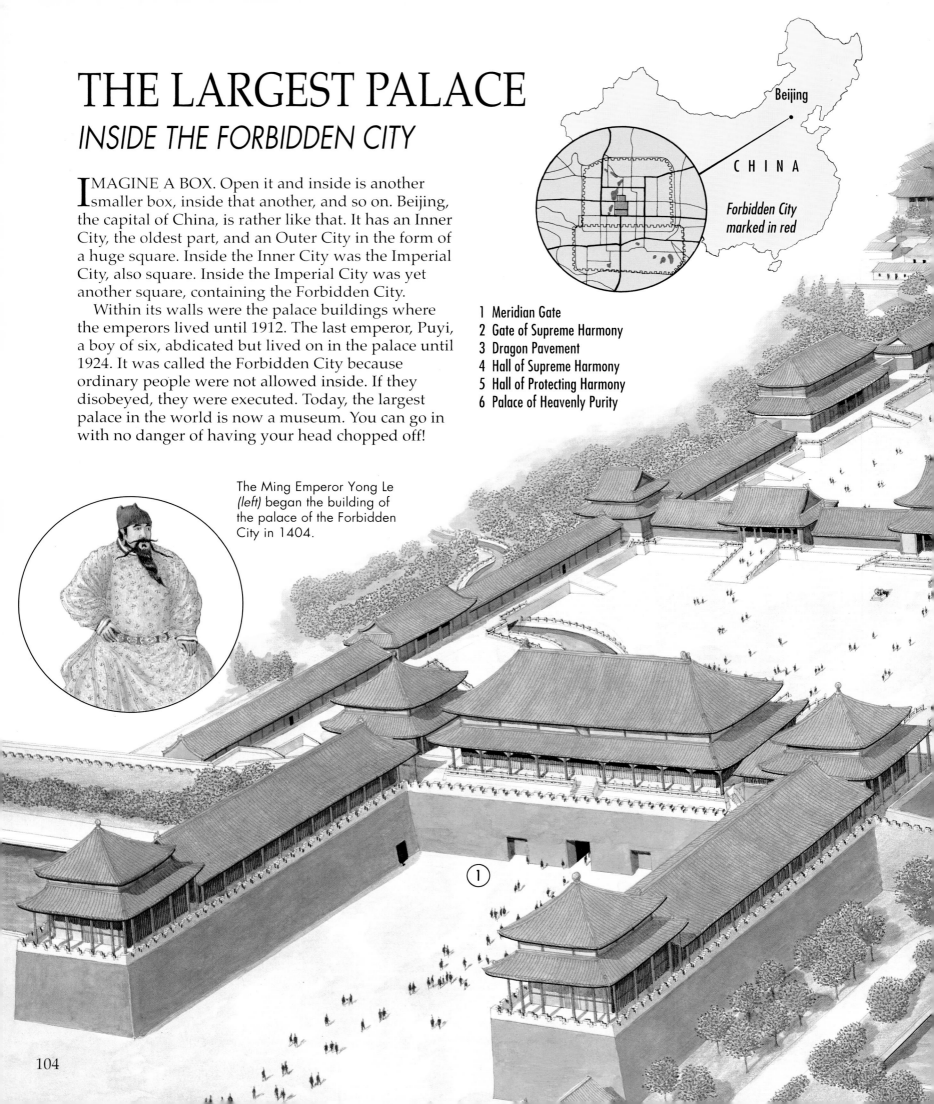

104

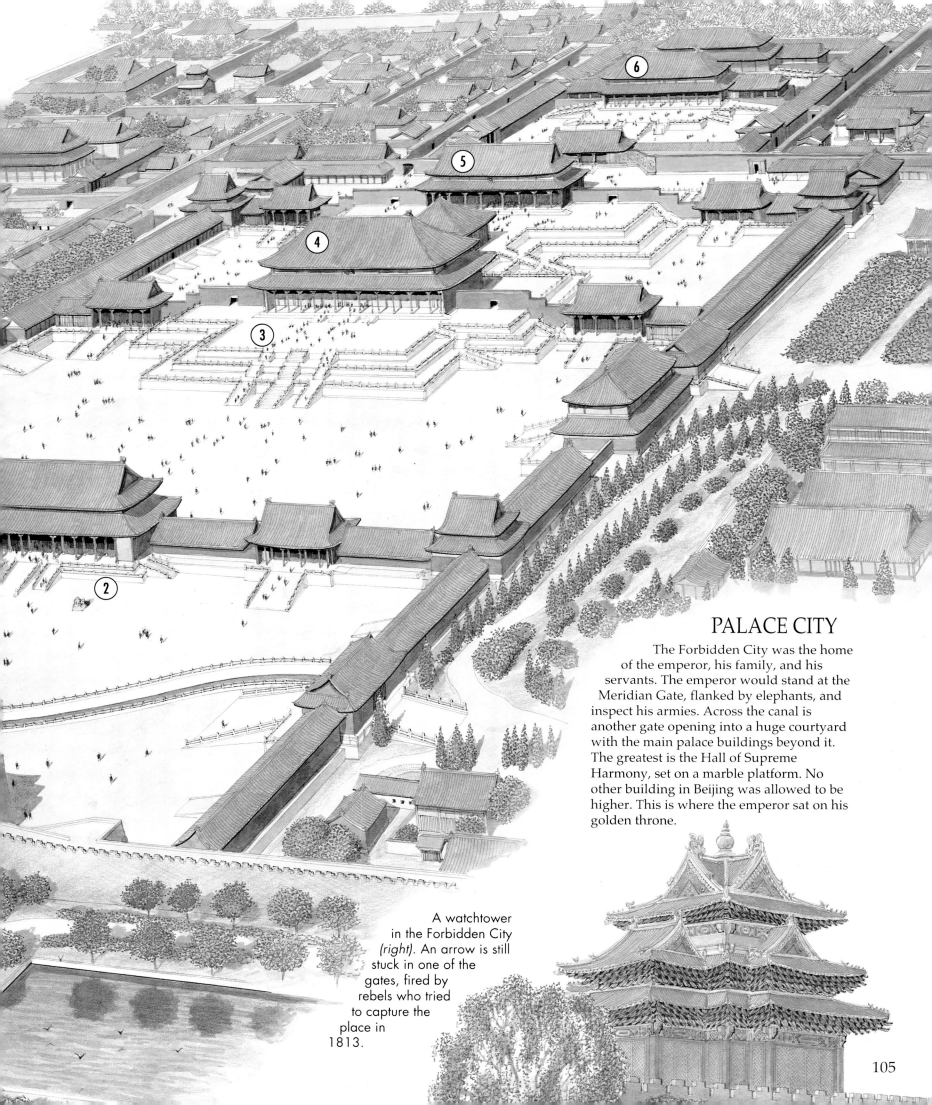

PALACE CITY

The Forbidden City was the home of the emperor, his family, and his servants. The emperor would stand at the Meridian Gate, flanked by elephants, and inspect his armies. Across the canal is another gate opening into a huge courtyard with the main palace buildings beyond it. The greatest is the Hall of Supreme Harmony, set on a marble platform. No other building in Beijing was allowed to be higher. This is where the emperor sat on his golden throne.

A watchtower in the Forbidden City *(right)*. An arrow is still stuck in one of the gates, fired by rebels who tried to capture the place in 1813.

THE LONGEST WALL
THE GREAT WALL OF CHINA

The Chinese thought of the Great Wall as a dragon *(right)* defending their country against the warlike tribes who lived to the north.

DEFENDING THE WALL

The soldiers who guarded the wall lived in the towers. When an attack came they lit a fire as a signal. More soldiers from other parts of the wall rushed to help them. Protected by battlements, they fired their arrows down on the enemy warriors trying to climb the wall. They also had giant catapults for hurling stones. In more peaceful times, the soldiers repaired the wall or worked in the fields close by.

THE FIRST GREAT WALL

Great Wall

CHINA

TEN THOUSAND YEARS AGO, nearly all human beings were nomads. They moved from place to place with their herds, living off the land. In a few places, people learned to grow crops. They were able to settle down in villages. They built permanent houses, learned new crafts such as metalwork, and traded with other villages. What we call civilization had begun (*see page 95*). To others who were still nomads, the villages were a tempting target. They raided them for food, killing the people and burning the houses. So villagers built walls around their settlements, to keep the raiders out.

One of the earliest centers of civilization was northern China. By 200 BC, a large region was ruled by the emperors of the Qin dynasty. It was often raided by the Huns, a fierce race of nomads to the north. The Qin emperors decided to build one long wall to keep them out. This was the first Great Wall of China. It ran from the Yellow Sea to the deserts of Central Asia.

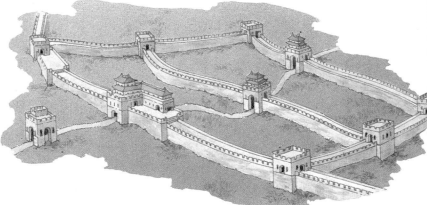

The wall snakes across China's mountains and valleys. In some places extra defenses were needed. This is the gate at Xifengkou Pass, near the eastern end, where there were three lines of wall.

BUILDING THE WALL

The Great Wall is the largest construction ever built. But it was not built all at once. Work went on for centuries. Most of the present wall was built in the 14th-16th centuries. Millions of men worked on it, carrying the stone in baskets (*right*). The final length was over 3,700 miles (more than two-thirds the distance across the United States). It is almost 30 feet high, with towers every 650 feet. Ten men can march side by side along the top.

THE OLDEST MONARCHY
JAPAN'S EMPERORS

THE PEOPLE OF ANCIENT JAPAN believed their islands were created by the goddess of the Sun. A child of the Sun goddess, Jimmu, united the people under his rule and became the first emperor.

When did all this happen? The legends say Jimmu's rule began in 660 BC. Modern historians are not so sure. They think Jimmu may have lived hundreds of years later, from about 40 BC to 10 BC. In any event, the same imperial family has ruled Japan to the present day. No other monarchy in the world has lasted so long.

Japan has always had an emperor, or sometimes an empress, who was looked upon as a god as well as a monarch. But the god-emperor was not always a powerful ruler. For hundreds of years other great families, stronger than the royal family, fought for control. Japan was torn by civil wars.

Japan became a settled, peaceful country again in the 16th century. The men who brought peace were the *shoguns*, or "governors," of the Tokugawa family. Though loyal to the emperor, they held all the power. For 200 years they shut the country down. Few foreign visitors were allowed in and no Japanese were allowed out. Japan was cut off from the rest of the world, but at least there was peace. Warlike nobles were kept in their own castles. The emperors lived quietly in their palace in Kyoto.

Emperor Jimmu *(right)* and his descendants united the Japanese islands over 2,000 years ago. His life and deeds belong to legend.

Prince Shotoku built the first Buddhist monasteries. This one, the Horyuji at Nara *(right)*, is the oldest surviving wooden building in the world.

The Japanese religion of Shinto was founded by the Emperor Suinin about 1,500 years ago. This is the first Shinto shrine, or temple, at Ise *(left)*. The Emperor Suinin built it for the Sun goddess. Inside the building, he placed her sacred mirror. It is still there today.

PRINCE SHOTOKU

Prince Shotoku (AD 572-622, *bottom*) was born in a stable but grew up to become one of the great men of Japan. He lived at a time when the religion of Buddhism was spreading to Japan from China. Shotoku also wrote the first Japanese constitution, setting down the laws and rules of government.

MODERN JAPAN

Under the Tokugawa shoguns, Japan was isolated from the rest of the world. The visit of an American expedition led by Commodore Perry in 1854 began to change things. Japan started to trade with the United States and other Western countries. At the same time, ordinary people protested over their poor working conditions. The last Tokugawa was forced to resign in 1867 and the Emperor Meiji took over the government. He moved into the shoguns' old palace and began a program to make Japan a modern state.

The Japanese people saw themselves as a great nation led by their god-emperor. They caught up fast. Soon they had a strong army, a powerful navy, modern factories, and banks full of money. They fought a war with Russia and won. They were on the winning side in World War I. In World War II they conquered an empire in the Far East, but were driven back and defeated by the Americans in 1945.

The Emperor Hirohito (reigned 1926-89, the longest reign in Japanese history) was a quiet man who liked to study shellfish. After Japan's defeat, he announced that he was not a god. It was the end of a tradition that had lasted 2,000 years. When Hirohito died, he was succeeded by his son, Akihito.

JAPAN

Kyoto

Nara   Ise

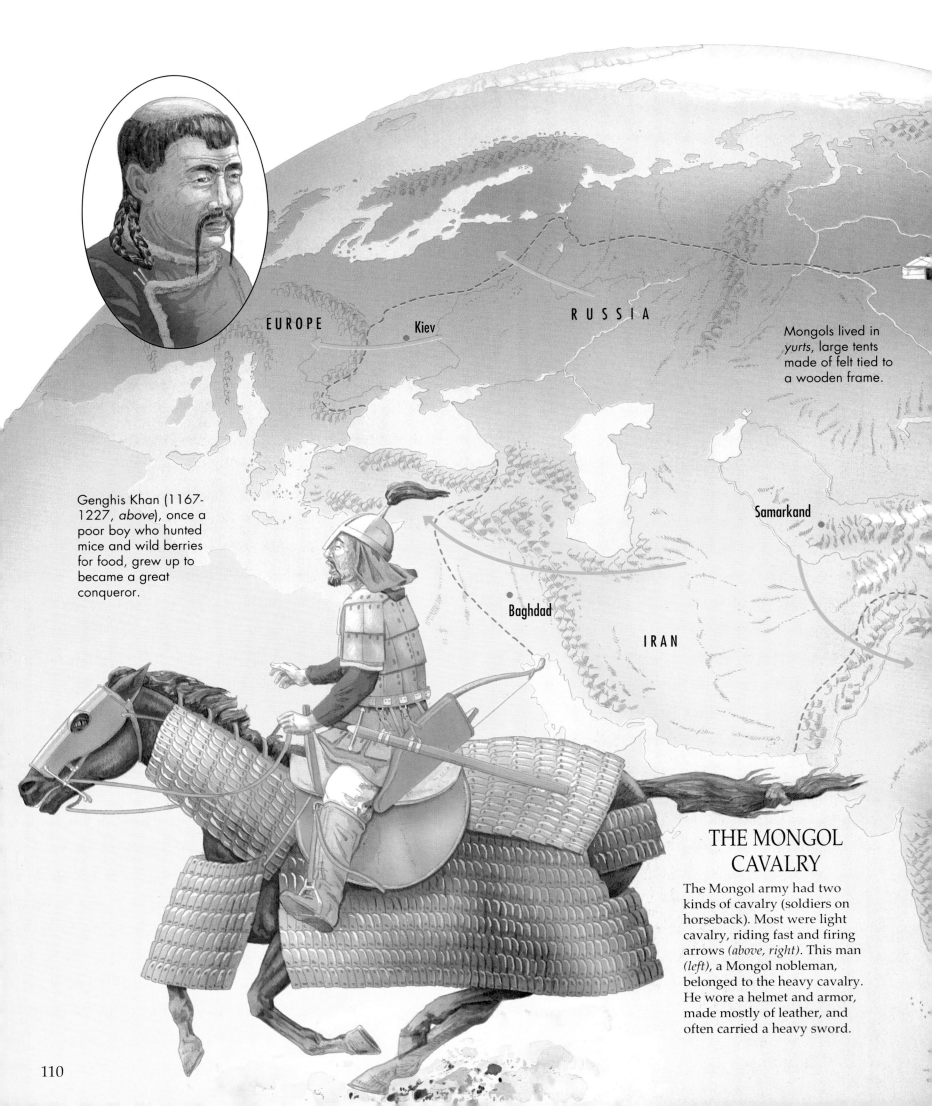

EUROPE

Kiev

RUSSIA

Mongols lived in *yurts*, large tents made of felt tied to a wooden frame.

Genghis Khan (1167-1227, *above*), once a poor boy who hunted mice and wild berries for food, grew up to became a great conqueror.

Samarkand

Baghdad

IRAN

THE MONGOL CAVALRY

The Mongol army had two kinds of cavalry (soldiers on horseback). Most were light cavalry, riding fast and firing arrows (*above, right*). This man (*left*), a Mongol nobleman, belonged to the heavy cavalry. He wore a helmet and armor, made mostly of leather, and often carried a heavy sword.

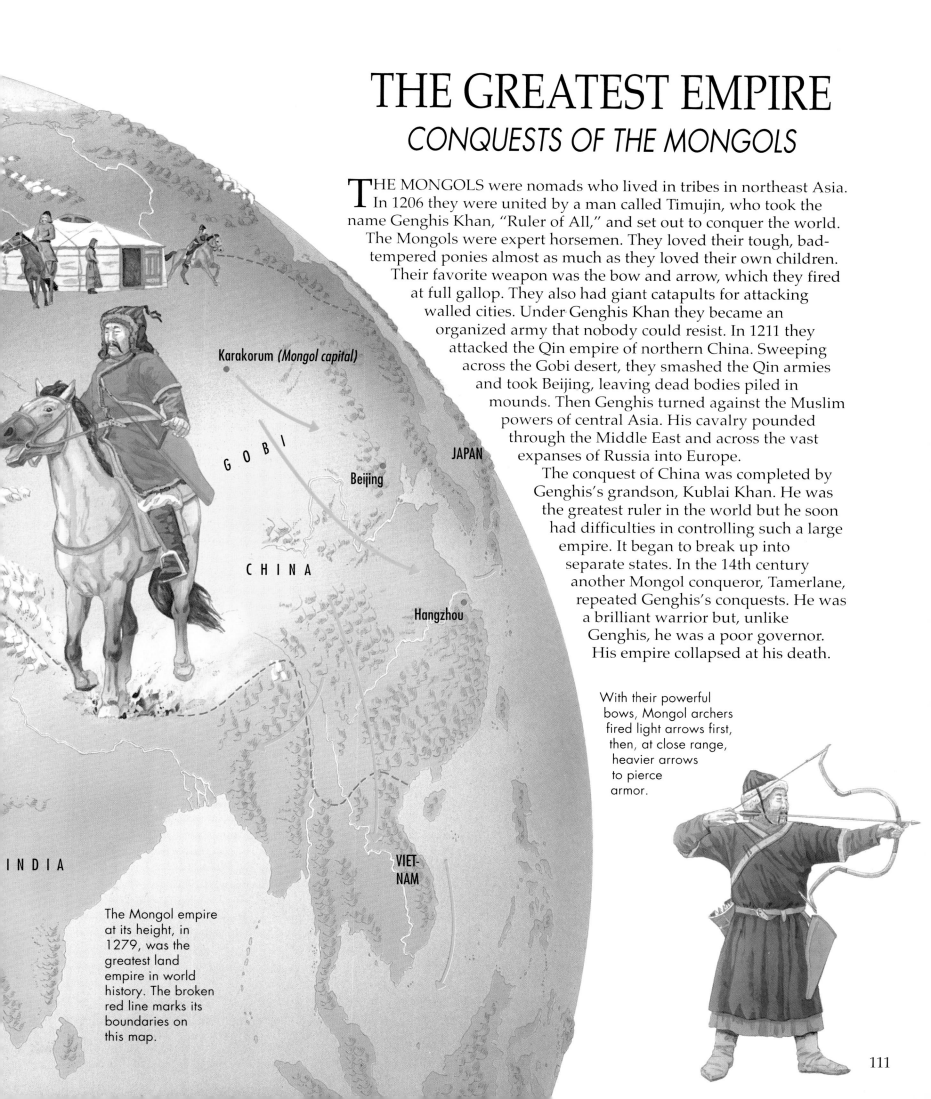

THE GREATEST EMPIRE
CONQUESTS OF THE MONGOLS

THE MONGOLS were nomads who lived in tribes in northeast Asia. In 1206 they were united by a man called Timujin, who took the name Genghis Khan, "Ruler of All," and set out to conquer the world. The Mongols were expert horsemen. They loved their tough, bad-tempered ponies almost as much as they loved their own children. Their favorite weapon was the bow and arrow, which they fired at full gallop. They also had giant catapults for attacking walled cities. Under Genghis Khan they became an organized army that nobody could resist. In 1211 they attacked the Qin empire of northern China. Sweeping across the Gobi desert, they smashed the Qin armies and took Beijing, leaving dead bodies piled in mounds. Then Genghis turned against the Muslim powers of central Asia. His cavalry pounded through the Middle East and across the vast expanses of Russia into Europe.

The conquest of China was completed by Genghis's grandson, Kublai Khan. He was the greatest ruler in the world but he soon had difficulties in controlling such a large empire. It began to break up into separate states. In the 14th century another Mongol conqueror, Tamerlane, repeated Genghis's conquests. He was a brilliant warrior but, unlike Genghis, he was a poor governor. His empire collapsed at his death.

With their powerful bows, Mongol archers fired light arrows first, then, at close range, heavier arrows to pierce armor.

Karakorum *(Mongol capital)*

G O B I

JAPAN

Beijing

C H I N A

Hangzhou

I N D I A

VIET-NAM

The Mongol empire at its height, in 1279, was the greatest land empire in world history. The broken red line marks its boundaries on this map.

THE LARGEST CASTLE
PRAGUE CASTLE, HEART OF THE CZECH LANDS

PRAGUE CASTLE is the Czechs' greatest national monument. It is also the largest ancient castle in the world. Known to the Czechs as Hradcany, it was founded by a prince in the 9th century. It has been rebuilt and enlarged many times since then. Today, it has an area of 66 acres. The "castle" is like a town inside a town. There are a whole group of buildings – palaces, churches, houses, towers – all built in different centuries.

Saint Vaclav, the patron saint of the Czechs, also known as the famous "Good King Wenceslas," is buried there.

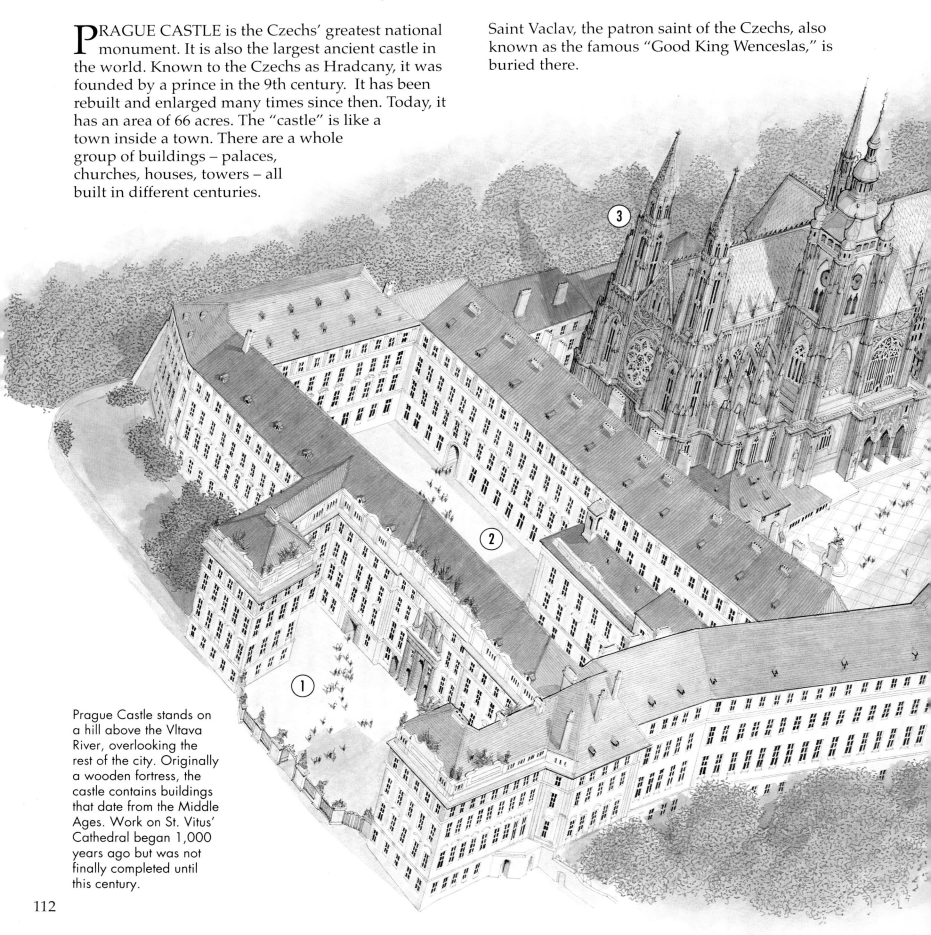

Prague Castle stands on a hill above the Vltava River, overlooking the rest of the city. Originally a wooden fortress, the castle contains buildings that date from the Middle Ages. Work on St. Vitus' Cathedral began 1,000 years ago but was not finally completed until this century.

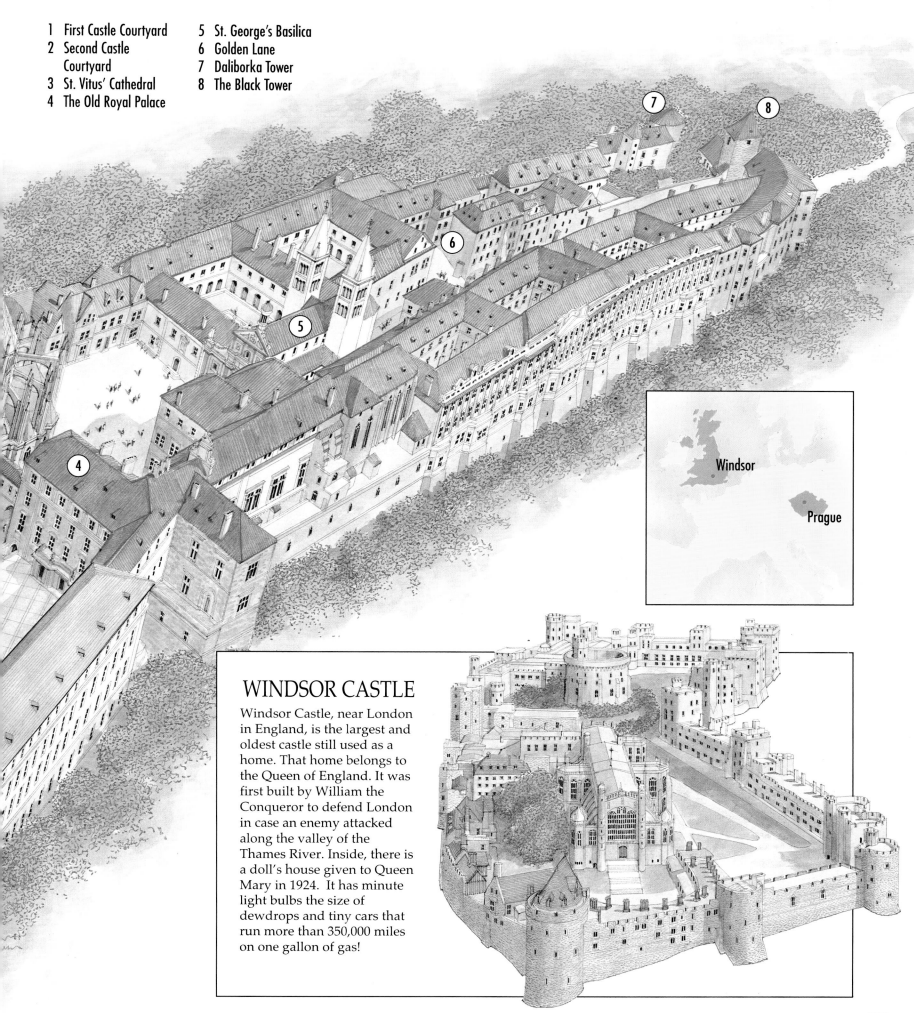

1 First Castle Courtyard
2 Second Castle Courtyard
3 St. Vitus' Cathedral
4 The Old Royal Palace
5 St. George's Basilica
6 Golden Lane
7 Daliborka Tower
8 The Black Tower

Windsor

Prague

WINDSOR CASTLE

Windsor Castle, near London in England, is the largest and oldest castle still used as a home. That home belongs to the Queen of England. It was first built by William the Conqueror to defend London in case an enemy attacked along the valley of the Thames River. Inside, there is a doll's house given to Queen Mary in 1924. It has minute light bulbs the size of dewdrops and tiny cars that run more than 350,000 miles on one gallon of gas!

THE SMALLEST COUNTRY
VATICAN CITY STATE

THE VATICAN CITY is all that remains of lands belonging to the Pope that, until 1870, included most of central Italy. Under an agreement made with the Italian government in 1929, the Vatican became a fully independent state with its own government. With an area of only 109 acres (about one-eighth the size of Central Park, New York), it is the smallest independent country in the world.

The Vatican is the center of the Roman Catholic Church, which numbers nearly 900 million followers. It is home to the Pope, who is head of the Church, and a population of about 800, the smallest of any nation.

This tiny country is dominated by the magnificent St. Peter's Basilica (not a cathedral, but an important Roman Catholic church), and its square. Within its walls there are a number of palaces, museums, colleges, two churches besides St. Peter's, and a railroad station. It runs its own bank, post office, and newspaper, and issues its own stamps and coins.

The Vatican City State is located on the west bank of the Tiber River in Rome, capital city of Italy.

VATICAN CITY STATE

Tiber

EUROPE

ITALY

Rome

THE OLDEST ARMY

The Swiss Guard was founded in 1506, making it the oldest existing army in the world. It is also the smallest, numbering 100. Members of the Guard must have completed their training in the Swiss army. Only once did they go into battle. In 1527 they defended the Pope from the forces of the Emperor Charles V.

THE LARGEST CHURCH

Where St. Peter's stands today was, in Roman times, the Gardens of Nero. Here, many Christians were put to death. They included St. Peter, one of Jesus's apostles, who died around the year AD 67. A church was later built over St. Peter's tomb. It stood for a thousand years before the Popes decided they needed a new church to replace the old one, now crumbling into ruin. The greatest architects of the time, including Michelangelo, were hired to design and build the new St. Peter's. Begun in 1507, it took more than 150 years to complete. A new church, The Basilica of Our Lady of Peace, built in Ivory Coast, Africa, in 1989, is taller but not as large as St. Peter's.

Today, crowds gather in St. Peter's Square every week to receive the Pope's blessing which he delivers from a balcony overlooking the square.

1 Vatican Radio
2 Government Palace
3 Railroad station
4 Vatican museums
5 St. Peter's Basilica
6 Sistine Chapel

7 Apostolic Palace
8 Pope's apartments
9 Audience hall
10 Barracks of Swiss Guard
11 Palace of the Holy Office
12 St. Peter's Square

THE SMALLEST COUNTRIES

1	Vatican City	0.17
2	Monaco	0.73
3	Nauru	8
4	Tuvalu	10
5	San Marino	24
6	Liechtenstein	62
7	St. Kitts & Nevis	104
8	Maldives	115
9	Malta	122
10	Grenada	133

areas are given in square miles

REACHING FOR THE SKIES
THE TALLEST BUILDINGS IN HISTORY

For NEARLY 4,000 YEARS, the Great Pyramid of Giza looked down on all the other great pyramids of ancient Egypt – and on every other building in the world. The only one of the Seven Wonders of the World to survive largely intact, it lost 33 feet off its height when the topmost stones fell away (*see page 99*).

It was not until the time when the great cathedrals of medieval Europe were built that its record was broken. In 1311 the central tower of Lincoln Cathedral in England, topped by a lead-covered wooden spire, finally outreached the Great Pyramid. Although the spire was blown down in a storm in 1549, no higher building was erected until the Washington Monument, built in 1884 to commemorate the first US president, George Washington, was completed.

Just five years later, the record returned to Europe. Gustav Eiffel's iron tower, the marvel of the 1889 Paris International Exhibition, astonished the world. It took 230 men just over two years to build it, hammering together 18,000 pieces of iron using 2,500,000 rivets. Extended in 1959 by a 66-foot TV antenna, the Eiffel Tower can sway up to five inches in high winds. In hot weather the metal expands and the tower grows another seven inches taller.

The coming of the skyscraper, made possible by the use of steel building frames and the invention of hydraulic elevators, meant that sooner or later one would take over the mantle as the world's tallest building. The Chrysler Building duly did so in 1930, only to be overtaken by another New York skyscraper, the Empire State Building, a few months later. The Empire State's spire, extended by a TV mast twenty years later, was originally intended to be a mooring post for airships. It remained the world's highest building until 1973, when the twin towers of the World Trade Center, also in New York City, were built.

The record quickly changed hands twice more. Chicago took the record from New York with its Sears Tower. Then, in 1976, the CN Tower in Toronto became the world's tallest self-supporting structure. It is as high as five football fields stacked end to end!

The illustrations are approximately to scale

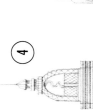

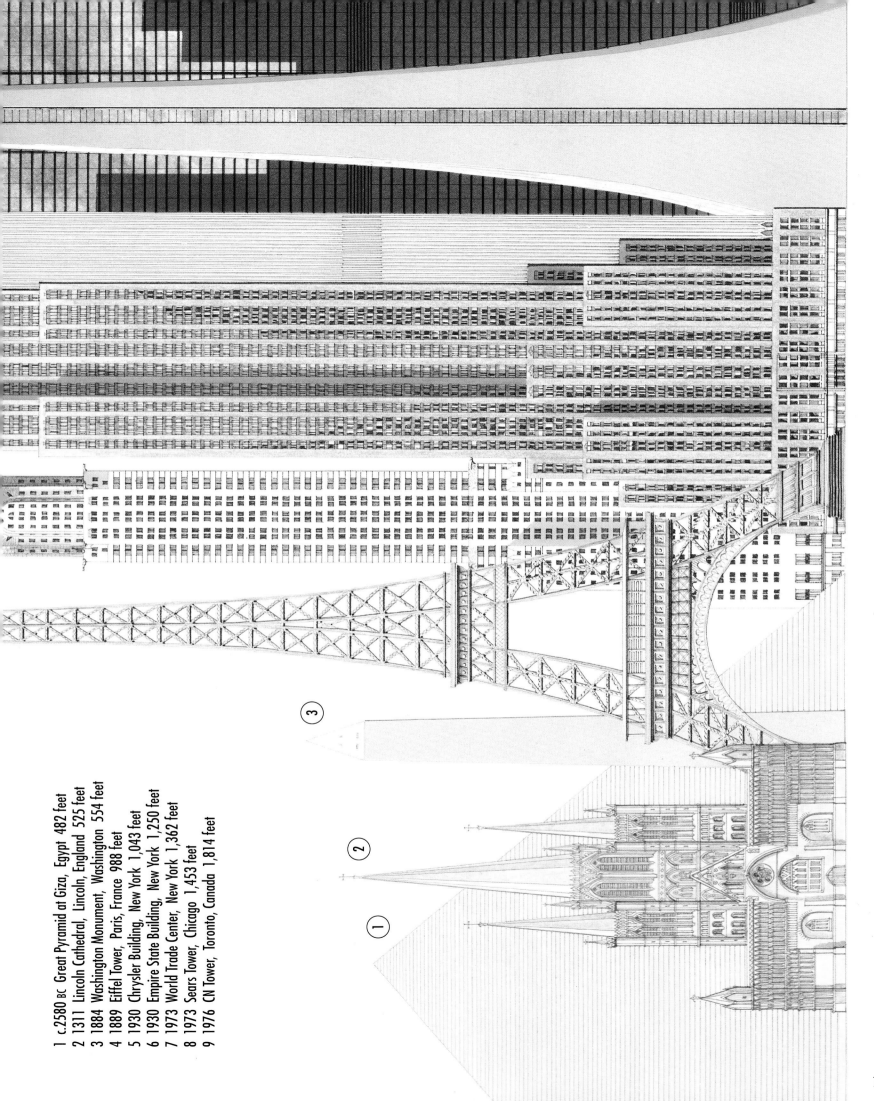

1 c.2580 BC Great Pyramid at Giza, Egypt 482 feet
2 1311 Lincoln Cathedral, Lincoln, England 525 feet
3 1884 Washington Monument, Washington 554 feet
4 1889 Eiffel Tower, Paris, France 988 feet
5 1930 Chrysler Building, New York 1,043 feet
6 1930 Empire State Building, New York 1,250 feet
7 1973 World Trade Center, New York 1,362 feet
8 1973 Sears Tower, Chicago 1,453 feet
9 1976 CN Tower, Toronto, Canada 1,814 feet

117

THE HIGHEST MONUMENTS
AND THE TALLEST STEEPLE

G ATEWAY ARCH, the highest monument in the world, stands on the banks of the Mississippi River in the city of St. Louis, Missouri. Built in 1965, the 630-foot-high stainless steel arch was designed in the shape of a rainbow. The arch is hollow inside. Elevators go up to the top where there are portholes to look through.

The Gateway Arch marks St. Louis' historic role as "gateway to the West." In the mid-nineteenth century, hopeful farmers, their wagon trains laden with all their possessions and drawn by oxen, set out from St. Louis bound for Oregon and California and a better life in the West.

The illustrations are approximately to scale

The Cathedral, or Munster, at Ulm, Germany, holds the record for the tallest church steeple. From the laying of its foundations to the completion of its spire, the building took 500 years to complete.

The tallest statue in the world, the bronze Amida Buddha in Ushiku City, Japan, stands 394 feet tall and weighs over 1000 tons. Inside the statue are rooms for meditation and spiritual learning. You can climb a stairway and look out of the statue's chest on to the gardens below.

THE LARGEST SCULPTURE

In the Black Hills of South Dakota, four gigantic stone heads look out from a high granite cliff on Mount Rushmore. The heads represent four famous American presidents: George Washington, Thomas Jefferson, Theodore Roosevelt, and Abraham Lincoln. The heads are each about 65 feet high, and were designed over 50 years ago by the sculptor Gutzon Borglum. Miners and quarrymen spent 15 years chiselling and drilling to carve the faces out of the mountain. Finishing touches, like the dark shadows at the center of the eyes, were added at the end.

Only a short distance from Mount Rushmore, a new, even larger sculpture is being blasted out of the mountains. The figure of the American Indian Chief Crazy Horse was begun in 1948 by sculptor Korczak Ziolkowski. So far, only the face has been carved out. The whole statue will stand 654 feet high when it is eventually completed.

The highest column in the world is at San Jacinto, Texas (left). It is 570 feet high. The Texas star at the top alone weighs nearly 220 tons. The column was built in 1936 to commemorate a battle fought 100 years earlier. Then, in a fierce attack lasting only 18 minutes, Texan soldiers defeated the Mexican army. For the next nine years, until 1845, Texas was an independent nation.

GATEWAY ARCH

ULM CATHEDRAL

SAN JACINTO MONUMENT

GREAT PYRAMID AT GIZA 482 feet
Tallest pyramid

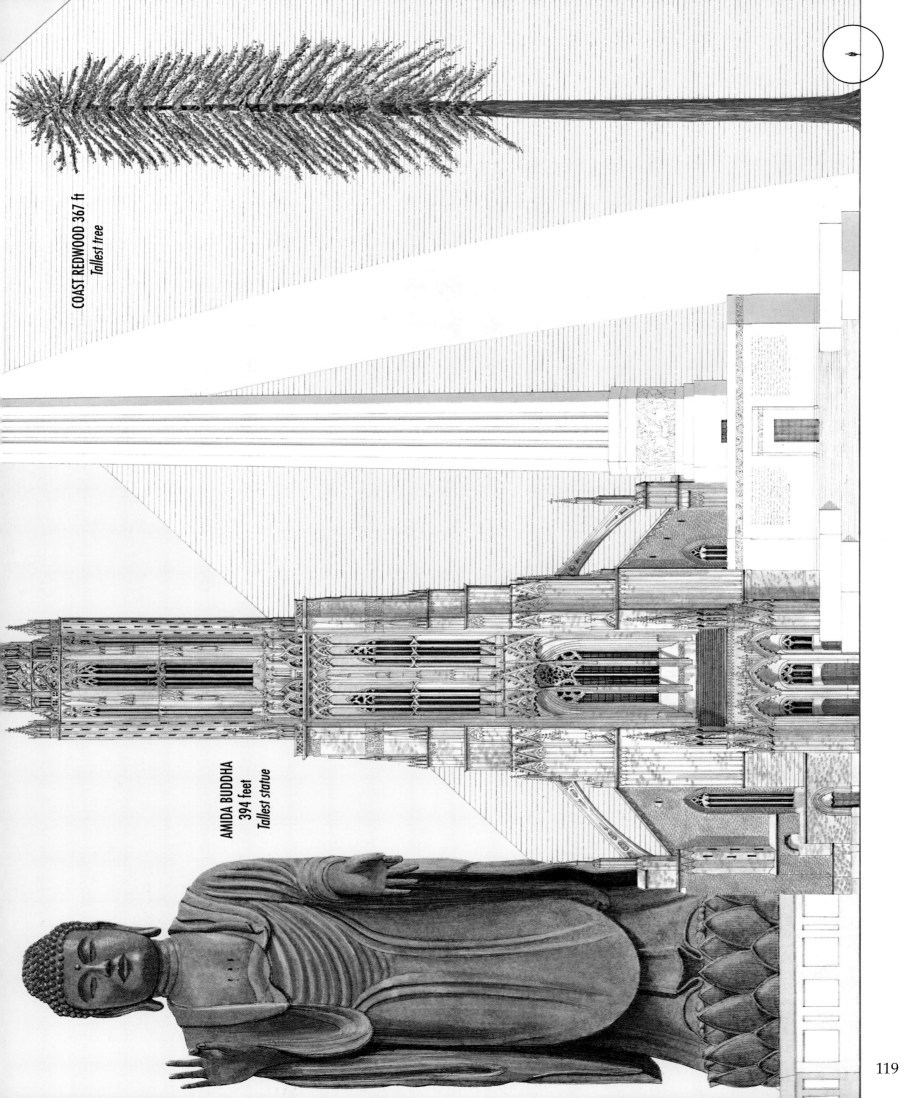

COAST REDWOOD 367 ft
Tallest tree

AMIDA BUDDHA
394 feet
Tallest statue

119

THE LONGEST BRIDGE

JAPAN'S HONSHU-SHIKOKU BRIDGE PROJECT

JAPAN IS A COUNTRY of islands. It has four large islands, and hundreds of small ones. The Honshu-Shikoku Bridge Project allows people to drive or travel by train to all four main islands. They are all linked by bridges or tunnels.

The project consists of not one, but three crossings, each made up of a number of bridges linked together in a chain (*see inset*). The three bridges were completed at the end of the 1990s. One of the three includes the Akashi-Kaikyo Bridge. Completed in 1998, it is now the longest suspension bridge in the world, taking the record held by the Humber Bridge in England.

The stretch of water that the bridges cross is called the Seto Inland Sea. It has many small islands, some of which have been used as "stepping stones" for the bridge supports. As the seabed is hard granite, supports can also be built in the water.

Japan often suffers from earthquakes and typhoons. The bridges must be able to stand up against these fierce forces of nature, as well as strong tidal currents in the Seto Inland Sea. The bridge engineers also had to keep in mind that this region is a national park where some rare and beautiful plants and animals live. They had to plan the bridges and their roads in a way that would damage the environment as little as possible.

JAPAN

Area of inset (*below*)

Minami Bisan-seto Bridge

Kita Bisan-seto Bridge

Yoshima Viaduct

Yoshima Bridge

Iwakurojima Bridge

OSAKA

KOBE

SETO INLAND SEA

Akashi-Kaikyo Bridge

Seto-Ohashi Bridge

HONSHU

SHIKOKU

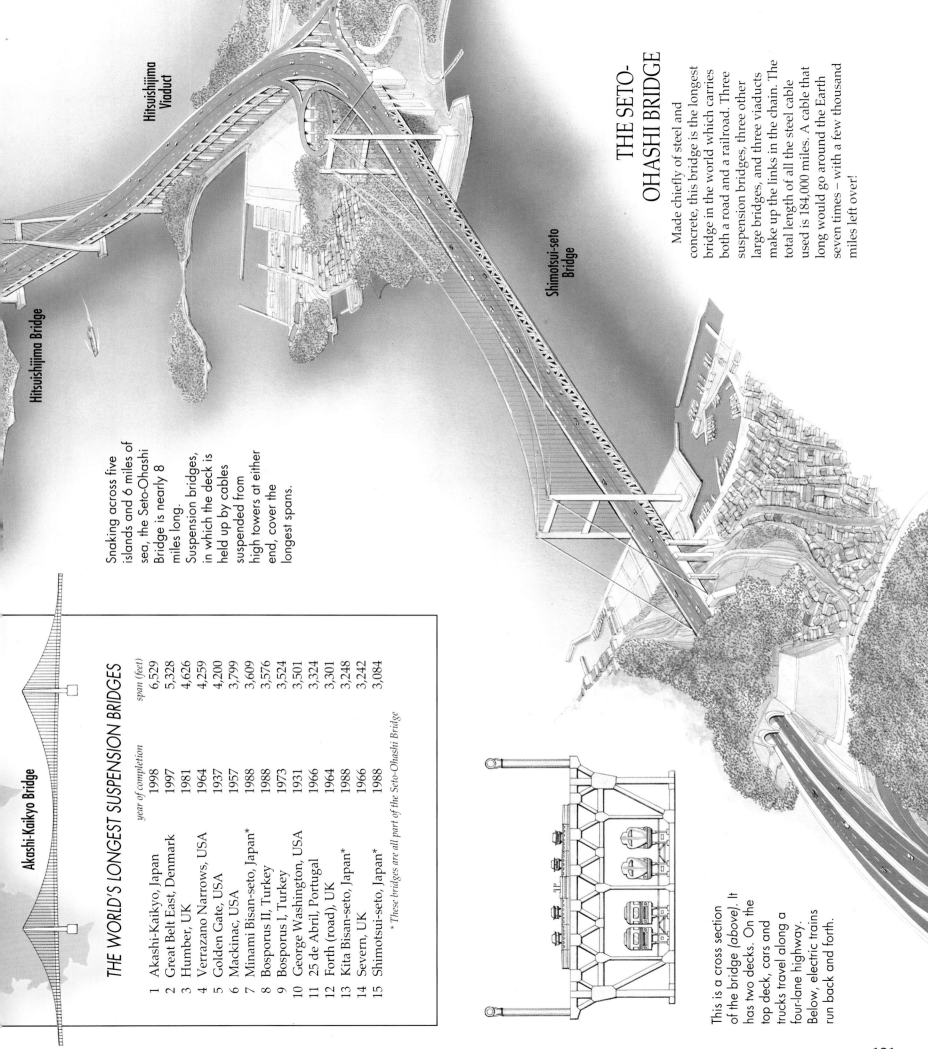

Hitsuishijima Viaduct

Hitsuishijima Bridge

Shimotsui-seto Bridge

THE SETO-OHASHI BRIDGE

Made chiefly of steel and concrete, this bridge is the longest bridge in the world which carries both a road and a railroad. Three suspension bridges, three other large bridges, and three viaducts make up the links in the chain. The total length of all the steel cable used is 184,000 miles. A cable that long would go around the Earth seven times – with a few thousand miles left over!

Snaking across five islands and 6 miles of sea, the Seto-Ohashi Bridge is nearly 8 miles long. Suspension bridges, in which the deck is held up by cables suspended from high towers at either end, cover the longest spans.

Akashi-Kaikyo Bridge

THE WORLD'S LONGEST SUSPENSION BRIDGES

		year of completion	span (feet)
1	Akashi-Kaikyo, Japan	1998	6,529
2	Great Belt East, Denmark	1997	5,328
3	Humber, UK	1981	4,626
4	Verrazano Narrows, USA	1964	4,259
5	Golden Gate, USA	1937	4,200
6	Mackinac, USA	1957	3,799
7	Minami Bisan-seto, Japan*	1988	3,609
8	Bosporus II, Turkey	1988	3,576
9	Bosporus I, Turkey	1973	3,524
10	George Washington, USA	1931	3,501
11	25 de Abril, Portugal	1966	3,324
12	Forth (road), UK	1964	3,301
13	Kita Bisan-seto, Japan*	1988	3,248
14	Severn, UK	1966	3,242
15	Shimotsui-seto, Japan*	1988	3,084

* These bridges are all part of the Seto-Ohashi Bridge

This is a cross section of the bridge (above). It has two decks. On the top deck, cars and trucks travel along a four-lane highway. Below, electric trains run back and forth.

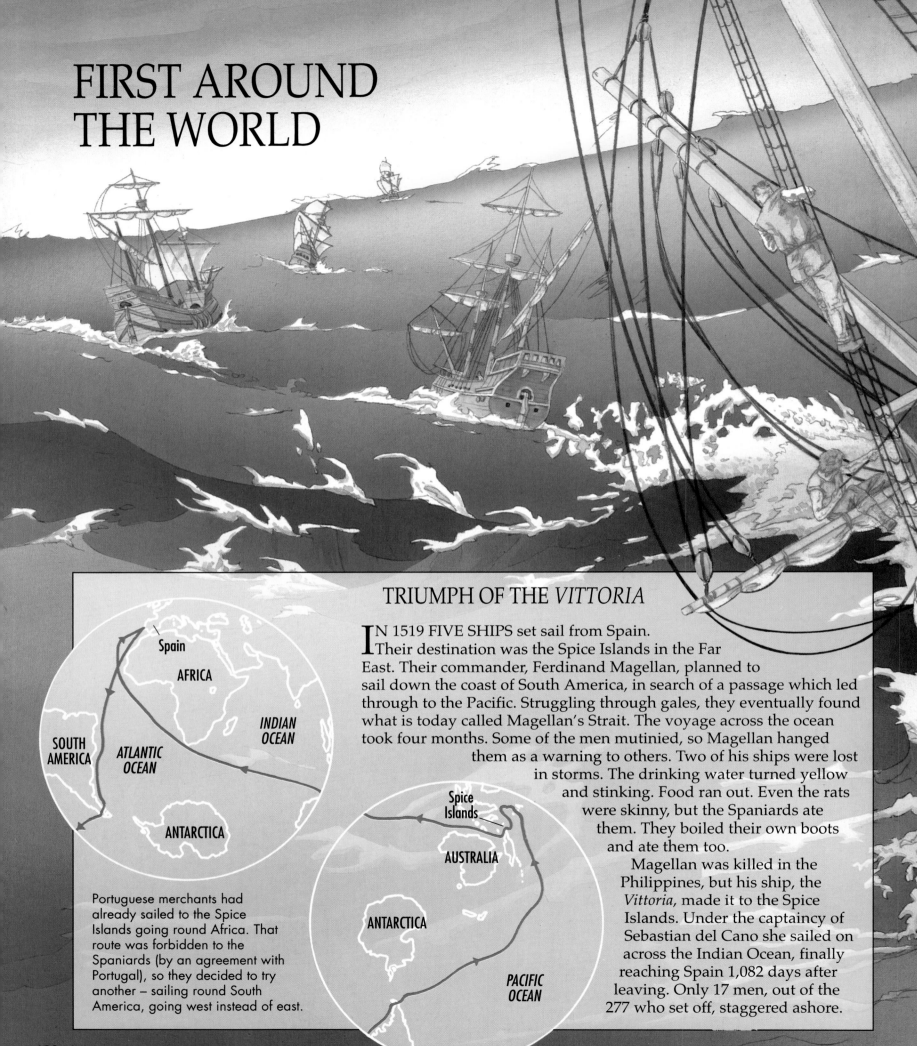

FIRST AROUND THE WORLD

TRIUMPH OF THE *VITTORIA*

IN 1519 FIVE SHIPS set sail from Spain. Their destination was the Spice Islands in the Far East. Their commander, Ferdinand Magellan, planned to sail down the coast of South America, in search of a passage which led through to the Pacific. Struggling through gales, they eventually found what is today called Magellan's Strait. The voyage across the ocean took four months. Some of the men mutinied, so Magellan hanged them as a warning to others. Two of his ships were lost in storms. The drinking water turned yellow and stinking. Food ran out. Even the rats were skinny, but the Spaniards ate them. They boiled their own boots and ate them too.

Magellan was killed in the Philippines, but his ship, the *Vittoria*, made it to the Spice Islands. Under the captaincy of Sebastian del Cano she sailed on across the Indian Ocean, finally reaching Spain 1,082 days after leaving. Only 17 men, out of the 277 who set off, staggered ashore.

Portuguese merchants had already sailed to the Spice Islands going round Africa. That route was forbidden to the Spaniards (by an agreement with Portugal), so they decided to try another – sailing round South America, going west instead of east.

ARCTIC
OCEAN

North
Pole

GREENLAND

Peary's
route
1908-9

Robert E. Peary (1856-1920) helped to build the Panama Canal before he became a polar explorer. He spent years with the Inuit (Eskimos) learning how to live in the Arctic.

Peary and his companions pose for a photograph at the place Peary claimed to be the North Pole. The US flag, the "Stars and Stripes," is planted in a mound of snow on the spot.

IN 1909 AMERICAN EXPLORER Robert Peary began his eighth Arctic expedition. It would surely be his last. He was 52 years old and he had lost all his toes through frostbite. But he was determined to reach the North Pole. Nothing else in his life mattered so much.

From his base on Cape Columbia in the Canadian Arctic, he set out with 19 dog sleds across the shifting, broken ice of the Arctic Ocean. Though often held up by stretches of open water, he advanced at a brisk rate of 15 miles a day. Other members of the expedition had gone ahead to leave supplies of fuel and food before turning back. He made the final dash to the Pole with his old friend, Matthew Henson, and four Inuit. On April 6, they reached the Pole.

No one had ever traveled so fast across the Arctic ice. In that final dash he covered more than 180 miles in four days. Indeed, doubts over his incredible speed have made some people think that Peary never reached the Pole at all.

FIRST TO THE POLES
PEARY AND AMUNDSEN REACH THE ENDS OF THE EARTH

NORWEGIAN EXPLORER Roald Amundsen wanted to be the first man to reach the North Pole. When he heard that Peary (*opposite*) had got there first, he switched to the South Pole. His ship, the *Fram*, specially built for polar voyages, carried his expedition to the Bay of Whales. In October 1911 he set out with four men and four sleds, pulled by 52 dogs.

The first stage was across the Ross Ice Shelf. They made good progress across the flat ice, stopping for supplies already placed along part of the route by an advance party. Next came the climb up the rough ice of the Axel Heiberg Glacier. Terrible cold (-60°F), gales and blizzards, hidden cracks in the ice – dangers loomed at all times. But Amundsen was confident and on December 14, they reached the South Pole and raised the Norwegian flag. By January 25, they were back at their ship.

The Norwegians were not the only men in Antarctica during this time. A British team, led by Captain Robert F. Scott, was also trying to reach the Pole. They followed a longer route. On January 17, they found the Norwegian flag already flying at the Pole. Tired and sad, Scott's men turned back. On the Ross Ice Shelf they were caught in terrible blizzards. Not one of them survived.

Amundsen's journey to the South Pole was a well-planned expedition. Dogs pulled their sleds loaded with supplies while Amundsen's men walked across the ice.

ANTARCTICA

South Pole

Ross Ice Shelf

SOUTHERN OCEAN

Amundsen's route 1911

The Norwegian Roald Amundsen (1872-1928) gave up his medical studies to be an explorer. Besides his polar conquest, he was the first to sail through the North-west Passage, in Arctic Canada.

TO THE HIGHEST POINT ON EARTH

HILLARY AND TENZING CLIMB MOUNT EVEREST

PEOPLE FIRST BEGAN CLIMBING mountains about 200 years ago, but not until the twentieth century did anyone try to climb Mount Everest, the highest mountain in the world (29,080 feet *see page 33*). Two British mountaineers, George Mallory and Andrew Irvine, *may* have got there in 1924. They were last seen 800 feet from the top. Then they disappeared.

The Tibetans call Everest Qomolangma, "Mother Goddess of the World." Gales blow at more than 90 miles an hour and the air is so thin that most climbers take oxygen tanks.

In 1953 a British and Commonwealth expedition led by Colonel John Hunt set out to climb Everest. Two men reached the South Summit but had to return. Colonel Hunt chose two others to make a second attempt. They were Edmund Hillary, a New Zealander, and Tenzing Norgay. Tenzing was a Sherpa, one of the peoples who live in mountainous Nepal. On May 29, they reached the top. Worried that their oxygen might run out, they stayed only 15 minutes. After taking photographs they made their way, weary but triumphant, back down the mountain.

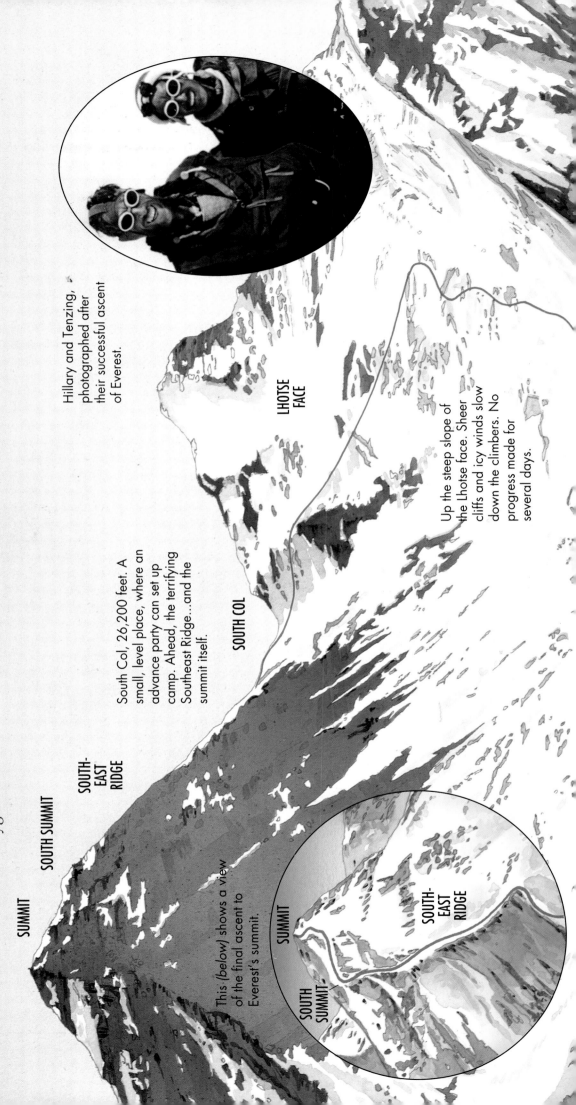

Hillary and Tenzing, photographed after their successful ascent of Everest.

LHOTSE FACE

SOUTH COL

South Col, 26,200 feet. A small, level place, where an advance party can set up camp. Ahead, the terrifying Southeast Ridge...and the summit itself.

Up the steep slope of the Lhotse face. Sheer cliffs and icy winds slow down the climbers. No progress made for several days.

SUMMIT

SOUTH SUMMIT

SOUTH-EAST RIDGE

This *(below)* shows a view of the final ascent to Everest's summit.

SUMMIT

SOUTH SUMMIT

SOUTH-EAST RIDGE

WESTERN CWM

Up the sloping valley called the Western Cwm. Several camps are established on the slopes. This route had been used only once before.

KHUMBU ICEFALL

CHINA

Tibet

Mt. Everest

BURMA

NEPAL

INDIA

PAKISTAN

Base Camp is set up on the Khumbu Glacier at a height of 17,572 feet. It is a long hard climb to get this far! Ahead lies the dangerous Khumbu icefall.

KHUMBU GLACIER

NEARLY THERE!

On the Southeast Ridge, Hillary and Tenzing cut out a ledge where they could pitch camp. Hillary slept sitting up to stop the tent blowing away. Next morning the wind dropped and the sun shone. By 9 a.m. they were on the South Summit. Ahead was a rock wall, 40 feet straight up. They hauled themselves up and stood on top of the world.

FIRST IN SPACE

FROM GAGARIN TO THE SPACE WALKERS

PEOPLE DREAMED of traveling in outer space long before rockets were invented. In 1865 the French science fiction writer Jules Verne wrote a story about travelers to the Moon. They got there in something that looked like a train!

The secret of space travel was the rocket – gasoline or jet engines do not work in space. The first man who suggested that rockets might be used for space flight was a Russian teacher, Konstantin Tsiolkovsky, in 1903. No one took much notice then but the American scientist, Robert H. Goddard, built the first successful rocket, using liquid fuel, in 1926 *(see pages 162-163)*.

The Space Age really began on October 4, 1957, when the Soviet Union launched Sputnik 1, the first man-made satellite to orbit (travel around) Earth. A dog called Laika was the first living thing in space, closely followed by the first human being, Soviet cosmonaut ("sailor of the universe") Yuri Gagarin, on April 12, 1961. His spacecraft, Vostok 1, made one orbit of Earth in a flight that lasted 108 minutes. The descent capsule, which measured just 7.5 feet across, landed in Russia but Gagarin was not in it: He had parachuted out at 22,000 feet.

Yuri Gagarin was the first human being to travel outside Earth's atmosphere.

THE FIRST SPACE WALK

Aleksei Leonov, Soviet ex-fighter pilot, trained as a cosmonaut and became the first human to walk in space in 1965. He left his spacecraft, Voskhod 2, via an airlock. With the door to the spacecraft shut behind him, the airlock was depressurized. He then opened the exit hatch and entered space. Tied to the craft by a cable, Leonov spent ten minutes alone in space, taking pictures with a portable television camera.

In 1984, US astronaut Captain Bruce McCandless was the first person to go "outside" into space with no link to a spacecraft. He was the first human satellite. He and Colonel Bob Stewart were out on "extra-vehicular activity" for five hours, traveling in little vehicles like armchairs fitted with gas-powered thrusters. Thrilled at the experience, they called each other "Flash Gordon" and "Buck Rogers!"

A YEAR IN SPACE

In the 1970s the Soviets and the Americans began building large space stations. Much larger than the tiny capsules of Gagarin and Glenn, they allowed crews to spend time carrying out scientific research. In 1987-88 Soviet cosmonauts Musa Manarov and Vladimir Titov spent just short of 366 days in the *Mir* space station. Their record was broken by Valeri Poliakov in 1995. He now also holds the record for the longest distance traveled. On board *Mir,* he has flown about 250 million miles, well over the equivalent of a return trip to the Sun.

The first woman in space was 26-year-old Valentina Tereshkova from the Soviet Union *(right)*. She orbited Earth in Vostok 6 48 times in 1963.

SPACE FIRSTS

October 4, 1957 Soviets launch Sputnik 1, first man-made satellite

April 12, 1961 Soviet cosmonaut Yuri Gagarin makes first flight in manned spacecraft, Vostok 1

May 5, 1961 First US astronaut Alan Shepard makes 15-minute flight

February 20, 1962 John Glenn becomes first US astronaut to orbit Earth

June 16, 1963 Soviet cosmonaut Valentina Tereshkova becomes first woman in space

March 18, 1965 Soviet cosmonaut Aleksei Leonov makes first space walk

July 21, 1969 US astronaut Neil Armstrong is the first man to walk on the Moon

February 7, 1984 US astronaut Bruce McCandless performs first untethered space walk

1994-95 Russian doctor Valeri Poliakov spends a record 437 days in space

Soviet Air Force Major Yuri Gagarin (1934-1968) *(right)*, a carpenter's son, made the first-ever manned space flight in Vostok 1 in April 1961.

Neil Armstrong, *(right)* the first person to set foot on the Moon

Machines and Inventions

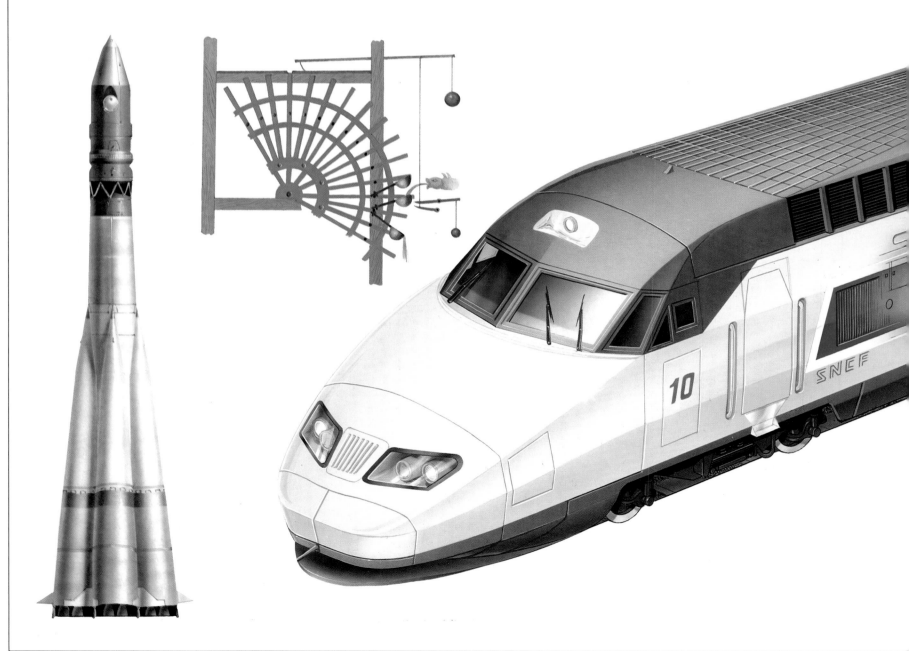

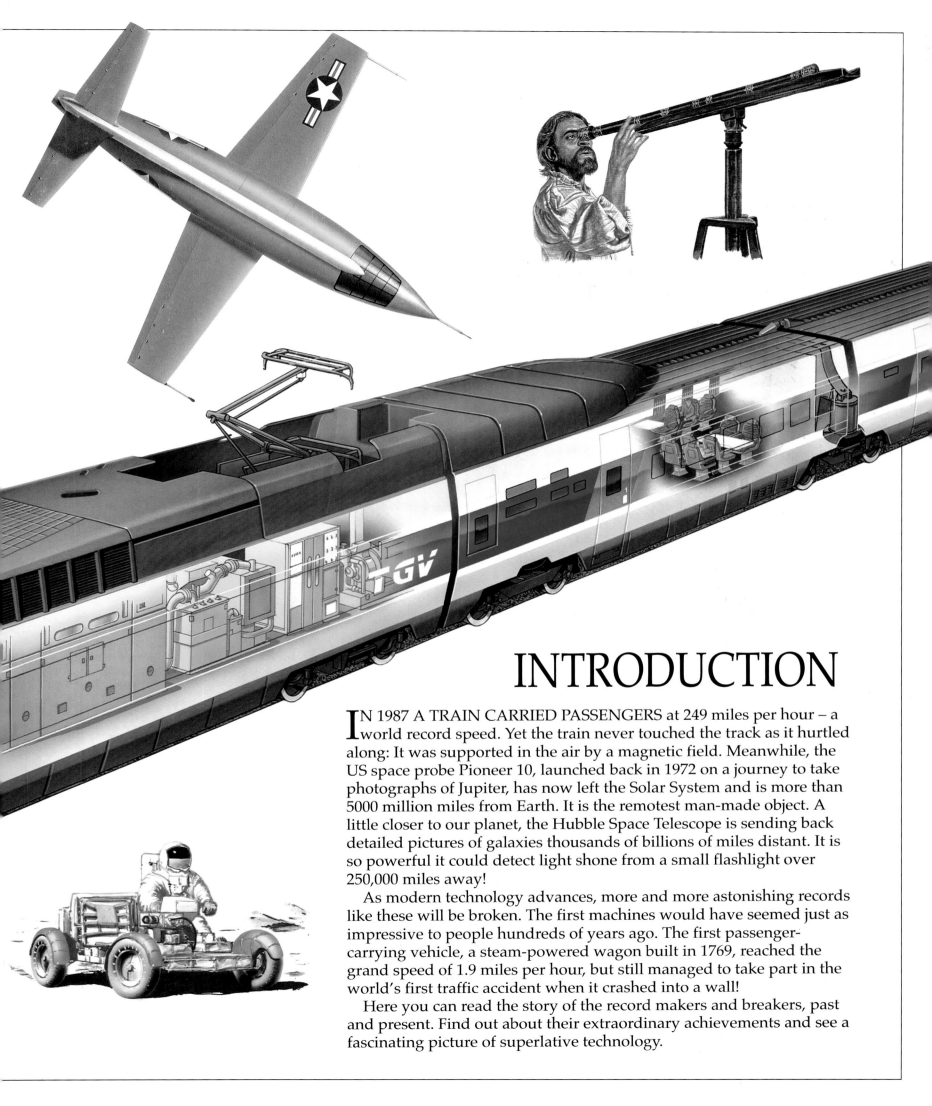

INTRODUCTION

IN 1987 A TRAIN CARRIED PASSENGERS at 249 miles per hour – a world record speed. Yet the train never touched the track as it hurtled along: It was supported in the air by a magnetic field. Meanwhile, the US space probe Pioneer 10, launched back in 1972 on a journey to take photographs of Jupiter, has now left the Solar System and is more than 5000 million miles from Earth. It is the remotest man-made object. A little closer to our planet, the Hubble Space Telescope is sending back detailed pictures of galaxies thousands of billions of miles distant. It is so powerful it could detect light shone from a small flashlight over 250,000 miles away!

As modern technology advances, more and more astonishing records like these will be broken. The first machines would have seemed just as impressive to people hundreds of years ago. The first passenger-carrying vehicle, a steam-powered wagon built in 1769, reached the grand speed of 1.9 miles per hour, but still managed to take part in the world's first traffic accident when it crashed into a wall!

Here you can read the story of the record makers and breakers, past and present. Find out about their extraordinary achievements and see a fascinating picture of superlative technology.

THE FIRST MECHANICAL CLOCK
AND OTHER GREAT CHINESE INVENTIONS

IF YOU GO OUT and buy this book with paper money, if you put up an umbrella, strike a match, fly a kite, or push a wheelbarrow, you have the Chinese to thank. These things are so familiar to us today we scarcely wonder where they came from. But it was the Chinese who first invented them.

The iron plow, steel manufacturing, printing, the rocket, and many more important inventions were all thought up by the Chinese many centuries before they appeared in the West. The mechanical clock (see opposite), magnetic compass, suspension bridge, playing cards, parachute, paddle-wheel boats, even the decimal system – all first appeared in China.

Some of these inventions found their way to Europe through reports from travelers, while others were later "invented" by Europeans unaware that they were already in existence. Without inventions that had had their origins in China, Europe in the Middle Ages might have been a very different place. Seed drills, iron plows, collar harnesses, and the technique of growing crops in rows – ideas imported to Europe from China – helped farmers. The magnetic compass, the ship's rudder, and other nautical improvements guided European explorers across the world's oceans in the 15th century. Gunpowder greatly strengthened armies. Printing presses spread learning around the world.

From late medieval times, far fewer inventions came out of China. Since then, most technological advances have been made in Europe, North America, or Japan.

The first machine to record earthquakes, called a *seismograph*, was invented in AD 132. When it is shaken, a rod inside the machine swings and opens one of eight dragons' jaws. A ball drops into the toad's mouth below, recording the direction of the earthquake.

Invented in the first century BC, the Chinese wheelbarrow needs much less effort to move it than modern designs. The weight is balanced evenly on either side of the wheel.

GREAT CHINESE FIRSTS

Magnetic compass **4th century** BC
  Known in Europe 11th century
Paper **2nd century** BC *First paper made in
  Europe in 12th century*
Rudder **1st century** AD *Adopted by Europeans in
  about 1180*
Suspension bridge **1st century** AD *Suspension bridge
  built in United States 1801*
Fishing-reel **3rd century** AD *Known in Europe 17th century*
Umbrella **4th century** AD *Known in Europe 18th century*
Matches **6th century** AD *Made in Europe 19th century*
Printing **8th century** AD *First European presses in 14th century*
Playing-cards **9th century** AD *Known in Europe 13th century*
Paper money **9th century** AD *Made in Sweden in 1661*
Gunpowder **9th century** AD *Used in Europe 13th century*
Rocket **12th century** AD *Made in Europe 14th century*

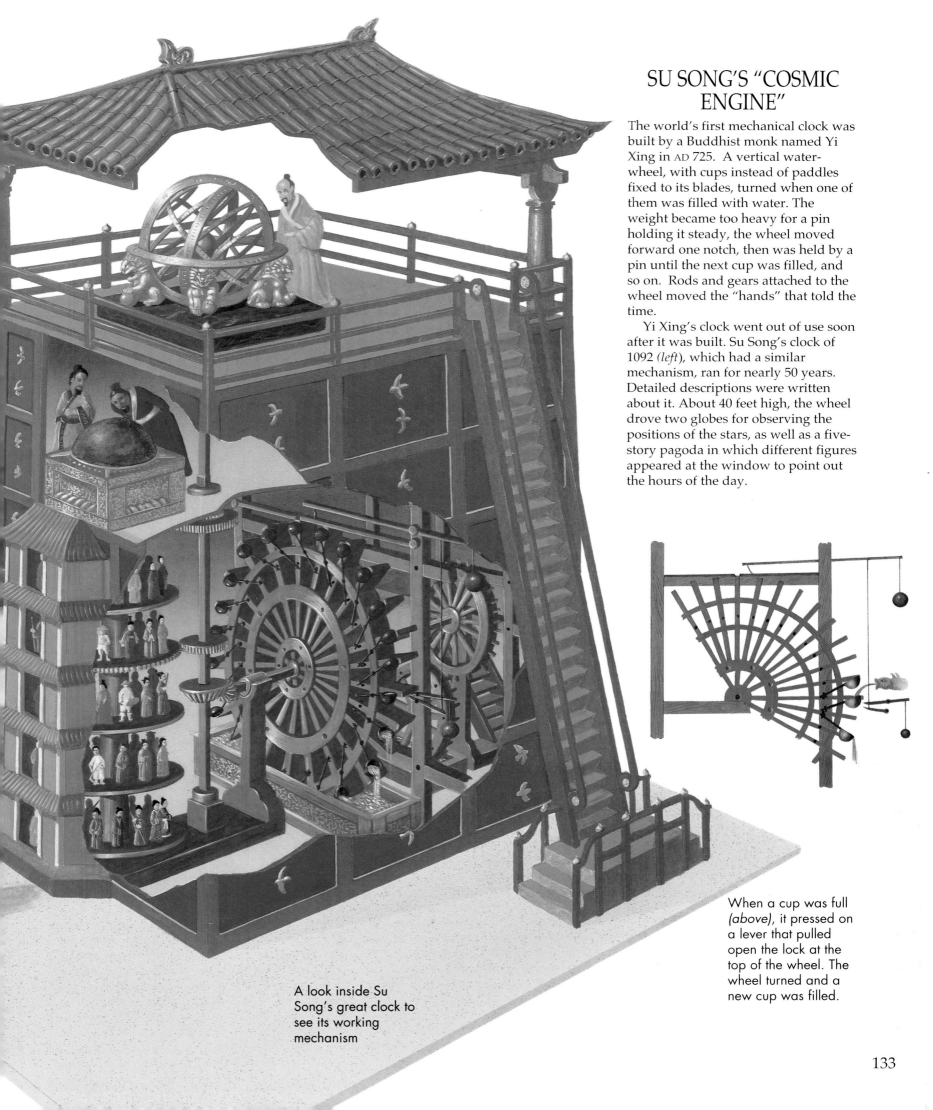

SU SONG'S "COSMIC ENGINE"

The world's first mechanical clock was built by a Buddhist monk named Yi Xing in AD 725. A vertical water-wheel, with cups instead of paddles fixed to its blades, turned when one of them was filled with water. The weight became too heavy for a pin holding it steady, the wheel moved forward one notch, then was held by a pin until the next cup was filled, and so on. Rods and gears attached to the wheel moved the "hands" that told the time.

Yi Xing's clock went out of use soon after it was built. Su Song's clock of 1092 (left), which had a similar mechanism, ran for nearly 50 years. Detailed descriptions were written about it. About 40 feet high, the wheel drove two globes for observing the positions of the stars, as well as a five-story pagoda in which different figures appeared at the window to point out the hours of the day.

When a cup was full (above), it pressed on a lever that pulled open the lock at the top of the wheel. The wheel turned and a new cup was filled.

A look inside Su Song's great clock to see its working mechanism

133

THE FIRST PHOTOGRAPH
NIÉPCE'S HISTORIC IMAGE

THE EARLIEST PHOTOGRAPH that survives today was taken in 1827 by a Frenchman Joseph Nicéphore Niépce. Simple cameras, in which rays of light reflected from an object passed through a pinhole in a dark box to make an upside-down image on a screen inside, had been invented centuries earlier. The problem was how to make the image permanent. Niépce solved it by fitting his camera with a metal plate coated with a thin layer of bitumen (the substance used to surface roads) and oil. After eight hours, a ghostly image formed on the plate. The quality of photographic images was soon improved by another Frenchman, Louis Daguerre, and an Englishman, William Fox Talbot.

X-rays were discovered – accidentally – by German scientist Wilhelm Röntgen in 1895. These invisible rays can pass through many materials, such as flesh, but not through metal or bone. Röntgen made the first X-ray photograph *(right)* of his wife's hand in 1896. Her ring is clearly visible.

The earliest surviving photograph was a view taken in 1827 by Nicéphore Niépce from the window of his home at Chalon-sur-Saône, near Beaune, France.

Daguerre's photograph of an artist's studio, the world's first fully successful photograph (1837). It was called a daguerrotype, a photograph on a copper plate fixed with ordinary salt.

American inventor George Eastman introduced the easy-to-use Kodak camera *(right)* in 1888 and photography soon became popular. Eastman also produced the first roll films.

THE FIRST MOVIES

In 1891 American inventor Thomas Alva Edison *(see page 136)* built a machine called the Kinetoscope. It was the first successful moving-picture machine, although only one person at a time could view through an eyepiece as the sequence of photographs on a strip of film wound past. Just four years later, two brothers, Auguste and Louis Lumière gave the first public cinema show in a cafe in Paris. The films showed scenes of everyday life in the city.

These five photographs *(below)* are milestones in the early history of photography.

Fox Talbot's 1835 photograph of a window at Lacock Abbey. It was the first photograph made by the negative-positive process, that allows many copies to be made.

The first color photograph was made in 1861 by the Scottish physicist James Clerk Maxwell.

Frenchman Hippolyte Bayard discovered how to make positive images directly on paper. He took this photo of windmills in Montmartre, Paris, in 1839.

THE FASTEST CAMERA

The fastest production camera is the image converter, or Imacon camera. It is used in scientific and industrial research. The image converter camera can reveal what happens when a high-speed bullet hits a target, for example. Light entering the camera is converted into an electron beam (like the inside of a television camera tube). This forms an image that can be recorded on film. There is less than one billionth of a second between each image, which means that a sequence of a billion images could be taken in one second!

TALKING MACHINES

In March 1876, American inventor Alexander Graham Bell made the world's first telephone call. His assistant, Tom Watson, in the next room, heard the words "Mr Watson, come here, I want to see you." In Bell's telephone, there was a steel strip that vibrated when someone spoke close to it. These vibrations could be sent along a wire with an electric current and make another strip vibrate, reproducing the original sounds. These were not very clear: Users of the first telephones had to shout to make themselves heard!

The telephone was improved by another American inventor, Thomas Alva Edison, so that it could be used over long distances. Some of its parts he also adapted to produce the first recording machine, which he called the phonograph. The first recorded sound was heard in 1877, when Edison listened to his own voice saying "Halloo, Halloo!"

His phonograph was like a telephone, only with the vibrating parts connected to a steel needle. As Edison spoke into a horn, the needle "wrote" the pattern of vibrations on a piece of tinfoil wrapped around a drum, which was turned at the same time. When the needle was returned to the beginning of its written message and the drum turned again, the pattern cut in the foil made it vibrate in the same way. The telephone parts also vibrated and the sound came back out of the drum.

In this imaginary scene, five great inventors sit around a table, each with their famous inventions in front of them.

ALEXANDER GRAHAM BELL
First telephone (1876)

THOMAS EDISON
First recording machine (1877)

First electric light bulb (1879) (also invented by Joseph Swan)

GUGLIELMO MARCONI (right)
First radio transmission across Atlantic (1901)

MESSAGES WITHOUT WIRES

Radio waves, which carry radio sounds and television pictures, move through the air at the speed of light. Heinrich Hertz, a German physicist, sent the first radio signals over a short distance in 1887. Italian inventor Guglielmo Marconi showed that radio messages could be sent across the world. In 1901, Marconi sent the first transatlantic radio signal – the three dots of S in Morse code – from Cornwall, England, to Newfoundland in Canada, a distance of 2,187 miles.

FIRST WITH THE NEWS
GREAT ELECTRICAL INVENTIONS

THE TELEPHONE, television, and radio are all so important to our daily lives it is difficult to imagine what we would do without them. Yet not much longer than 150 years ago, they did not even exist. The very first machine for sending messages was not electrical at all, but a tower with great mechanical arms fixed on top of it. The arms could be moved into different positions, each standing for a different word or number. Series of towers were built within sight of one another between two places, their operators relaying a message from one tower to the next. Called a semaphore telegraph, it first appeared in France in the 1790s.

*First electric telegraph
that recorded messages
on paper (1838)*

JOHN LOGIE BAIRD *(below, left)*
First television pictures (1926)

The Scottish inventor John Logie Baird was the first to give a demonstration of television in 1926. His camera used a spinning disk pierced with holes and an electronic "eye." The eye recorded the brightness of different parts of the image — the head of a ventriloquist's dummy — and transmitted what it "saw" to a screen.

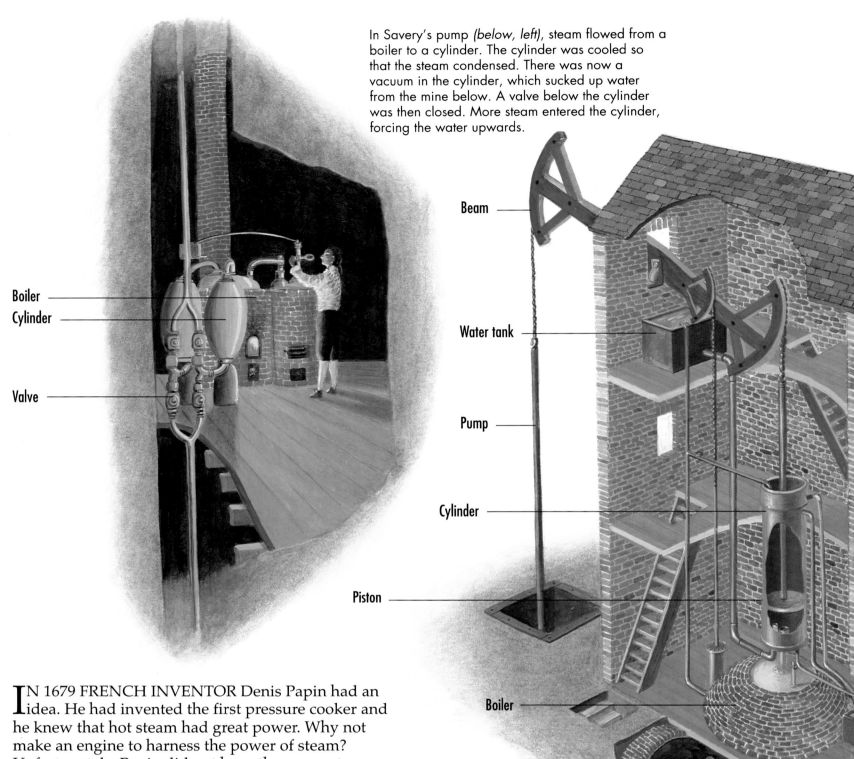

In Savery's pump *(below, left)*, steam flowed from a boiler to a cylinder. The cylinder was cooled so that the steam condensed. There was now a vacuum in the cylinder, which sucked up water from the mine below. A valve below the cylinder was then closed. More steam entered the cylinder, forcing the water upwards.

Boiler

Cylinder

Valve

Beam

Water tank

Pump

Cylinder

Piston

Boiler

IN 1679 FRENCH INVENTOR Denis Papin had an idea. He had invented the first pressure cooker and he knew that hot steam had great power. Why not make an engine to harness the power of steam? Unfortunately, Papin did not have the money to develop his idea. He died in poverty in 1714.

The first steam engine was designed in 1698 by Thomas Savery, an English engineer. It was called "the miner's friend" because it was built to pump water out of mines. Its only known successful use, however, was in lifting water at large houses in London, England.

The first working steam engine was built in 1712 by the Cornish engineer Thomas Newcomen. A large beam rocked back and forth 16 times a minute as it pumped water. In 1776 James Watt, a Scottish instrument maker, improved the Newcomen engine. His engines did not waste as much heat and made better use of the power of steam.

For his engine *(above, right)*, Newcomen used atmospheric pressure not to suck up water but to drive down a piston. Steam was admitted to a cylinder at a pressure high enough to push up the piston inside it. The steam was then condensed by a spray of water, a vacuum was created, and atmospheric pressure drove the piston downwards. The movement of the piston rocked the beam back and forth and worked the pump.

THE FIRST STEAM ENGINES
DRIVING FORCE OF THE INDUSTRIAL REVOLUTION

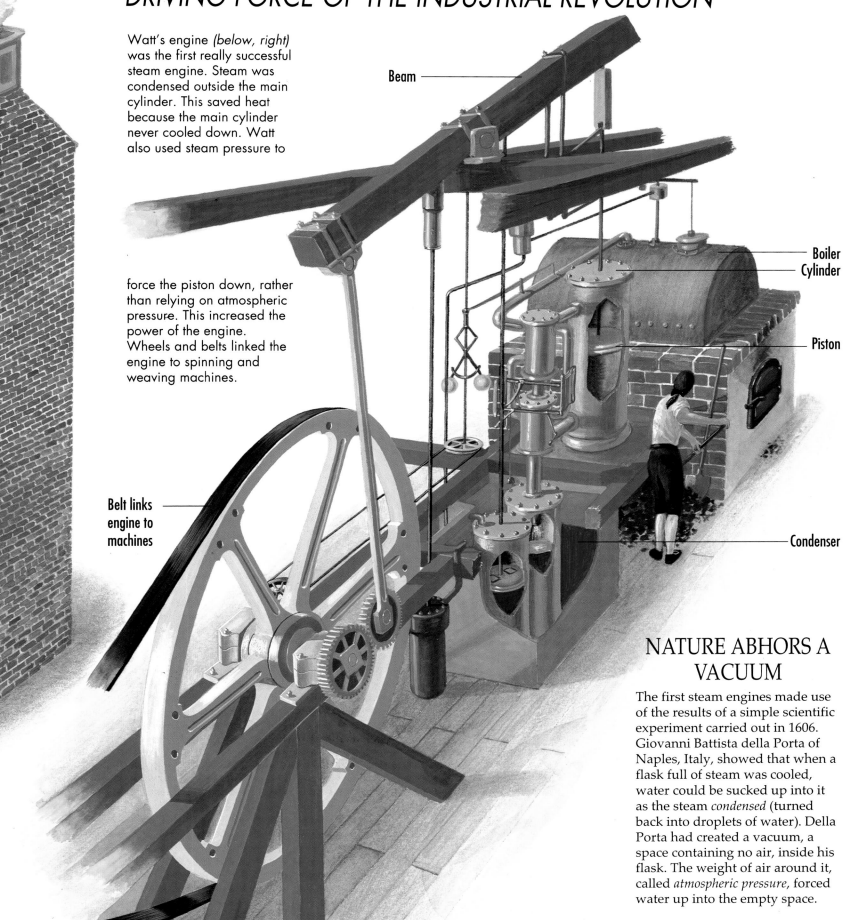

Watt's engine *(below, right)* was the first really successful steam engine. Steam was condensed outside the main cylinder. This saved heat because the main cylinder never cooled down. Watt also used steam pressure to force the piston down, rather than relying on atmospheric pressure. This increased the power of the engine. Wheels and belts linked the engine to spinning and weaving machines.

Beam

Boiler

Cylinder

Piston

Condenser

Belt links engine to machines

NATURE ABHORS A VACUUM

The first steam engines made use of the results of a simple scientific experiment carried out in 1606. Giovanni Battista della Porta of Naples, Italy, showed that when a flask full of steam was cooled, water could be sucked up into it as the steam *condensed* (turned back into droplets of water). Della Porta had created a vacuum, a space containing no air, inside his flask. The weight of air around it, called *atmospheric pressure*, forced water up into the empty space.

139

THE LARGEST LOCOMOTIVE
UNION PACIFIC'S "BIG BOY"

THE LARGEST, HEAVIEST, and most powerful railroad locomotive that ever pulled a train was the "Big Boy." Between 1941 and 1945, 25 of these giants were built by the American Locomotive Company of Schenectady, New York for the Union Pacific Railroad. They were 130 feet long (about one-and-a-half times the length of a basketball court) and weighed more than 600 tons. Each locomotive was able to haul a load six times its own weight up a steep gradient in the mountains of the western United States.

Big Boys had two sets of eight driving wheels. The front set were specially designed to swivel to enable the giant locomotive to go around bends on the twisting mountain railroad. No fireman could shovel coal fast enough to keep the furnace stoked up, so a mechanical stoker was used. This machine could deliver 24 tons of coal an hour to the firebox. The Big Boys used up a lot of water, too. At top speed they guzzled 55 tons of water an hour – about a saucepanful every second!

The illustrations are approximately to scale

The Big Boy locomotives hauled ore trains with more than 70 wagons between Wyoming and Utah, across the Wasatch Mountains.

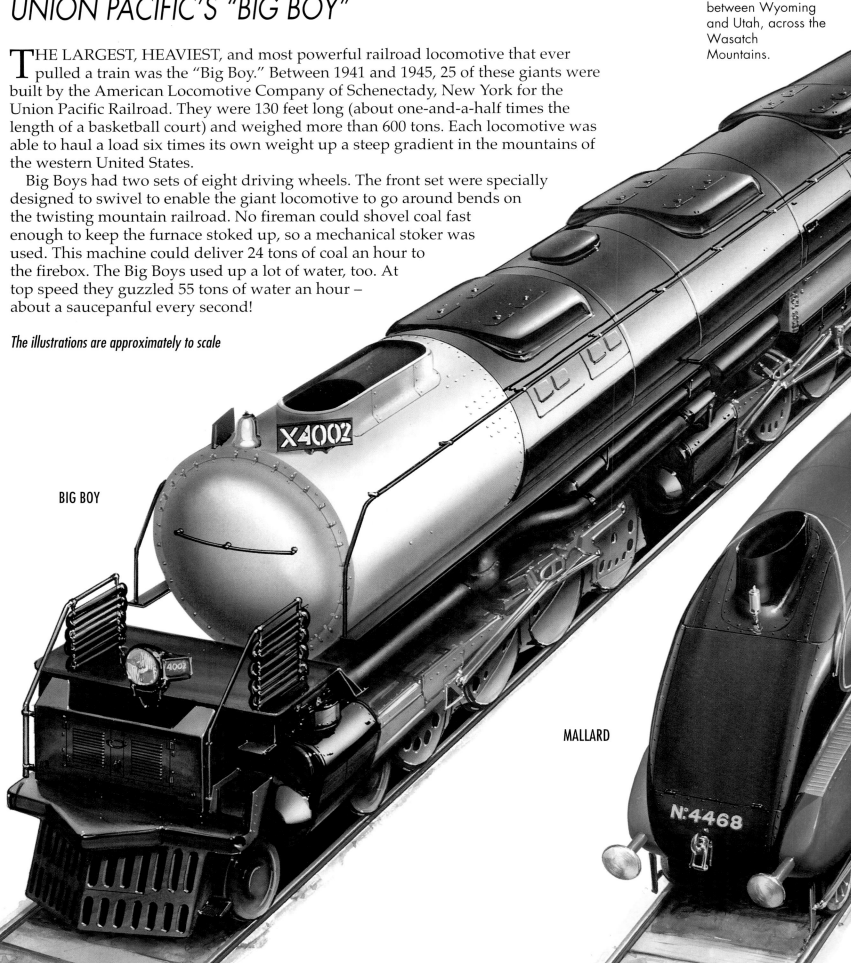

BIG BOY

X4002

MALLARD

N° 4468

THE FASTEST STEAM LOCOMOTIVE

A new world record speed for a steam locomotive was set on July 3, 1938. The *Mallard*, a new engine fitted with a streamlined casing, was chosen for the honor. Pulling a seven-coach train between Grantham and Peterborough, England, *Mallard* was timed at a speed of 125 miles per hour over a distance of about 1,310 feet. It was damaged during the run, but was repaired and placed in the Railway Museum, York, England. Its record has stood to this day.

TREVITHICK'S LOCOMOTIVE

THE FIRST TRAINS

The first steam locomotive to run on rails was built by Cornish engineer Richard Trevithick. His four-wheel locomotive made a demonstration run on February 22, 1804, reaching 12 miles per hour when empty and 5 miles per hour (a brisk walking-pace) when loaded. Unfortunately, the weight of the train broke the rails! By 1812, stronger tracks had been built between Middleton Colliery and Leeds, England. They carried the first successful steam locomotives.

In 1829, while the new Liverpool and Manchester Railway was being built in northern England, a competition was held to find the best locomotive to run along it. The £500 prize was won easily by the *Rocket*, entered by George and Robert Stephenson. It reached the then breathtaking speed of 29 miles per hour, a world record. For the first time, people would be able to travel on land faster than by horse.

This illustration *(below)* shows the inside of a steam locomotive. Water is heated by the fire tubes in the boiler. The steam is forced into a cylinder where it pushes a piston linked to the driving wheels. When the piston reaches the end of the cylinder, steam is let into the other side, pushing the piston back again.

ROCKET

Boiler   Steam   Piston

Fire-box   Driving wheels   Cylinder

THE FASTEST TRAIN
FRANCE'S ROCKET ON RAILS

THE FRENCH HIGH-SPEED TRAIN, the *Train à Grande Vitesse* or TGV, holds the world speed record for a train traveling on rails. During a test run without passengers between Paris and Tours in 1990, the TGV reached a speed of 320 miles per hour – half as fast again as a Formula 1 racing car *(see page 170)*. Even in regular service, the TGV easily outpaces any other train. The 264-mile journey from Paris to Lyon takes about 2 hours.

The TGV is powered by electric current from an overhead cable. The two locomotives, one at either end of the train, together with its eight passenger cars, are all carefully streamlined, so the train uses up no more fuel than an ordinary train.

Back in the age of steam, if you found yourself in the driver's cab, you would be faced by an array of dials and levers, you would feel the searing heat from the firebox,

and your ears would be deafened by the pounding noise. The TGV driver's cab is more like a modern office, the noise of the speeding locomotive barely rising above the level of whirring computers. Computers effectively drive the train. The driver checks the train's progress on a computer screen and gives instructions by using a keyboard. A radio links on-board computers with the signaling center and other trains on the track. Computers also operate the brakes, air-conditioning, and other equipment.

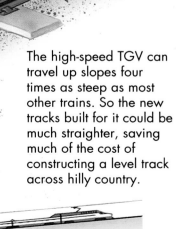

The high-speed TGV can travel up slopes four times as steep as most other trains. So the new tracks built for it could be much straighter, saving much of the cost of constructing a level track across hilly country.

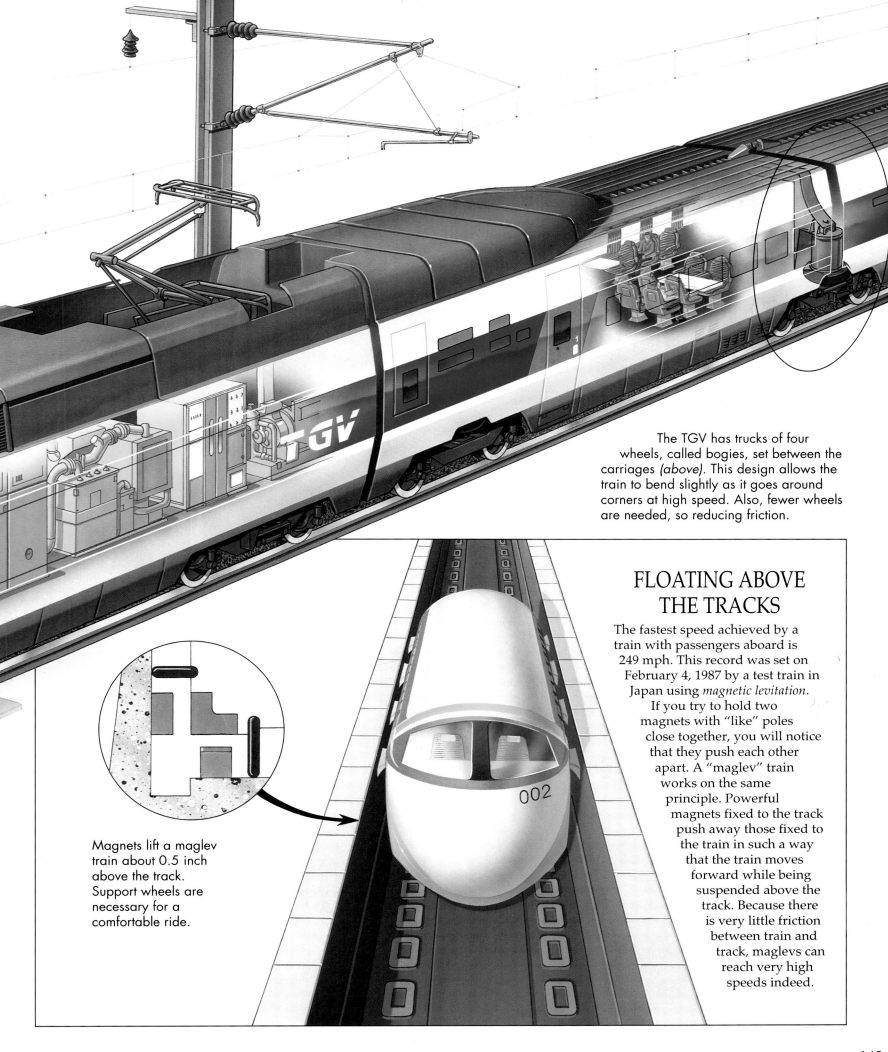

The TGV has trucks of four wheels, called bogies, set between the carriages *(above)*. This design allows the train to bend slightly as it goes around corners at high speed. Also, fewer wheels are needed, so reducing friction.

FLOATING ABOVE THE TRACKS

The fastest speed achieved by a train with passengers aboard is 249 mph. This record was set on February 4, 1987 by a test train in Japan using *magnetic levitation.* If you try to hold two magnets with "like" poles close together, you will notice that they push each other apart. A "maglev" train works on the same principle. Powerful magnets fixed to the track push away those fixed to the train in such a way that the train moves forward while being suspended above the track. Because there is very little friction between train and track, maglevs can reach very high speeds indeed.

Magnets lift a maglev train about 0.5 inch above the track. Support wheels are necessary for a comfortable ride.

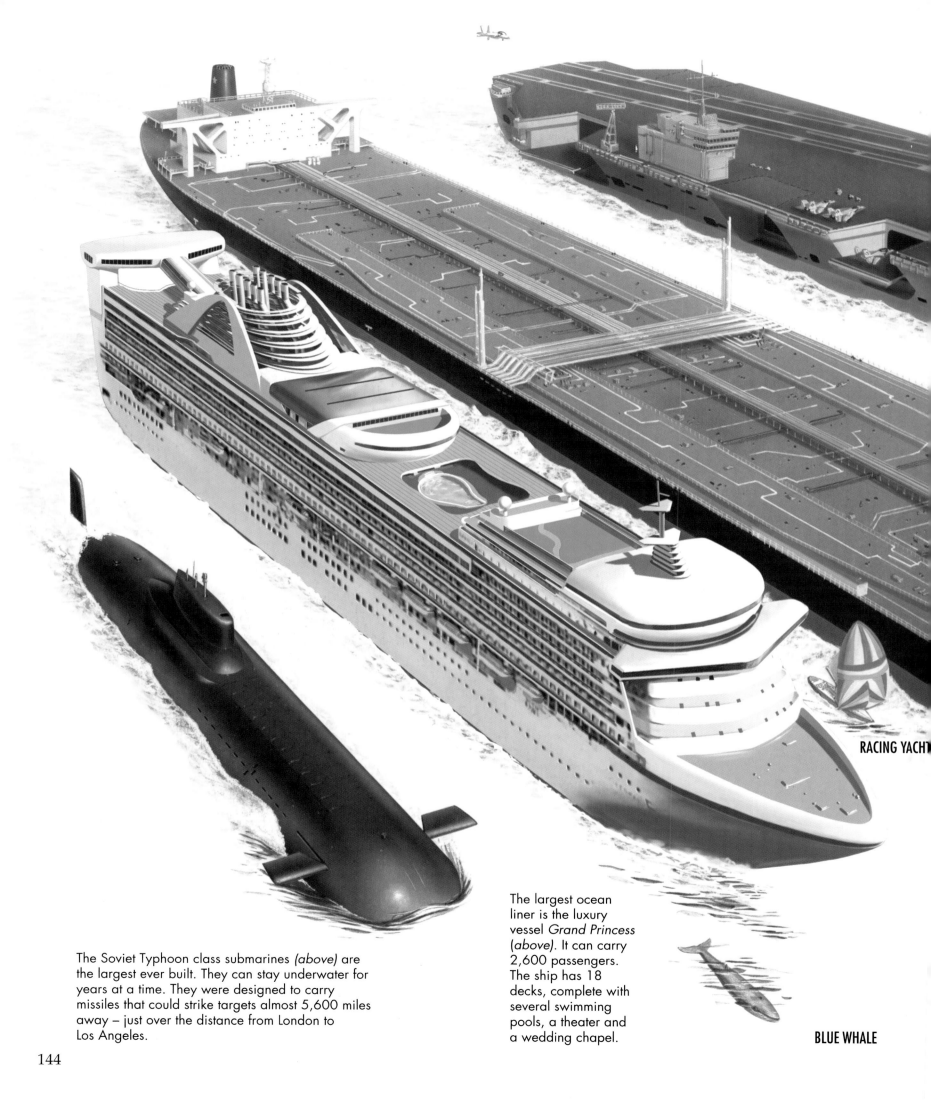

RACING YACHT

The Soviet Typhoon class submarines (above) are the largest ever built. They can stay underwater for years at a time. They were designed to carry missiles that could strike targets almost 5,600 miles away – just over the distance from London to Los Angeles.

The largest ocean liner is the luxury vessel *Grand Princess* (above). It can carry 2,600 passengers. The ship has 18 decks, complete with several swimming pools, a theater and a wedding chapel.

BLUE WHALE

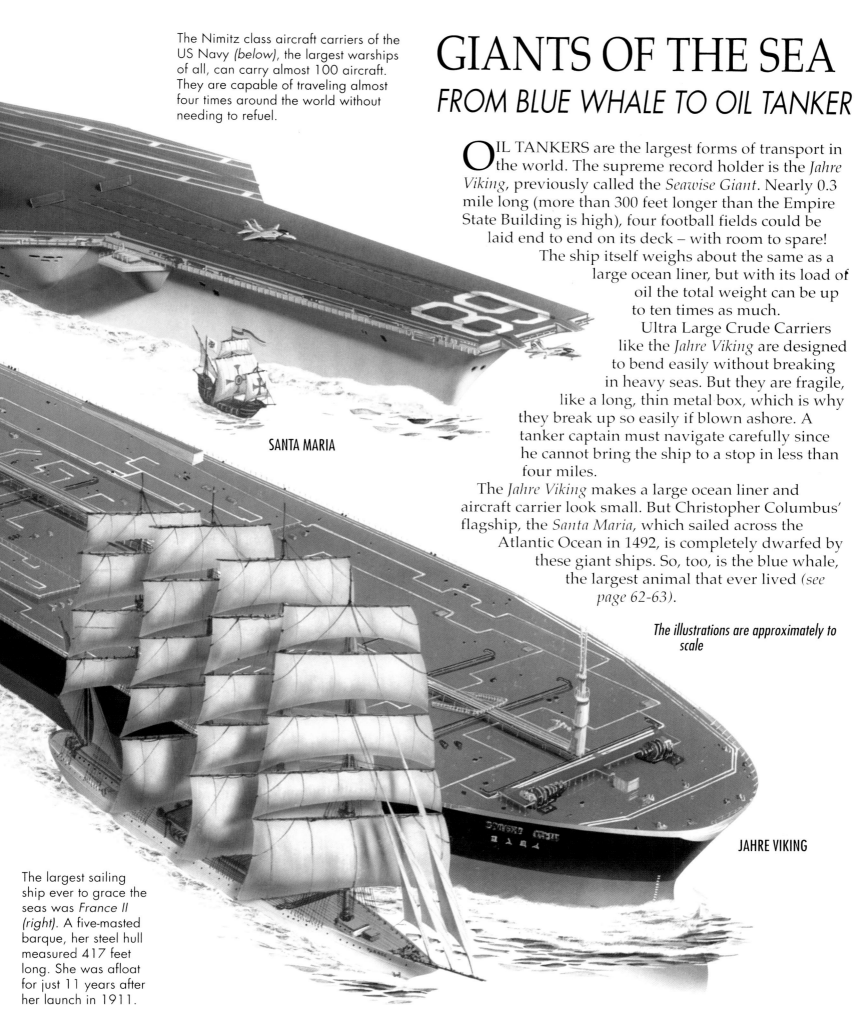

The Nimitz class aircraft carriers of the US Navy *(below)*, the largest warships of all, can carry almost 100 aircraft. They are capable of traveling almost four times around the world without needing to refuel.

GIANTS OF THE SEA
FROM BLUE WHALE TO OIL TANKER

OIL TANKERS are the largest forms of transport in the world. The supreme record holder is the *Jahre Viking*, previously called the *Seawise Giant*. Nearly 0.3 mile long (more than 300 feet longer than the Empire State Building is high), four football fields could be laid end to end on its deck – with room to spare! The ship itself weighs about the same as a large ocean liner, but with its load of oil the total weight can be up to ten times as much.

Ultra Large Crude Carriers like the *Jahre Viking* are designed to bend easily without breaking in heavy seas. But they are fragile, like a long, thin metal box, which is why they break up so easily if blown ashore. A tanker captain must navigate carefully since he cannot bring the ship to a stop in less than four miles.

The *Jahre Viking* makes a large ocean liner and aircraft carrier look small. But Christopher Columbus' flagship, the *Santa Maria*, which sailed across the Atlantic Ocean in 1492, is completely dwarfed by these giant ships. So, too, is the blue whale, the largest animal that ever lived *(see page 62-63)*.

The illustrations are approximately to scale

SANTA MARIA

JAHRE VIKING

The largest sailing ship ever to grace the seas was *France II (right)*. A five-masted barque, her steel hull measured 417 feet long. She was afloat for just 11 years after her launch in 1911.

HUMAN-POWERED VEHICLES
FROM RUNNING MACHINE TO FLYING MACHINE

PEOPLE FLED IN TERROR and horses bolted when Baron von Drais first rode his "running machine" in 1817. The German inventor sat astride his *draisienne*, which consisted of two wheels, one behind the other, connected by a wooden frame, and moved forward simply by pushing on the ground with his feet. On good roads, this machine was faster than a horse. It was the fastest land vehicle of its time.

The *draisienne* was the first of a long line of human-powered vehicles, eventually leading to the first human-powered aircraft. In 1839 a Scottish blacksmith, Kirkpatrick Macmillan, built the first real bicycle – one that could be driven without the rider's feet touching the ground – with pedals which turned the back wheel. He was fined five shillings by Glasgow

magistrates when he knocked over a child during a ride around the city streets.

The first really successful pedal-powered bicycle was made in Paris in 1861 by a coach repairer, Pierre Michaux and his son, Ernest. They fitted two pedals to the front wheel of a *draisienne*. The new machine, known as a "boneshaker," became popular. English inventor James Starley designed a famous version of it in 1870. This became known as the Penny Farthing, for its enormous front wheel (5 feet across) and much smaller rear wheel.

Starley's nephew, John, later built the Rover safety bicycle in 1885. With its strong diamond-shaped frame, equal-sized wheels, and geared chain drive, it was the forerunner of all modern bicycles.

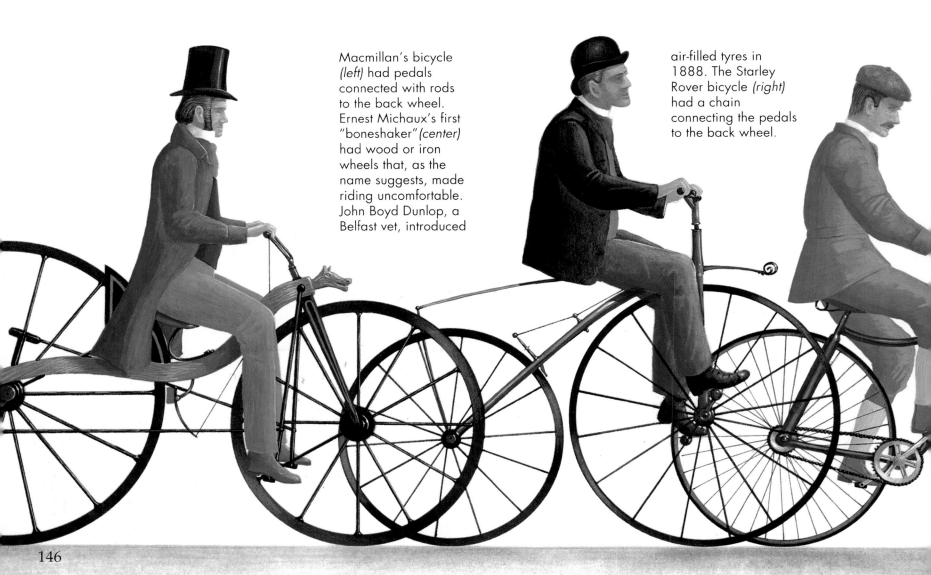

Macmillan's bicycle *(left)* had pedals connected with rods to the back wheel. Ernest Michaux's first "boneshaker" *(center)* had wood or iron wheels that, as the name suggests, made riding uncomfortable. John Boyd Dunlop, a Belfast vet, introduced air-filled tyres in 1888. The Starley Rover bicycle *(right)* had a chain connecting the pedals to the back wheel.

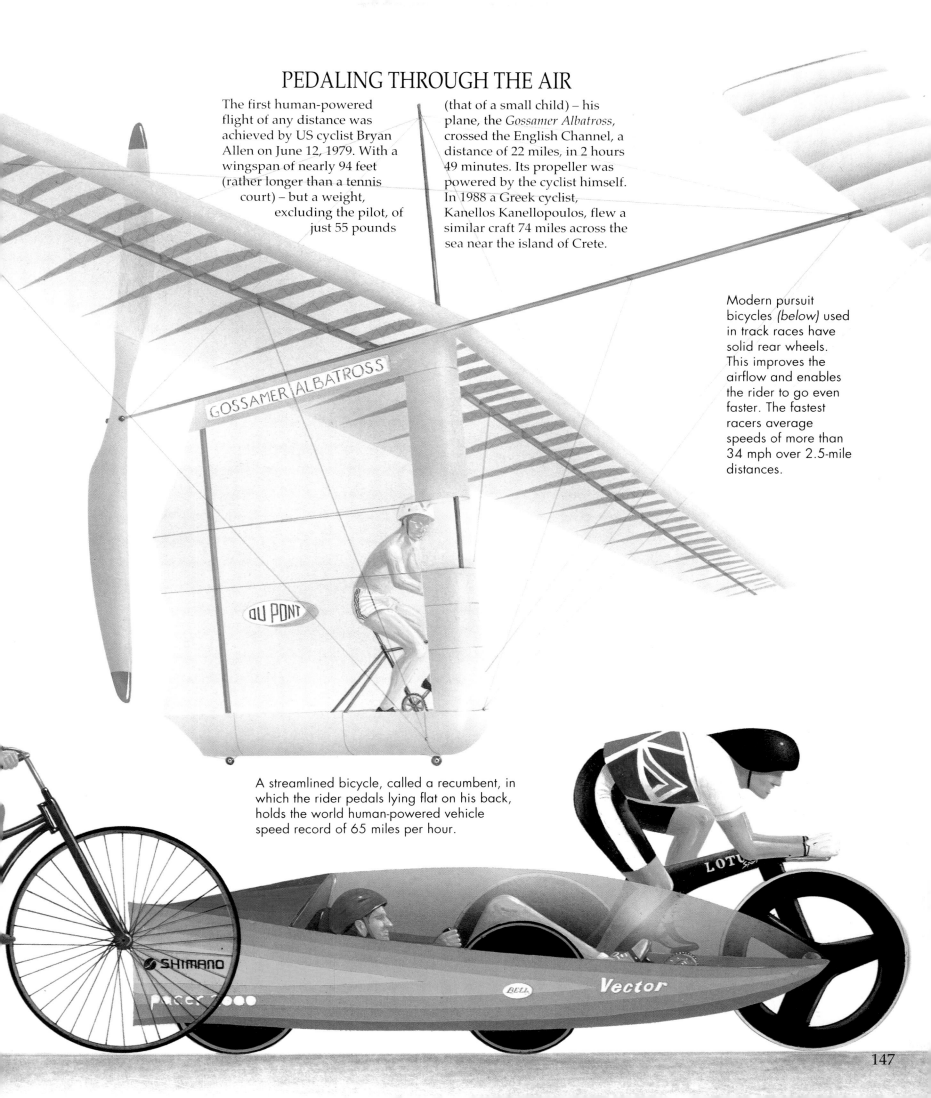

PEDALING THROUGH THE AIR

The first human-powered flight of any distance was achieved by US cyclist Bryan Allen on June 12, 1979. With a wingspan of nearly 94 feet (rather longer than a tennis court) – but a weight, excluding the pilot, of just 55 pounds (that of a small child) – his plane, the *Gossamer Albatross*, crossed the English Channel, a distance of 22 miles, in 2 hours 49 minutes. Its propeller was powered by the cyclist himself. In 1988 a Greek cyclist, Kanellos Kanellopoulos, flew a similar craft 74 miles across the sea near the island of Crete.

Modern pursuit bicycles *(below)* used in track races have solid rear wheels. This improves the airflow and enables the rider to go even faster. The fastest racers average speeds of more than 34 mph over 2.5-mile distances.

A streamlined bicycle, called a recumbent, in which the rider pedals lying flat on his back, holds the world human-powered vehicle speed record of 65 miles per hour.

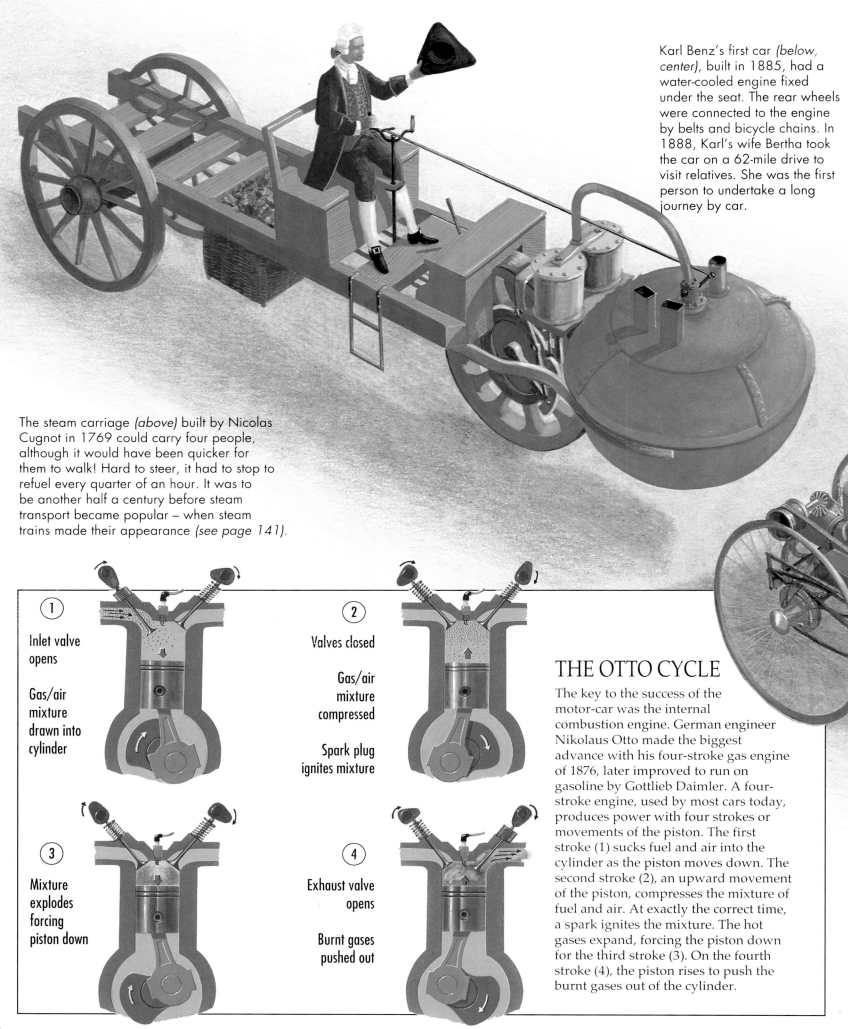

Karl Benz's first car (below, center), built in 1885, had a water-cooled engine fixed under the seat. The rear wheels were connected to the engine by belts and bicycle chains. In 1888, Karl's wife Bertha took the car on a 62-mile drive to visit relatives. She was the first person to undertake a long journey by car.

The steam carriage (above) built by Nicolas Cugnot in 1769 could carry four people, although it would have been quicker for them to walk! Hard to steer, it had to stop to refuel every quarter of an hour. It was to be another half a century before steam transport became popular – when steam trains made their appearance (see page 141).

① Inlet valve opens

Gas/air mixture drawn into cylinder

② Valves closed

Gas/air mixture compressed

Spark plug ignites mixture

③ Mixture explodes forcing piston down

④ Exhaust valve opens

Burnt gases pushed out

THE OTTO CYCLE

The key to the success of the motor-car was the internal combustion engine. German engineer Nikolaus Otto made the biggest advance with his four-stroke gas engine of 1876, later improved to run on gasoline by Gottlieb Daimler. A four-stroke engine, used by most cars today, produces power with four strokes or movements of the piston. The first stroke (1) sucks fuel and air into the cylinder as the piston moves down. The second stroke (2), an upward movement of the piston, compresses the mixture of fuel and air. At exactly the correct time, a spark ignites the mixture. The hot gases expand, forcing the piston down for the third stroke (3). On the fourth stroke (4), the piston rises to push the burnt gases out of the cylinder.

In 1885, a few months before Benz produced his motor-car, Gottlieb Daimler attached a gasoline engine to a wooden-framed bicycle *(below, right)*. His son Paul rode the world's first motor vehicle about 10 miles around the streets of Cannstatt, Germany. During the trip, the saddle, fitted too close to the top of the engine, burst into flames!

THE FIRST CARS
ENTER THE HORSELESS CARRIAGE

THE FIRST SELF-PROPELLED land vehicles were powered by steam engines *(see page 138)*. Frenchman Nicolas Cugnot built the first steam carriage in 1769. Designed to pull heavy guns, it caused the world's first motor accident when it crashed into a wall at its top speed of 3 miles per hour!

The age of the automobile really began in 1885 when German engineer Karl Benz successfully fitted a gasoline engine to a three-wheeled tricycle. To begin with, his new car lurched and spluttered dangerously around the streets of Mannheim, but a smooth ride was soon achieved. The local newspaper reported: "Without the aid of any human element, the vehicle rolled onward, taking bends in its stride and avoiding all oncoming traffic and pedestrians. It was followed by a crowd of running and breathless youngsters."

Meanwhile, another German engineer, Gottlieb Daimler was hard at work. He had already invented a gasoline-driven motorcycle and was, in 1886, to build the first four-wheeled car, a "horseless carriage" fitted with a powerful gasoline engine.

In 1890, two French machine toolmakers, René Panhard and Emile Levassor, began making cars using Daimler engines. The following year they produced a model *(right)* that can be described as the first modern car. Fitted beneath a square hood at the front, its engine was connected to the rear wheels by a clutch and gears. Other modern devices made their first appearances in early French designs: Hollow rubber tyres were first used on a 1895 Peugeot and a propeller shaft replaced chain drive in the first Renault built in 1898.

GOING FOR THE LAND SPEED RECORD

FROM EARLY ELECTRICS TO MODERN JETS

THE FIRST WORLD LAND SPEED RECORD was set at Achères near Paris, France, in 1898, just 13 years after the motor car had been first invented. Count Gaston de Chasseloup-Laubat drove an electric car, the *Jeantaud*, at a speed of 57.6 mph. Medical experts at the time declared it would be impossible to breathe at these speeds, and that the driver's heart would surely stop! Chasseloup-Laubat improved on his own record a year later, taking it up to 58.2 mph. In the same year, Camille Jenatzy became the first motorist to exceed 100 km/h. His bullet-shaped electric car, called *La Jamais Contente* ("never-satisfied") held the record for three years. A spectator described the car as moving "with a subdued noise like the rustling of wings, scarcely seeming to touch the ground."

Steam-powered cars were among the early land speed record holders. One reached a speed of 75 mph in 1902 but they were soon to give way to faster gasoline-engined cars. The *Mors*, the first of the breed, broke the record in 1902. In 1927, the 300 km/h barrier was breached by the first car specially built for the record attempt, the *Sunbeam*. This streamlined vehicle, driven by Englishman Henry Segrave, was powered by two aircraft engines. The record was then pushed steadily higher by a series of cars with more and more powerful engines. The largest of these, the *Thunderbolt*, reached 345 mph in 1939.

In 1964, however, the gasoline engine faced a new type of competition. Jet and rocket-powered cars were allowed to enter the speed contest for the first time. A jet-engined car, the *Spirit of America*, soon took the record to over 500 mph in that year. The first rocket-powered car, *Blue Flame*, driven by American Gary Gabelich shot past 1,000 km/h in 1970.

The land speed racers of the early 1900s were the fastest vehicles on Earth, faster even than the primitive aircraft that were taking to the skies at the time. Racing at speeds we would consider even today extremely fast (more than 90 miles per hour) on bumpy road surfaces, many of the drivers risked their lives.

JEANTAUD
March 1899
57.6 mph
First electric-powered record holder

SERPOLLET
April 1902 75 mph
First steam-powered record holder

GOBRON-BRILLIÉ
July 1904
103.6 mph
First record holder over 100 mph

LA JAMAIS CONTENTE
December 1899
65.8 mph
First record holder over 100 km/h

MORS
November 1902
77.1 mph
First gasoline-powered record holder

BLITZEN BENZ
November 1909
126 mph
First record holder over 200 km/h

SUNBEAM
March 1927
203 mph
First record holder over 200 mph and 300 km/h

BLUEBIRD
February 1932
254 mph
First record holder over 400 km/h

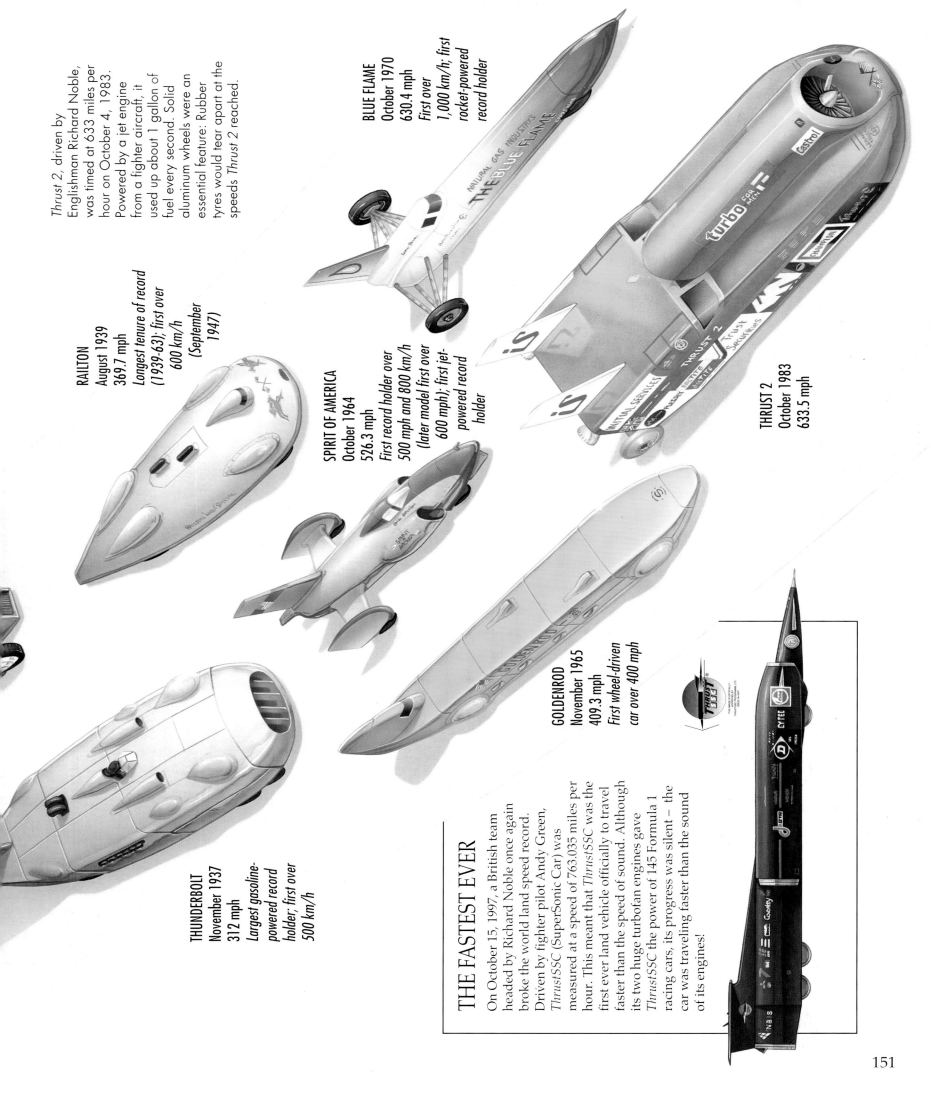

Thrust 2, driven by Englishman Richard Noble, was timed at 633 miles per hour on October 4, 1983. Powered by a jet engine from a fighter aircraft, it used up about 1 gallon of fuel every second. Solid aluminum wheels were an essential feature: Rubber tyres would tear apart at the speeds *Thrust 2* reached.

BLUE FLAME
October 1970
630.4 mph
*First over
1,000 km/h; first
rocket-powered
record holder*

RAILTON
August 1939
369.7 mph
*Longest tenure of record
(1939-63); first over
600 km/h
(September
1947)*

SPIRIT OF AMERICA
October 1964
526.3 mph
*First record holder over
500 mph and 800 km/h
(later model first over
600 mph); first jet-
powered record
holder*

THRUST 2
October 1983
633.5 mph

GOLDENROD
November 1965
409.3 mph
*First wheel-driven
car over 400 mph*

THUNDERBOLT
November 1937
312 mph
*Largest gasoline-
powered record
holder; first over
500 km/h*

THE FASTEST EVER

On October 15, 1997, a British team headed by Richard Noble once again broke the world land speed record. Driven by fighter pilot Andy Green, *ThrustSSC* (SuperSonic Car) was measured at a speed of 763.035 miles per hour. This meant that *ThrustSSC* was the first ever land vehicle officially to travel faster than the speed of sound. Although its two huge turbofan engines gave *ThrustSSC* the power of 145 Formula 1 racing cars, its progress was silent – the car was traveling faster than the sound of its engines!

151

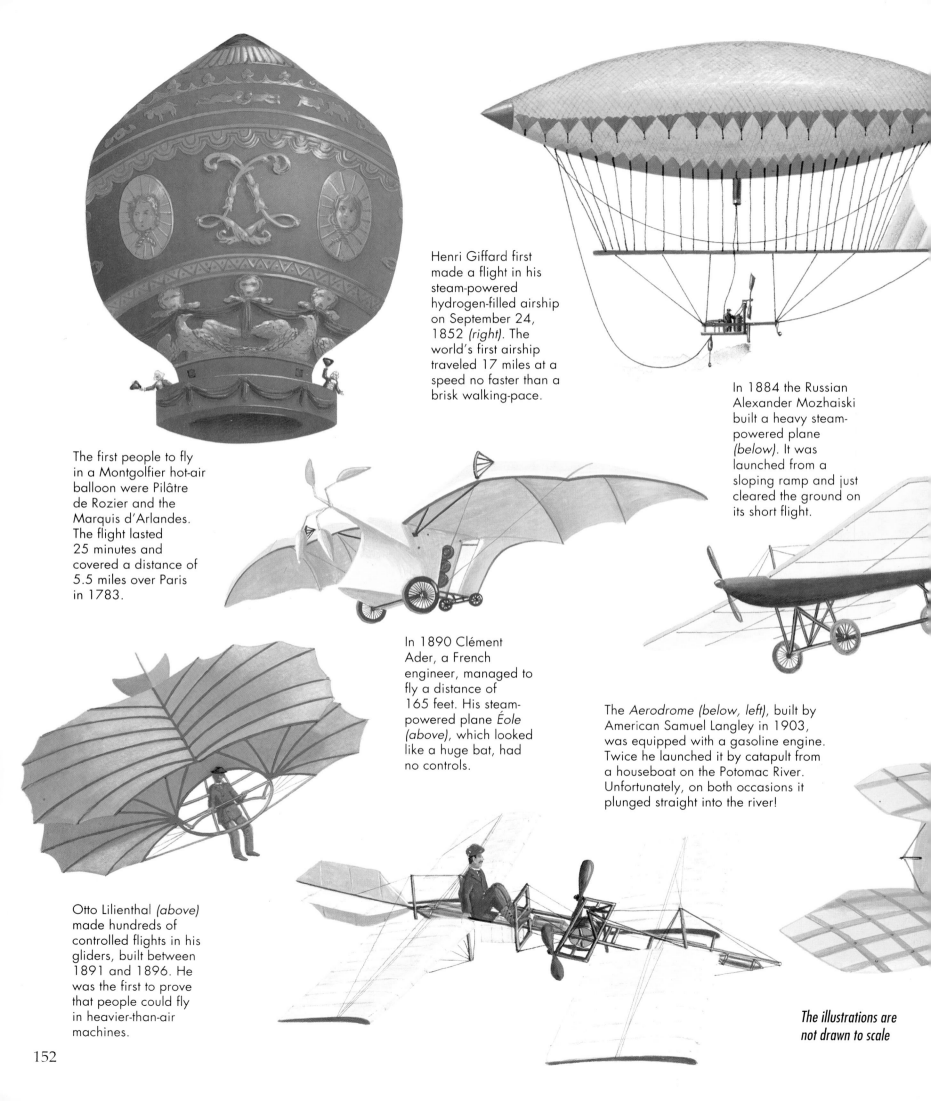

Henri Giffard first made a flight in his steam-powered hydrogen-filled airship on September 24, 1852 *(right)*. The world's first airship traveled 17 miles at a speed no faster than a brisk walking-pace.

In 1884 the Russian Alexander Mozhaiski built a heavy steam-powered plane *(below)*. It was launched from a sloping ramp and just cleared the ground on its short flight.

The first people to fly in a Montgolfier hot-air balloon were Pilâtre de Rozier and the Marquis d'Arlandes. The flight lasted 25 minutes and covered a distance of 5.5 miles over Paris in 1783.

In 1890 Clément Ader, a French engineer, managed to fly a distance of 165 feet. His steam-powered plane *Éole (above)*, which looked like a huge bat, had no controls.

The *Aerodrome (below, left)*, built by American Samuel Langley in 1903, was equipped with a gasoline engine. Twice he launched it by catapult from a houseboat on the Potomac River. Unfortunately, on both occasions it plunged straight into the river!

Otto Lilienthal *(above)* made hundreds of controlled flights in his gliders, built between 1891 and 1896. He was the first to prove that people could fly in heavier-than-air machines.

The illustrations are not drawn to scale

THE FIRST AIRCRAFT
THE QUEST FOR FLIGHT

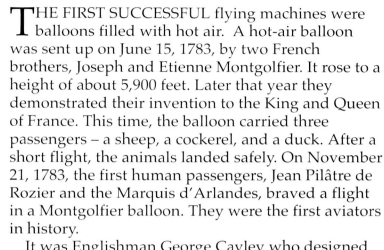

In 1849 a glider built by George Cayley *(right)* was launched from a hillside with a 10 year-old boy on board. It managed to travel about 1,641 feet.

Félix du Temple built the first powered airplane, a small model with a clockwork engine, in 1857. A full-sized steam-powered plane *(right)* took off from a steep ramp 17 years later. This was the first-known hop by a manned, powered airplane.

T HE FIRST SUCCESSFUL flying machines were balloons filled with hot air. A hot-air balloon was sent up on June 15, 1783, by two French brothers, Joseph and Etienne Montgolfier. It rose to a height of about 5,900 feet. Later that year they demonstrated their invention to the King and Queen of France. This time, the balloon carried three passengers – a sheep, a cockerel, and a duck. After a short flight, the animals landed safely. On November 21, 1783, the first human passengers, Jean Pilâtre de Rozier and the Marquis d'Arlandes, braved a flight in a Montgolfier balloon. They were the first aviators in history.

It was Englishman George Cayley who designed the modern airplane, with wings and a tail like those flying today. However, none of his machines ever flew for long: In the mid-19th century no engine yet invented was light enough to power a piloted flying machine.

The first people to fix a gasoline engine to an airplane and achieve a controlled flight were the American brothers, Wilbur and Orville Wright. Their aircraft *Flyer I* first flew on December 17, 1903.

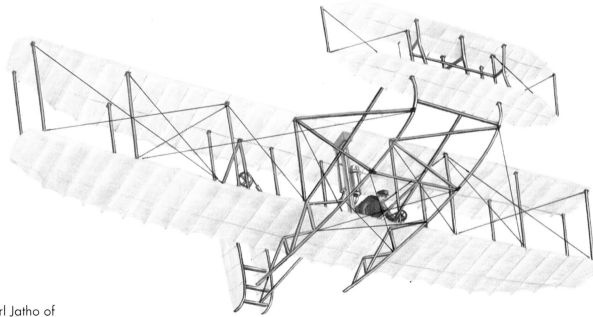

Karl Jatho of Germany came near to claiming the record for the first flight. Although it lacked controls, his kite-like airplane *(left)* made a number of flights of up to 197 feet.

FIRST CONTROLLED FLIGHT

The historic first flight of the Wright brothers' *Flyer I (above)* took place on sand dunes near Kitty Hawk, North Carolina. With Orville at the controls, *Flyer* remained aloft for about 12 seconds and flew a distance of just 118 feet, less than the wingspan of many modern airliners. By changing the angle of the wing tips (warping), the Wrights could control their aircraft. Theirs was indisputably the first controlled, powered flight.

THE FIRST HELICOPTERS
FROM FLYING TOP TO SIKORSKY

THE WAY IN WHICH a helicopter flies has been understood for many centuries. A flying top, invented by the Chinese around 500 BC, was a small propeller that flew upward when the stick on which it was balanced was spun rapidly. The propeller "bit" into the air, producing uplift. This method of flight worked well for small toys but how could a full-sized machine capable of carrying people through the air be built? Only when light gasoline engines *(see page 148)* became available in the early 1900s would the helicopter at last take to the skies.

The first take-off by a manned helicopter was achieved in 1907 by Frenchman Paul Cornu. However, he and other early helicopter pilots were not yet able to control their machines. They tended to twist in the opposite direction to the blades when the helicopter moved forward. The German aircraft designer Heinrich Focke and Russian-born American engineer Igor Sikorsky both came up with the answers. Fitting two rotors, each turning in opposite directions, solved the problem.

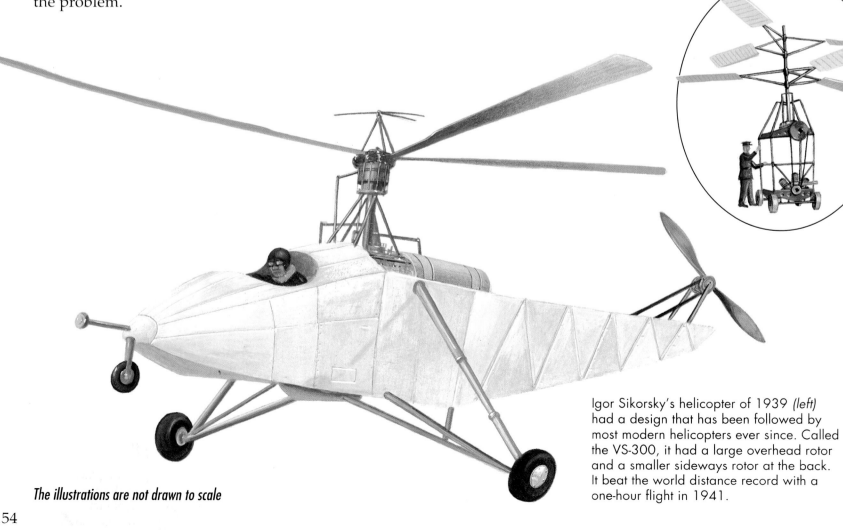

A FLYING TOP

Leonardo da Vinci, Italian painter, scientist and engineer was fascinated with the idea of helicopter flight. His design, produced around 1500, had a corkscrew-shaped rotor which, he thought, would soar upward through the air as it spun. To power the machine, the pilot simply pulled sharply on a rope wound around the central column – just as with a Chinese flying top. Not surprisingly, his machine never flew! Leonardo was, however, the first to use the word "helicopter," which he derived from the Greek for "spiral wing."

Igor Sikorsky's helicopter of 1939 *(left)* had a design that has been followed by most modern helicopters ever since. Called the VS-300, it had a large overhead rotor and a smaller sideways rotor at the back. It beat the world distance record with a one-hour flight in 1941.

The illustrations are not drawn to scale

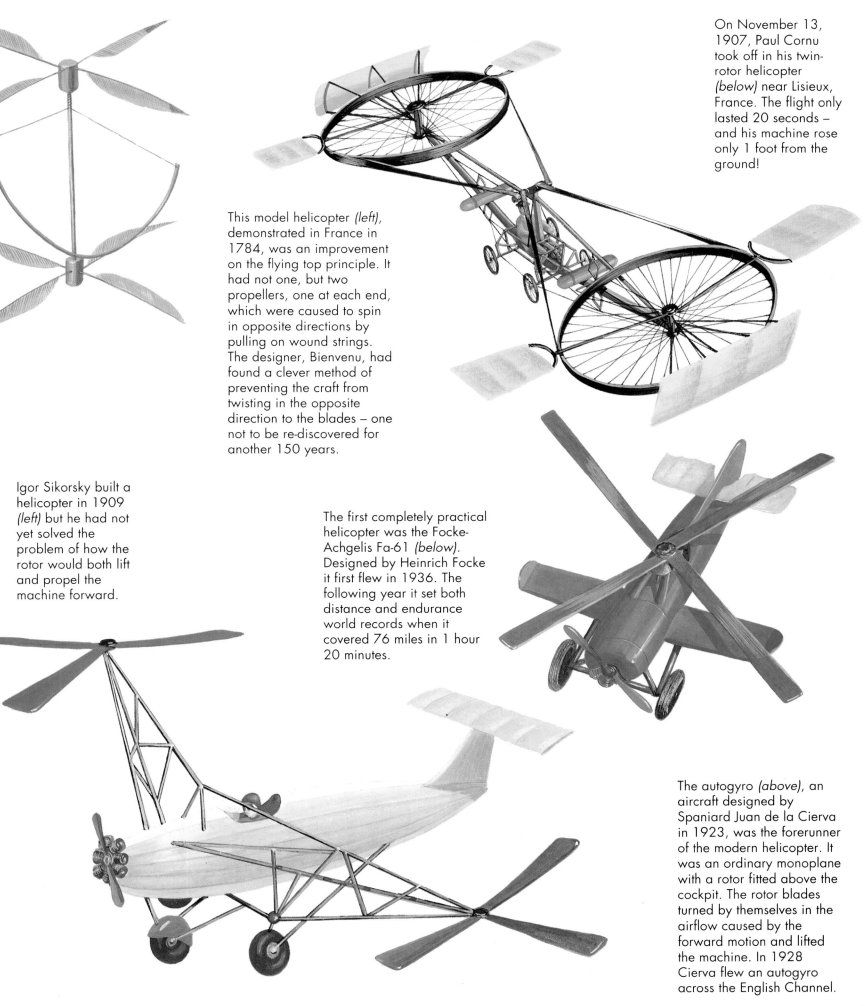

On November 13, 1907, Paul Cornu took off in his twin-rotor helicopter *(below)* near Lisieux, France. The flight only lasted 20 seconds – and his machine rose only 1 foot from the ground!

This model helicopter *(left)*, demonstrated in France in 1784, was an improvement on the flying top principle. It had not one, but two propellers, one at each end, which were caused to spin in opposite directions by pulling on wound strings. The designer, Bienvenu, had found a clever method of preventing the craft from twisting in the opposite direction to the blades – one not to be re-discovered for another 150 years.

Igor Sikorsky built a helicopter in 1909 *(left)* but he had not yet solved the problem of how the rotor would both lift and propel the machine forward.

The first completely practical helicopter was the Focke-Achgelis Fa-61 *(below)*. Designed by Heinrich Focke it first flew in 1936. The following year it set both distance and endurance world records when it covered 76 miles in 1 hour 20 minutes.

The autogyro *(above)*, an aircraft designed by Spaniard Juan de la Cierva in 1923, was the forerunner of the modern helicopter. It was an ordinary monoplane with a rotor fitted above the cockpit. The rotor blades turned by themselves in the airflow caused by the forward motion and lifted the machine. In 1928 Cierva flew an autogyro across the English Channel.

155

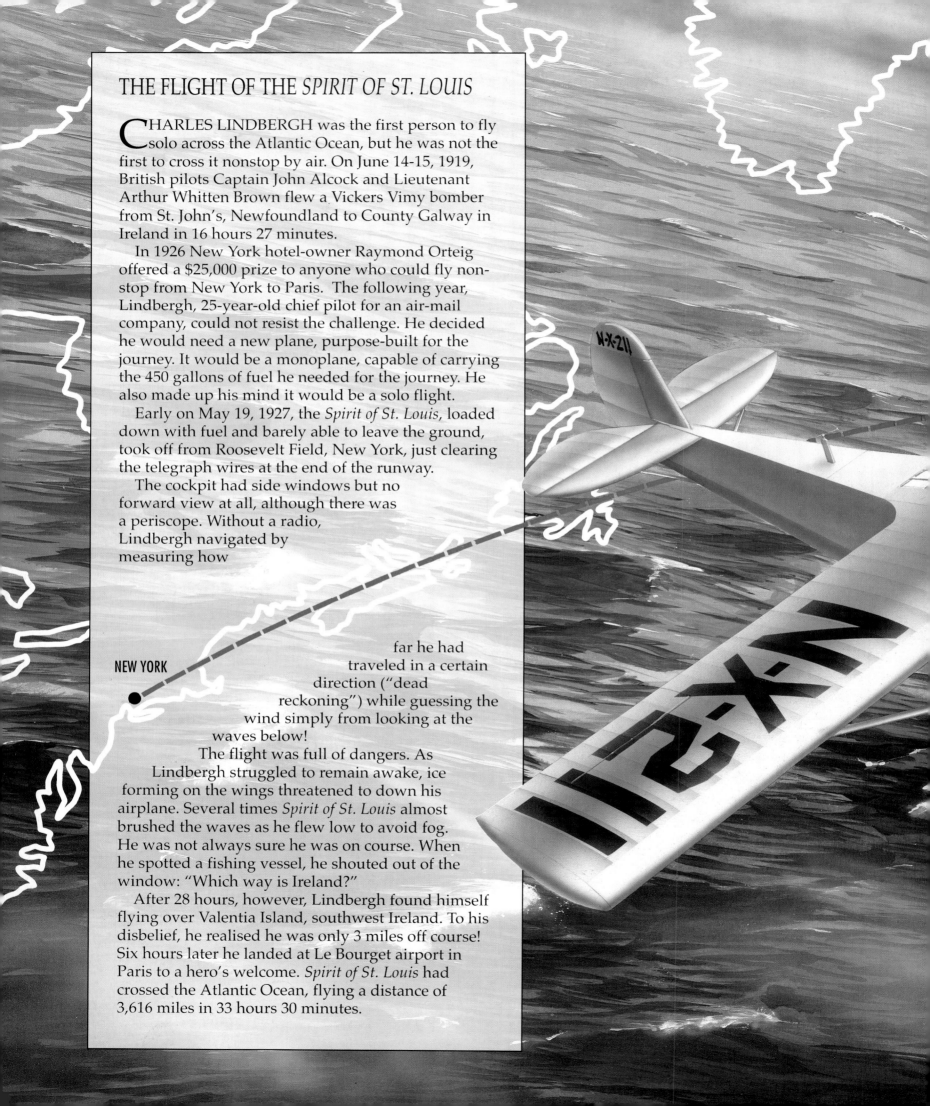

THE FLIGHT OF THE *SPIRIT OF ST. LOUIS*

CHARLES LINDBERGH was the first person to fly solo across the Atlantic Ocean, but he was not the first to cross it nonstop by air. On June 14-15, 1919, British pilots Captain John Alcock and Lieutenant Arthur Whitten Brown flew a Vickers Vimy bomber from St. John's, Newfoundland to County Galway in Ireland in 16 hours 27 minutes.

In 1926 New York hotel-owner Raymond Orteig offered a $25,000 prize to anyone who could fly non-stop from New York to Paris. The following year, Lindbergh, 25-year-old chief pilot for an air-mail company, could not resist the challenge. He decided he would need a new plane, purpose-built for the journey. It would be a monoplane, capable of carrying the 450 gallons of fuel he needed for the journey. He also made up his mind it would be a solo flight.

Early on May 19, 1927, the *Spirit of St. Louis*, loaded down with fuel and barely able to leave the ground, took off from Roosevelt Field, New York, just clearing the telegraph wires at the end of the runway.

The cockpit had side windows but no forward view at all, although there was a periscope. Without a radio, Lindbergh navigated by measuring how

NEW YORK

far he had traveled in a certain direction ("dead reckoning") while guessing the wind simply from looking at the waves below!

The flight was full of dangers. As Lindbergh struggled to remain awake, ice forming on the wings threatened to down his airplane. Several times *Spirit of St. Louis* almost brushed the waves as he flew low to avoid fog. He was not always sure he was on course. When he spotted a fishing vessel, he shouted out of the window: "Which way is Ireland?"

After 28 hours, however, Lindbergh found himself flying over Valentia Island, southwest Ireland. To his disbelief, he realised he was only 3 miles off course! Six hours later he landed at Le Bourget airport in Paris to a hero's welcome. *Spirit of St. Louis* had crossed the Atlantic Ocean, flying a distance of 3,616 miles in 33 hours 30 minutes.

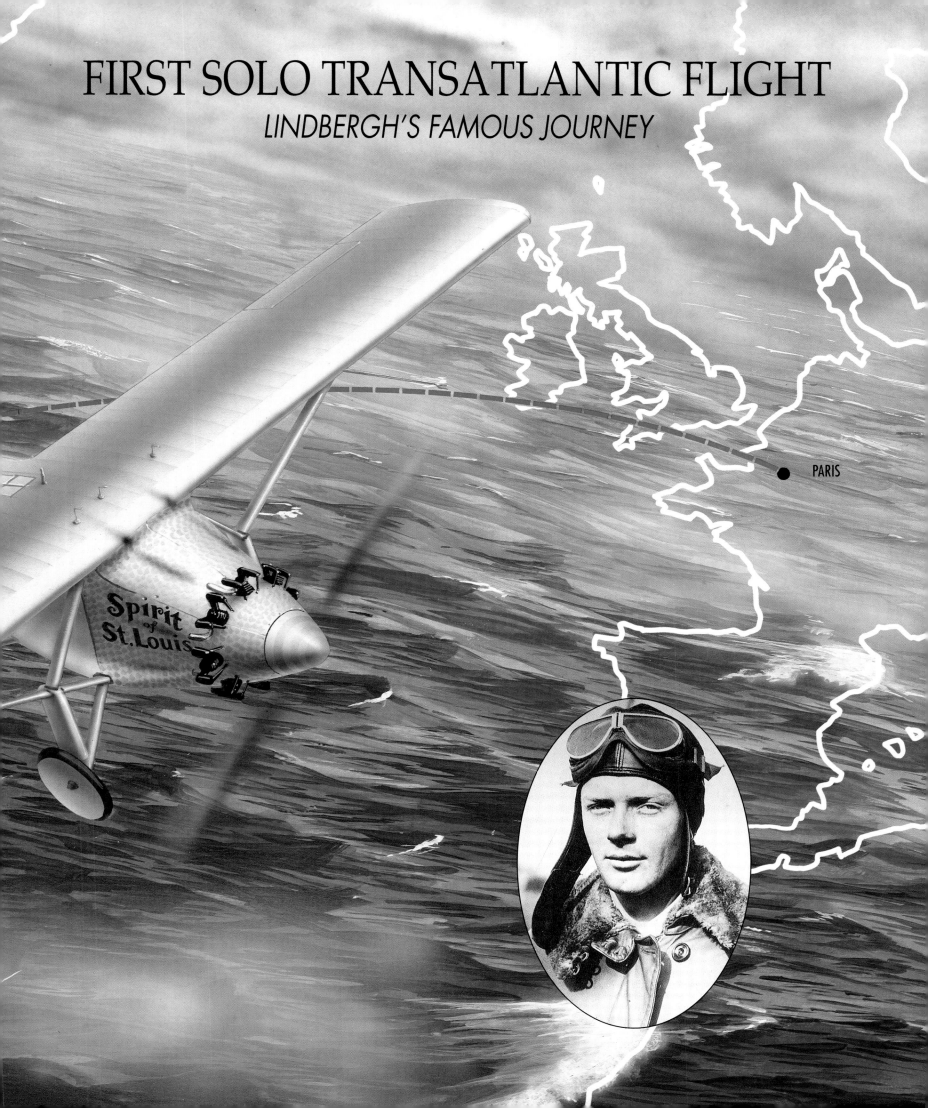

FIRST SOLO TRANSATLANTIC FLIGHT
LINDBERGH'S FAMOUS JOURNEY

PARIS

Spirit of St.Louis

THE FASTEST JET AIRCRAFT
LOCKHEED SR-71 BLACKBIRD

THE FASTEST JET AIRCRAFT ever to have flown was an American spyplane, the Lockheed SR-71. Known as "Blackbird" because of its sleek, black appearance, it was designed to fly fast and high over enemy territory photographing military bases on the ground. From a height of almost 15.5 miles, Blackbird's powerful cameras could take a clear shot of a car license plate!

Blackbird's top speed was 2,430 miles per hour – about three times the speed of sound. Its two engines produced more power than those of a large ocean liner. On September 1, 1974, it really showed what it could do. That day it made the fastest ever flight across the Atlantic Ocean, crossing from New York to London in just under 1 hour 55 minutes (a normal flight in an airliner takes around seven hours).

The Lockheed SR-71 was taken out of service in 1990. Some military experts think that the US Air Force may be developing an even faster jet. Called Aurora, it may be capable of flying nearly 19 miles high at twice Blackbird's speed!

The illustrations are approximately to scale

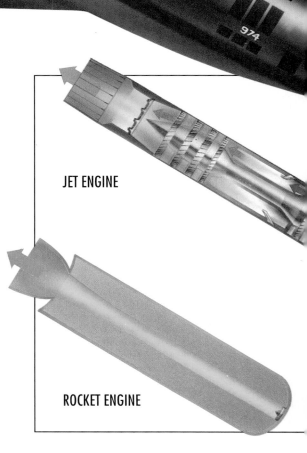

The first aircraft to fly faster than sound was a rocket-powered airplane called *Glamorous Glennis*. On October 14, 1947, Chuck Yeager of the US Air Force flew the X-1, as it was officially known, at a speed of 700 mph above the Mojave Desert in California.

JET ENGINE

ROCKET ENGINE

FASTEST OF ALL

On October 3, 1967, US pilot William Knight flew a rocket-powered plane at a speed of 4,520 mph – nearly seven times the speed of sound. This aircraft, the X-15 (left), could not take off from the ground and was carried aloft underneath a large transporter plane. When the transporter reached its maximum altitude, the X-15's rocket engines ignited and it blasted away to the record. Like Blackbird, the X-15 was built to withstand high temperatures generated at high speeds: Its outer skin became 14 times hotter than boiling water during flight.

The X-15 holds more than one record. Unlike jet engines, its rocket-powered engines did not need air to enable them to work. So the X-15 could fly much higher than jet aircraft, to levels of the atmosphere where the air is very thin indeed (see page 166). On August 22, 1963, the X-15 reached a height of 354,200 feet, a record altitude for any aircraft.

As thin as an aluminum can, Blackbird's metal skin was painted with a special heat-radiating black paint that could withstand temperatures of over 570° F – the sort of temperatures it experienced traveling at high speeds. As it sped along, it grew nearly 32 inches in length as the metal expanded.

JETS AND ROCKETS

In a jet engine, air enters a compressor, or fan, at its front end. The fan compresses the air (squeezes it into a smaller space) and feeds it through to the combustion chamber. Here, fuel is sprayed in and the mixture ignited. The hot gas produced expands and blasts out the rear of the engine. The gases streaming backward push the engine – and the aircraft attached to it – forward, just as when air is suddenly let out of a balloon, that flies forward, too.

A rocket can operate in space where there is no air. In a solid fuel rocket (left) the fuel burns rapidly, producing a large amount of hot gas. The gas blasts from the rear of the rocket, driving it forward, just as with a jet engine.

GIANTS OF THE AIR
TRANSPORTERS, HELICOPTERS, AIRLINERS, AND AIRSHIPS

THE BIGGEST FLYING MACHINES ever to take to the skies were the airships built in the 1920s and 1930s. These flying giants were the airliners of their day. They flew across the Atlantic – sometimes all the way around the world – but they were slow: The fastest airship could only reach a speed of 81 miles per hour. The first airship to cross the Atlantic Ocean was the British R-34: The trip took 90 hours. A modern airliner takes only about 7 hours to make the trip.

The largest airplane ever built is the Russian Antonov An-225. First flown in 1988, this giant plane is about 600 times the weight of a car. It was built to transport the Russian version of the space shuttle, known as Buran, to its launching-pad. Buran was not successful, so other tasks have had to be found to make use of its vast cargo compartments. It was pressed into service during the Gulf crisis of 1990-1, carrying refugees from Kuwait to safety.

The largest helicopter to ever fly, the Mil Mi-12 *(below)* from the former Soviet Union took to the skies for the first time in 1969. It looked like an airplane with rotor blades fixed to either end of its stubby wings. Capable of carrying loads of more than a third of its own weight, it was built to pick up and put down heavy loads in places where cargo planes could not land.

The wingspan of the Antonov An-225 *(above)* is 226 ft, nearly twice the distance of the Wright brothers' first flight!

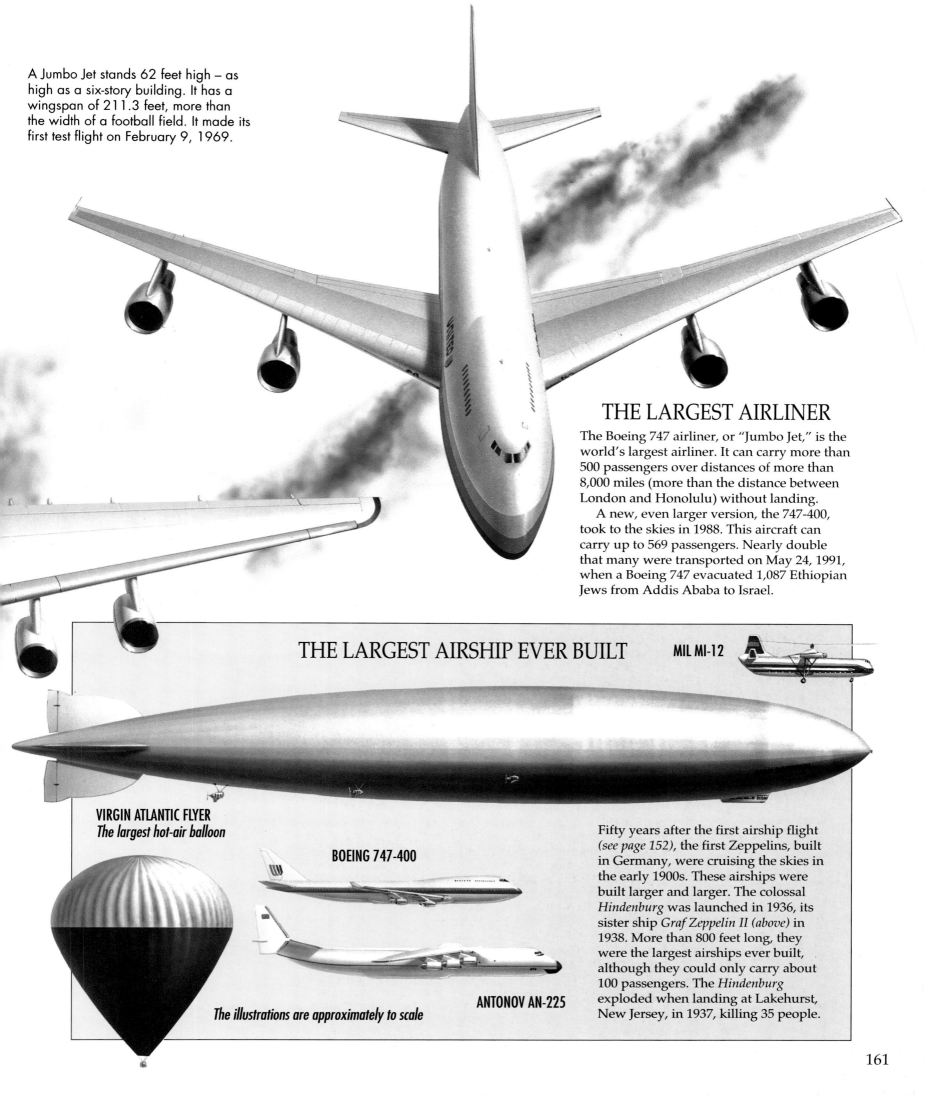

A Jumbo Jet stands 62 feet high – as high as a six-story building. It has a wingspan of 211.3 feet, more than the width of a football field. It made its first test flight on February 9, 1969.

THE LARGEST AIRLINER

The Boeing 747 airliner, or "Jumbo Jet," is the world's largest airliner. It can carry more than 500 passengers over distances of more than 8,000 miles (more than the distance between London and Honolulu) without landing.

A new, even larger version, the 747-400, took to the skies in 1988. This aircraft can carry up to 569 passengers. Nearly double that many were transported on May 24, 1991, when a Boeing 747 evacuated 1,087 Ethiopian Jews from Addis Ababa to Israel.

THE LARGEST AIRSHIP EVER BUILT

MIL MI-12

VIRGIN ATLANTIC FLYER
The largest hot-air balloon

BOEING 747-400

ANTONOV AN-225

The illustrations are approximately to scale

Fifty years after the first airship flight (*see page 152*), the first Zeppelins, built in Germany, were cruising the skies in the early 1900s. These airships were built larger and larger. The colossal *Hindenburg* was launched in 1936, its sister ship *Graf Zeppelin II (above)* in 1938. More than 800 feet long, they were the largest airships ever built, although they could only carry about 100 passengers. The *Hindenburg* exploded when landing at Lakehurst, New Jersey, in 1937, killing 35 people.

161

THE LARGEST ROCKET

AND FAMOUS FIRSTS IN SPACE TECHNOLOGY

TO GET INTO SPACE, a vehicle must overcome the pull of Earth's gravity. In practise, it must reach a speed of at least 17,500 miles per hour – or ten times the speed of a rifle bullet. Only immensely powerful rockets (*see page 159*) can achieve such speeds.

The first rockets, built by US inventor Robert Goddard in 1926, were only 3 feet tall. The Vostok rocket which put the first satellite into orbit more than 30 years later was 100 feet high. The Apollo astronauts were carried into space on their way to the Moon in 1969 in a Saturn V. As high as a 30-story skyscraper, the 364-foot rocket was the largest ever built. The open building used to house Saturn V was so vast that a special air-conditioning system was needed to stop clouds forming and rain falling inside!

Saturn V was 50 times as powerful as a Boeing 747 jumbo jet. The most powerful rocket today is the Russian *Energia*. Its four engines are capable of carrying a load as heavy as 24 family cars into orbit. Its original purpose was to launch a space shuttle and perhaps even to send a spaceship to Mars. The former Soviet Union's space program now faces an uncertain future, however.

The illustrations are approximately to scale

SPACE PIONEER

In January 1993, the US space probe Pioneer 10 (*right*) was 5 billion miles from Earth. Even at that distance, its radio signal can still be picked up by powerful receivers. It carries a plaque showing where it came from, should any intelligent life from another solar system come across it! Pioneer 10 is the most distant man-made object, a record that will one day be beaten by another space probe, Voyager 1, which is moving faster.

INSIDE SATURN V

Saturn V (*right*), like all launch vehicles, is made from several separate rockets, or stages, joined together. The first rocket is at the bottom and lifts the other stages into the air. When that first rocket runs out of fuel, it drops to the ground. Then the second stage rocket fires. The second stage, too, falls away when its fuel is gone. Then the third stage fires and lifts the spacecraft (in this case, the Apollo Command and Lunar Modules with astronauts on board) into orbit.

Command Module

Lunar Module

Third stage

Second stage

PIONEER 10

162

The US Space Shuttle *Columbia (left)* became the world's first reusable spacecraft when it made its second flight in November 1981.

The Soviet Vostok *(below)* rocket carried the first artificial satellite into orbit. Called Sputnik 1 *(below, left)*, the satellite was launched on October 4, 1957 and remained in orbit for 92 days.

The first-ever rocket was launched on March 16, 1926, by US inventor Robert Hutchings Goddard *(bottom, left)*. Using liquid gases for fuel, it reached a height of 41 feet.

The first long-range liquid-fuel rocket was the German V2 *(bottom, right)*, built in 1942. It was 47 feet long and had a range of 200 miles.

SPUTNIK I

V2 ROCKET

GODDARD'S ROCKET

16

FIRST TO THE MOON
THE FLIGHT OF APOLLO 11

THE FIRST LANDING by a manned spacecraft on another body in the Solar System took place on July 20, 1969, when Apollo 11 touched down on the surface of the Moon. A few hours later, US astronaut Neil Armstrong became the first person to step onto the lunar surface.

The spacecraft which took Armstrong and his fellow astronauts Edwin Aldrin and Michael Collins to the Moon was built in several sections, each with a different function. The Command Module (CM), located in the nose of Apollo 11, was both the control center and cramped living quarters for the crew. The Service Module (SM) contained the main rocket engine used to power the spacecraft. The Lunar Module (LM) was in two parts: Both would descend to the Moon itself, but only the upper section would lift off again.

Five more manned landings followed, the last in 1972. The Moon rocks collected were the most expensive rocks in history. The Apollo astronauts collected 842 pounds of rocks and soil from six different locations. With the whole Apollo programme costing $US 25 billion, a portion of Moon rock works out at $US 30 million a pound!

Watched by millions of television viewers, Armstrong and Aldrin spent 2¹/₂ hours gathering rock and soil samples. The footprints they left behind them will still be there 10 million years from now.

MOON LANDING
Once Apollo was in orbit around the Moon, one astronaut stayed in the CSM while the other two moved into the LM. The LM separated from the CSM (4) and descended to the Moon (5).

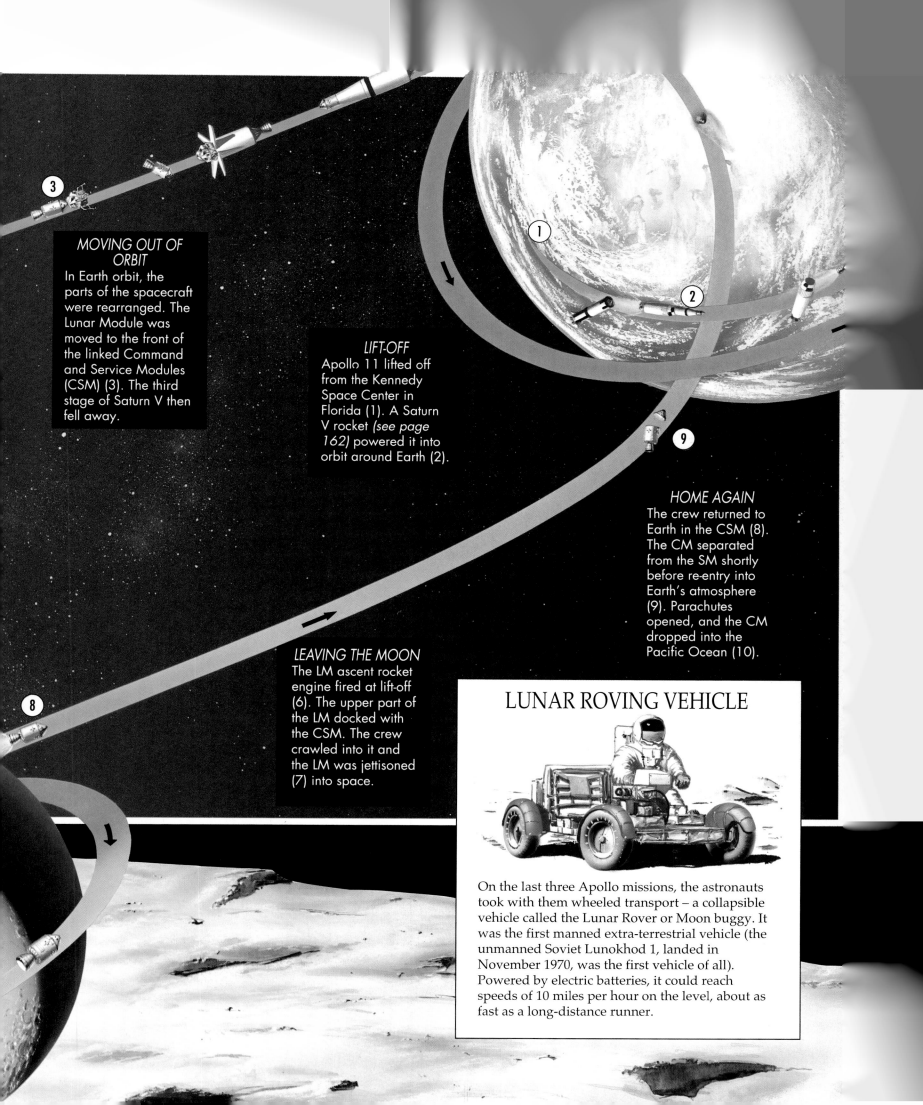

MOVING OUT OF ORBIT
In Earth orbit, the parts of the spacecraft were rearranged. The Lunar Module was moved to the front of the linked Command and Service Modules (CSM) (3). The third stage of Saturn V then fell away.

LIFT-OFF
Apollo 11 lifted off from the Kennedy Space Center in Florida (1). A Saturn V rocket *(see page 162)* powered it into orbit around Earth (2).

HOME AGAIN
The crew returned to Earth in the CSM (8). The CM separated from the SM shortly before re-entry into Earth's atmosphere (9). Parachutes opened, and the CM dropped into the Pacific Ocean (10).

LEAVING THE MOON
The LM ascent rocket engine fired at lift-off (6). The upper part of the LM docked with the CSM. The crew crawled into it and the LM was jettisoned (7) into space.

LUNAR ROVING VEHICLE

On the last three Apollo missions, the astronauts took with them wheeled transport – a collapsible vehicle called the Lunar Rover or Moon buggy. It was the first manned extra-terrestrial vehicle (the unmanned Soviet Lunokhod 1, landed in November 1970, was the first vehicle of all). Powered by electric batteries, it could reach speeds of 10 miles per hour on the level, about as fast as a long-distance runner.

HIGH FLYERS

HIGH ALTITUDE RECORD HOLDERS

MANY OF THE STARS we see in the sky are so far away we have to measure their distances in light-years. One light-year is the distance traveled by light, moving at 186,290 miles per second, in one year – that is, more than 6 trillion miles. Even the nearest star (apart from the Sun) is more than 4 light-years away. The farthest object ever detected may be more than 13 *billion* light-years distant!

By comparison, the greatest efforts made by humans to lift themselves clear of their home planet are humble indeed. The altitude record is held by the crew of Apollo 13, whose spacecraft reached a distance of just over 248,000 miles from Earth on April 15, 1970. It was, however, a major advance over the first ever manned space flight made by Yuri Gagarin, whose *Vostok 1* spacecraft climbed to an altitude of 203 miles just nine years earlier (*see page 128*).

Apart from spacecraft, the champion high-flyer is the US rocket-powered plane X-15, also famous for its speed records (*see page 159*). It could fly so high – more than 350,000 feet – its pilot was able to qualify as an astronaut! Jet-powered planes cannot ascend to such heights because they need air for their engines to work. A MiG fighter jet holds the altitude record at 123,524 feet.

HIGHEST IN A BALLOON

The greatest height ever reached by a manned balloon is 123,809 feet, achieved by Nicholas Piantanida in South Dakota in February 1966. Unfortunately, Piantanida did not survive the feat and his achievement is not recognized as a record.

The official altitude record is therefore still held by US Navy officers Malcolm Ross and Victor Prather, whose elongated balloon *Lee Lewis Memorial* lifted them to 113,739 feet above the Gulf of Mexico in 1961.

The all-time altitude record is held by the US astronauts aboard Apollo 13. Due to land on the Moon, an explosion caused the mission to be abandoned. Apollo 13 continued on around the Moon before returning to Earth.

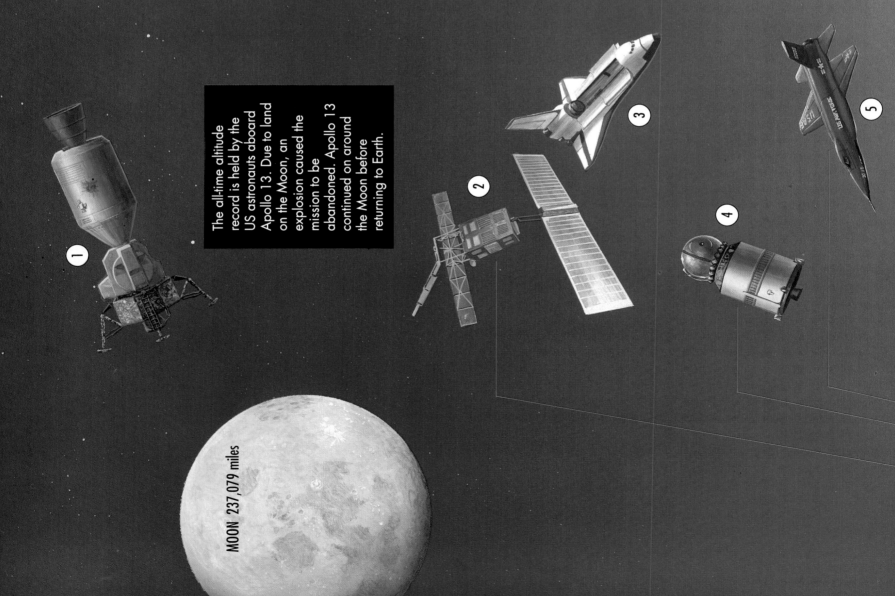

MOON 237,079 miles

MT. EVEREST *Highest mountain*
29,080 feet

KEY

1 Apollo 13 *Farthest manned flight* April 15, 1970 248,655 miles
2 Satellite 22,370 miles
3 Space Shuttle
4 Vostok 1 *First manned space flight* April 12, 1961 203 miles
5 X-15 *Highest flight by aircraft* August 22, 1963 354,200 feet
6 MiG 25 *Highest flight by jet aircraft* August 31, 1977 123,524 feet
7 Lee Lewis Memorial *Highest balloon flight* May 4, 1961 113,739 ft
8 Lockheed SR-71 Blackbird 98,430 feet
9 Concorde 59,000 feet
10 Aérospatiale SA315b Lama *Highest flight by helicopter*
    June 12, 1972 40,822 feet
11 Boeing 747 32,800 feet

The illustrations are not drawn to scale

167

HUBBLE SPACE TELESCOPE

GIANT STAR-WATCHER IN ORBIT

THE BEST TELESCOPES in the world all suffer from one thing: The air they must "see" through is polluted and tends to move about. Because of this, more distant stars appear faint or blurred, even if observatories are sited (as many are) on mountaintops far away from city lights and smog. So the best-performing telescopes would have to be located above Earth's atmosphere. That is exactly where the most powerful of them all, the Hubble Space Telescope, is to be found – orbiting 380 miles above Earth.

Like most modern large telescopes, the Hubble is a reflector: It uses mirrors to focus an image of the stars or galaxies it is pointed toward. Now, astronomers are able to see clearly stars 50 times fainter and 10 times farther away than they could using any of the best telescopes on the ground. The Hubble Space Telescope is so powerful it could detect light from a tiny flashlight over 250,000 miles away.

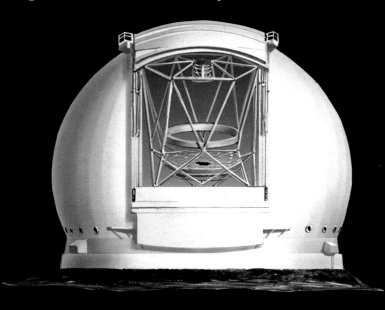

THE HONEYCOMB TELESCOPE

The Keck telescope, sitting atop the 13,796-foot peak of Mauna Kea on Hawaii, is the world's largest telescope. Its light-collecting mirror, measuring 32 feet across, consists of 36 hexagons fitted together in a honeycomb pattern. This is almost twice as large as a mirror in the world's next best telescope, the 16.6-foot Hale telescope at Mount Palomar, California. (The largest single-mirror instrument, on Mount Semirodriki, Russia, is not in a good observing site.) The Keck telescope is so sensitive that it could detect a candle shining more than 62,100 miles away!

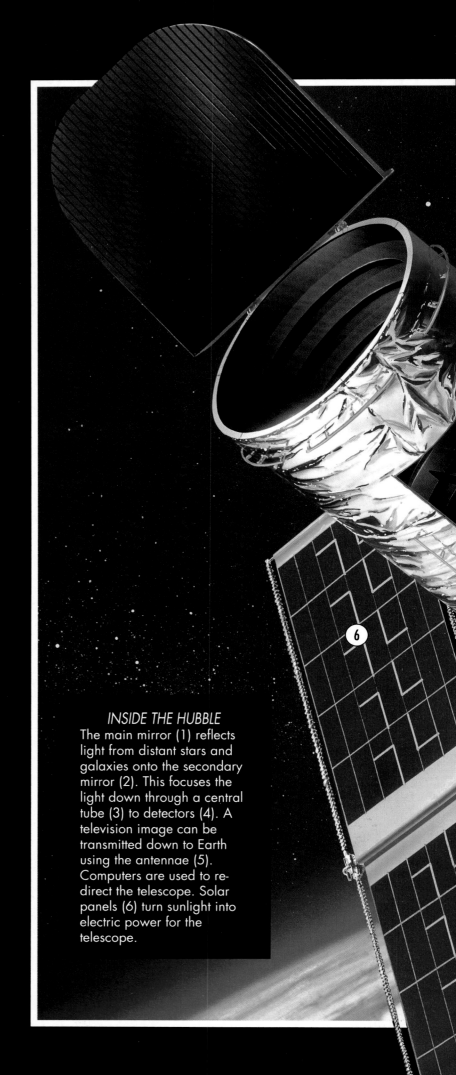

INSIDE THE HUBBLE
The main mirror (1) reflects light from distant stars and galaxies onto the secondary mirror (2). This focuses the light down through a central tube (3) to detectors (4). A television image can be transmitted down to Earth using the antennae (5). Computers are used to re-direct the telescope. Solar panels (6) turn sunlight into electric power for the telescope.

THE FIRST STARGAZER

In 1609 Italian scientist Galileo became the first person to gaze at the night sky through a telescope. To his amazement, he saw that the Moon had mountains and craters. Later, he found out that the planet Jupiter had several moons circling around it. Galileo also discovered many new stars, never before seen by humans.

THE RACE OF THE RECORD HOLDERS

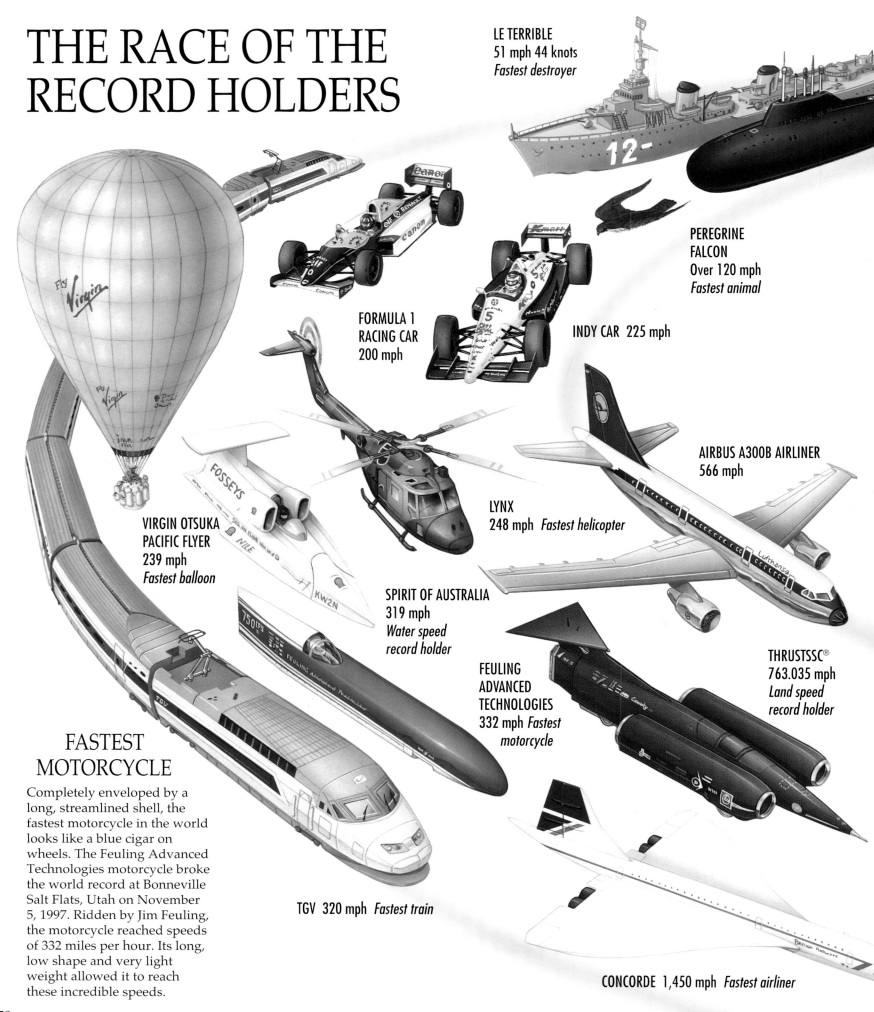

LE TERRIBLE
51 mph 44 knots
Fastest destroyer

PEREGRINE FALCON
Over 120 mph
Fastest animal

FORMULA 1 RACING CAR
200 mph

INDY CAR 225 mph

AIRBUS A300B AIRLINER
566 mph

VIRGIN OTSUKA PACIFIC FLYER
239 mph
Fastest balloon

LYNX
248 mph *Fastest helicopter*

SPIRIT OF AUSTRALIA
319 mph
Water speed record holder

FEULING ADVANCED TECHNOLOGIES
332 mph *Fastest motorcycle*

THRUSTSSC®
763.035 mph
Land speed record holder

FASTEST MOTORCYCLE

Completely enveloped by a long, streamlined shell, the fastest motorcycle in the world looks like a blue cigar on wheels. The Feuling Advanced Technologies motorcycle broke the world record at Bonneville Salt Flats, Utah on November 5, 1997. Ridden by Jim Feuling, the motorcycle reached speeds of 332 miles per hour. Its long, low shape and very light weight allowed it to reach these incredible speeds.

TGV 320 mph *Fastest train*

CONCORDE 1,450 mph *Fastest airliner*

RACING BICYCLE 45 mph

RACEHORSE 43 mph

ALFA CLASS SUBMARINE
51 mph 44 knots *Fastest submarine*

UNITED STATES
41 mph 36 knots
Fastest ocean liner

J CLASS RACING YACHT 35 mph 30 knots

THERMOPYLAE 24 mph
One of the fastest clippers

THE GREATEST SPEEDS achieved by manmade machines have all been reached in space, where there is no air to slow an object down. Even a satellite orbits Earth at twice the speed of the fastest aircraft. An unmanned space probe Helios B sent to observe the Sun holds the all-time speed record of 157,090 miles per hour. A spacecraft moving at that speed would travel from Earth to the Moon in an hour and a half! The crew of Apollo 10, US astronauts Thomas Stafford, Eugene Cernan, and John Young, hold the record for the fastest speed at which humans have traveled, when their command module returned from the Moon on May 26, 1969.

The illustrations are not drawn to scale

One hundred and fifty years ago, large sailing ships called clippers *(above)* vied with each other to be the quickest on the high seas. Loaded with tea and powered only by the wind, the clippers raced nonstop from China to Europe – more than halfway around the world – in about 100 days. But, apart from watercraft specially designed to break records, sea-going speed champions are well down the field when it comes to compare their speeds with others. A clipper never went faster than a human sprinter, and both a modern racing yacht and the fastest ocean liner (the *United States*) would be comfortably left behind by a racehorse. Only the quickest warships and submarines would outpace a racing cyclist, but any family car could easily overtake them all.

APOLLO 10 COMMAND MODULE
24,791 mph
Fastest speed at which humans have traveled

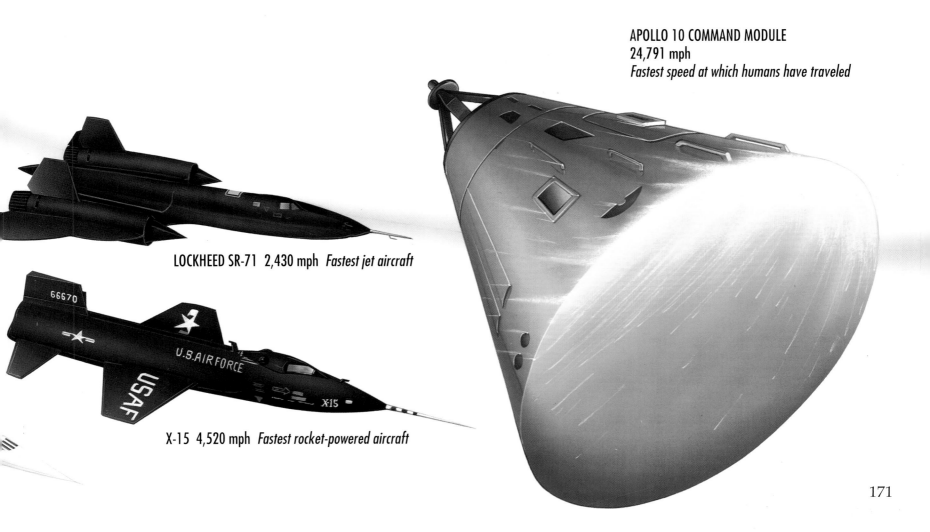

LOCKHEED SR-71 2,430 mph *Fastest jet aircraft*

66670

U.S.AIR FORCE

USAF

X-15

X-15 4,520 mph *Fastest rocket-powered aircraft*

INDEX

A

Aborigines 93
Achernar 6
Ader, Clément 152
Aegyptopithecus 58
Aerodrome, early aircraft 152
Aérospatiale SA315b *Lama*
  helicopter 167
Airbus A300B airliner 170
aircraft 147, 152-161, 166-167,
  171
  earliest 152-153
  fastest 158-159, 171
  first solo transatlantic flight
    156-157
  highest flying 166-167
  largest 160-161
aircraft carrier, largest 145
airliner 160-161, 170
  fastest 170
  largest 161
airport, most international
  traffic 90-91
airship 152, 160-161
  earliest 152
  largest 161
Akashi-Kaikyo Bridge 90-91,
  120-121
Akihito, Emperor 109
albacore 78-79
albatross, wandering 67, 74,
  76-77, 78-79
Alcock, Captain John 156
Aldrin, Edwin 164
Alpha Centauri 6
alphabet, first 97
Altair 6
Amazon Basin 26
Amenhotep II, King 102
amphibian
  earliest 49
  longest-lived 74
  rarest 83
  smallest 68
amphipod 76-77
Amun, Temple of 100-101
Amundsen, Roald 125
Andrewsarchus 56-57
Angel Falls 26
Angkor 90-91, 100-101
anglerfish 77
Annapurna 1 32
Antarctica 125
Antares 8
Antonov An-225 aircraft 160
Apollo spacecraft 162, 164-165,
  166-167, 171
arachnid (spider), fastest 73
Arandapsis 48
arch, longest natural 26
Archaeopteryx 49
archery 102, 111
archipelago, largest 26-27
archosaur 50-51

Arctic 124
Arcturus 6
Arlandes, Marquis d' 152-153
Armstrong, Neil 129, 164
army, oldest 114
Arsia Mons 20
art, earliest works of 92-93
Arun gorge 33
Ascraeus Mons 20
asteroids 14-15, 23
  largest 15
astronauts 129, 162, 164-166
Atacama Desert 26
atmosphere 18-19, 22, 26, 44
atmospheric pressure 138-139
atoll 29
  largest 29
Aurora aircraft 158
Australopithecus afarensis 58-59
autogyro 155
Ayers Rock (Uluru) 26-27

B

Baikal, Lake 26-27, 38-39
balloon 152, 161, 166, 170
  earliest 152
  fastest 170
  highest flight 166
  largest 161
Bambuti people 61, 90-91
banyan tree 85
baobab tree 85
bat
  farthest-traveled 80
  Kitti's hog-nosed 69
  noctule 80-81
  smallest 69
Bayard, Hippolyte 135
bear
  polar 66
  sun 69
beetle
  goliath 71
  heaviest 71
  jewel 74
Beijing 90-91, 104-105
Bell, Alexander Graham 136
Benz, Karl 148-149
Betelgeuse 6, 8
bicycles 146-147
  earliest 146
  fastest 147
Big Boy steam locomotive 140
bird
  deepest-diving 76-77
  earliest 49
  farthest-traveled 78-79
  fastest 72-73
  greatest wingspan 67
  heaviest flying 66
  largest 67
  longest-lived 74
  rarest 82
  smallest 68
  tallest-ever 52-53
black hole 9, 10-11
black smokers 30
Blitzen Benz car 150

Blue Flame car 150-151
Bluebird car 150
Boeing 747 "Jumbo jet" airliner
  161, 167
bone
  largest 60
  smallest 60
Borglum, Gutzon 118
Borobodur 90-91
Bouvet Island 30
boxing 103
Brachiosaurus 50-51, 52-53
Brassempouy 92-93
bridge 90-91, 120-121
  longest suspension 90-91,
    120-121
  widest long-span 90-91
brotulid 76-77
Brown, Lieutenant Arthur
  Whitten 157
Buddha statue 90-91, 119
Buddhism 109
building, tallest 90-91, 116-117
bustard, Kori 66
butterfly
  farthest-traveled 80-81
  largest 71
  monarch 80
  painted lady 81
  Queen Alexandra's birdwing
    71

C

Callisto 22-23
Cambodia 100-101
camera 134
Canaanite alphabet 97
Canada 116-117
Canopus 6
canyon 36-37
  largest in Solar System 21
  largest on Earth 26, 36-37
Capella 6
car 148-151, 170
  earliest 148-149
  fastest 151, 170
carbon dioxide 18, 21
caribou 80-81
carnivore
  largest-ever 56
  largest on land 66
  smallest 69
Caspian Sea 26-27
castle 90, 112-113
  largest ancient 90, 112-113
  largest residential 113
cat, rusty-spotted 69
Catal Huyuk 94
cathedral 90-91, 100, 114, 116-
  117, 118
  largest 90-91, 100
  tallest 116-117
  tallest steeple 90-91, 118
cave, longest 26
cave paintings 93
Cayley, George 153
Ceres 15
Charon 15

Chasseloup-Laubat, Count
  Gaston de 150
cheetah 72-73
chelonian
  deepest-diving 76-77
  largest 65
  longest-lived 75
Cherrapunji 26-27
China 90-91, 104-107
Chinese inventions 132, 154
Chinese writing 96
Cho Oyu 32-33
Choga Zanbil 98
Cholula pyramid 90, 98-99
Chrysler Building 116-117
church
  largest 115
  tallest steeple 90-91, 118
Cierva, Juan de la 155
cinema 134
city
  first 94-95
  highest capital 90
  largest 90
  oldest 90-91
civilizations, first 95, 96, 102-
  103, 107
clipper ship 171
clock 133
clouds 16-17, 18
  tallest 44
CN Tower 90, 116-117
coast redwood 119
cockroach
  fastest 73
  largest 70
Collins, Michael 164
color photograph 135
Colorado River 36-37
column, tallest 118-119
coma 25
comet 16, 24-25
  brightest short-period 24
  longest tail 24
Compsognathus 55
Concorde airliner 167, 170
constellation 6-7
  largest 6-7
  smallest 6
coral reef 29
  longest 26-27
Cornu, Paul 154-155
country
  highest birth rate 90-91
  largest 90-91
  largest population 90-91
  least densely populated 90
  most densely populated 91
  smallest 90-91, 114-115
crater 19
  most in Solar System 22
crocodile, estuarine 67
crop cultivation 94-95, 107
crustacean 77
Crux 6
Cugnot, Nicolas 148-149
cumulonimbus 44
cuneiform writing 96
cyclone *see* hurricane